WRITER: FRANK TIERI
ARTIST: JUAN ROMAN CANO SANTACRUZ
COLOR ARTIST: MOOSE BAUMANN
LETTERER: BILL TORTOLINI
COVER ARTIST: JOE JUSKO
EDITOR: CHARLIE BECKERMAN
SUPERVISING EDITOR: MARK PANICCIA

"AT THE SIGN OF THE LION"
FROM MARVEL TREASURY EDITION #26 (1980)
WRITER: MARY JO DUFFY
PENCILER: KEN LANDGRAF
INKER: GEORGE PÉREZ
COLORIST: GLYNIS WEIN
LETTERER: MICHAEL HIGGINS
EDITOR: JIM SHOOTER

COLLECTION EDITOR: CORY LEVINE
EDITORIAL ASSISTANTS: JAMES EMMETT & JOE HOCHSTEIN
ASSISTANT EDITORS: MATT MASDEU, ALEX STARBUCK & NELSON RIBEIRO
EDITORS, SPECIAL PROJECTS: JENNIFER GRÜNWALD & MARK D. BEAZLEY
SENIOR EDITOR, SPECIAL PROJECTS: JEFF YOUNGQUIST
SENIOR VICE PRESIDENT OF SALES: DAVID GABRIEL
SVP OF BRAND PLANNING & COMMUNICATIONS: MICHAEL PASCIULLO
BOOK DESIGN: SEAN BELLOWS

EDITOR IN CHIEF: AXEL ALONSO
CHIEF CREATIVE OFFICER: JOE QUESADA
PUBLISHER: DAN BUCKLEY
EXECUTIVE PRODUCER: ALAN FINE

WOLVERINE/HERCULES: MYTHS, MONSTERS & MUTANTS. Contains material originally published in magazine form as WOLVERINE/HERCULES: MYTHS, MONSTERS & MUTANTS #1-4 and MARVEL TREASURY EDITION #26. First printing 2011. ISBN# 978-0-7851-4110-5. Published by MARVEL WORLDWIDE, INC., a subsidiary of MARVEL ENTERTAINMENT, LLC. OFFICE OF PUBLICATION: 135 West 50th Street, New York, NY 10020. Copyright © 1980 and 2011 Marvel Characters, Inc. All rights reserved. $14.99 per copy in the U.S. and $16.50 in Canada (GST #R127032852); Canadian Agreement #40668537. All characters featured in this issue and the distinctive names and likenesses thereof, and all related indicia are trademarks of Marvel Characters, Inc. No similarity between any of the names, characters, persons, and/or institutions in this magazine with those of any living or dead person or institution is intended, and any such similarity which may exist is purely coincidental. **Printed in the U.S.A.** ALAN FINE, EVP - Office of the President, Marvel Worldwide, Inc. and EVP & CMO Marvel Characters B.V.; DAN BUCKLEY, Publisher & President - Print, Animation & Digital Divisions; JOE QUESADA, Chief Creative Officer; JIM SOKOLOWSKI, Chief Operating Officer; DAVID BOGART, SVP of Business Affairs & Talent Management; TOM BREVOORT, SVP of Publishing; C.B. CEBULSKI, SVP of Creator & Content Development; DAVID GABRIEL, SVP of Publishing Sales & Circulation; MICHAEL PASCIULLO, SVP of Brand Planning & Communications; JIM O'KEEFE, VP of Operations & Logistics; DAN CARR, Executive Director of Publishing Technology; JUSTIN F. GABRIE, Director of Publishing & Editorial Operations; SUSAN CRESPI, Editorial Operations Manager; ALEX MORALES, Publishing Operations Manager; STAN LEE, Chairman Emeritus. For information regarding advertising in Marvel Comics or on Marvel.com, please contact John Dokes, SVP Integrated Sales and Marketing, at jdokes@marvel.com. For Marvel subscription inquiries, please call 800-217-9158. **Manufactured between 7/7/2011 and 7/26/2011 by QUAD/GRAPHICS, DUBUQUE, IA, USA.**

10 9 8 7 6 5 4 3 2 1

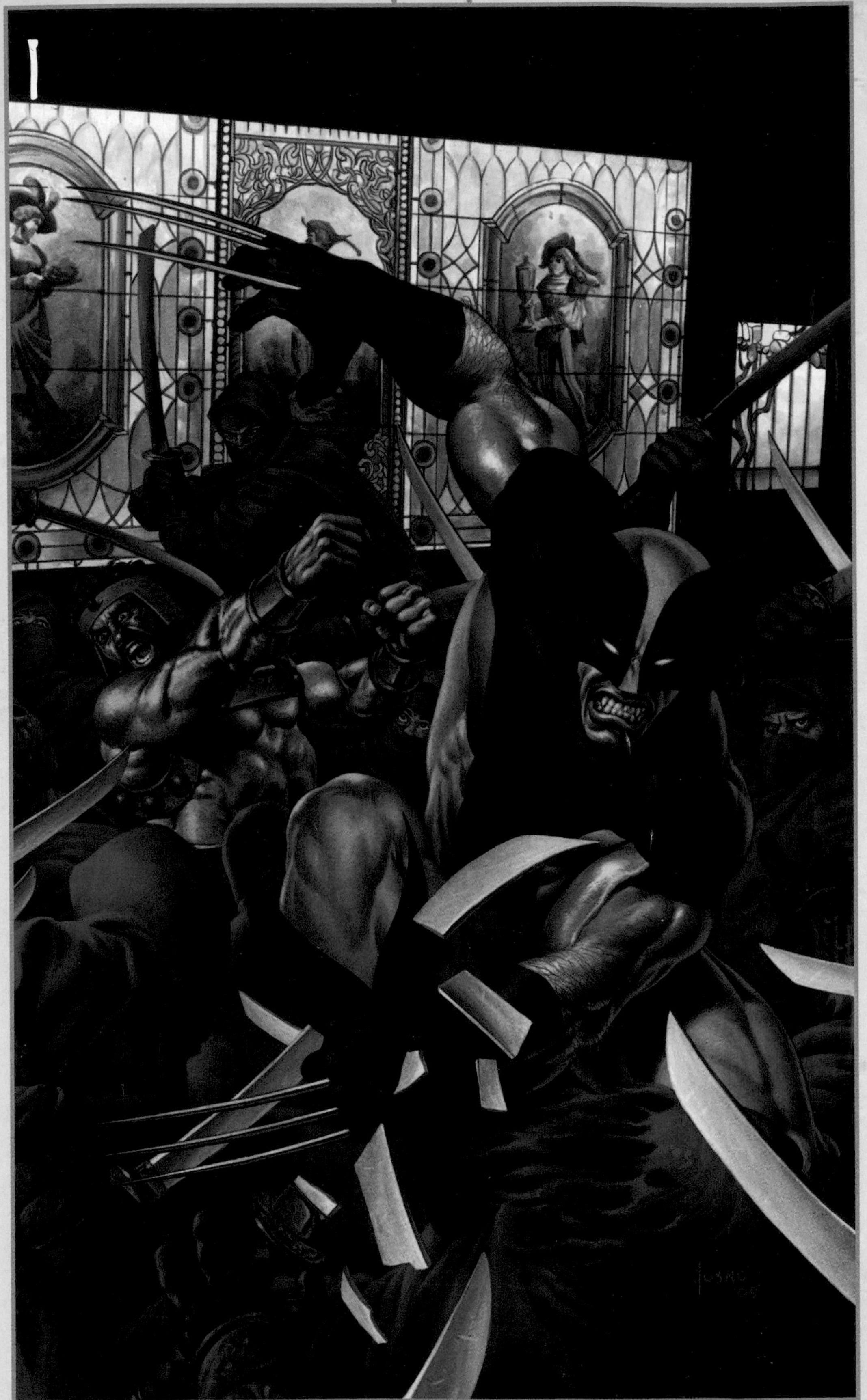

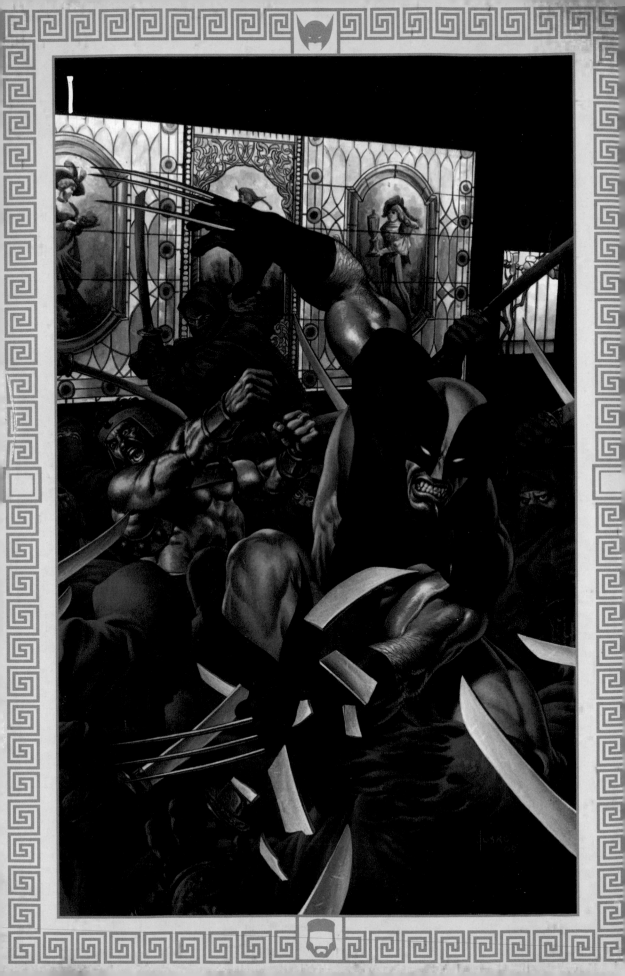

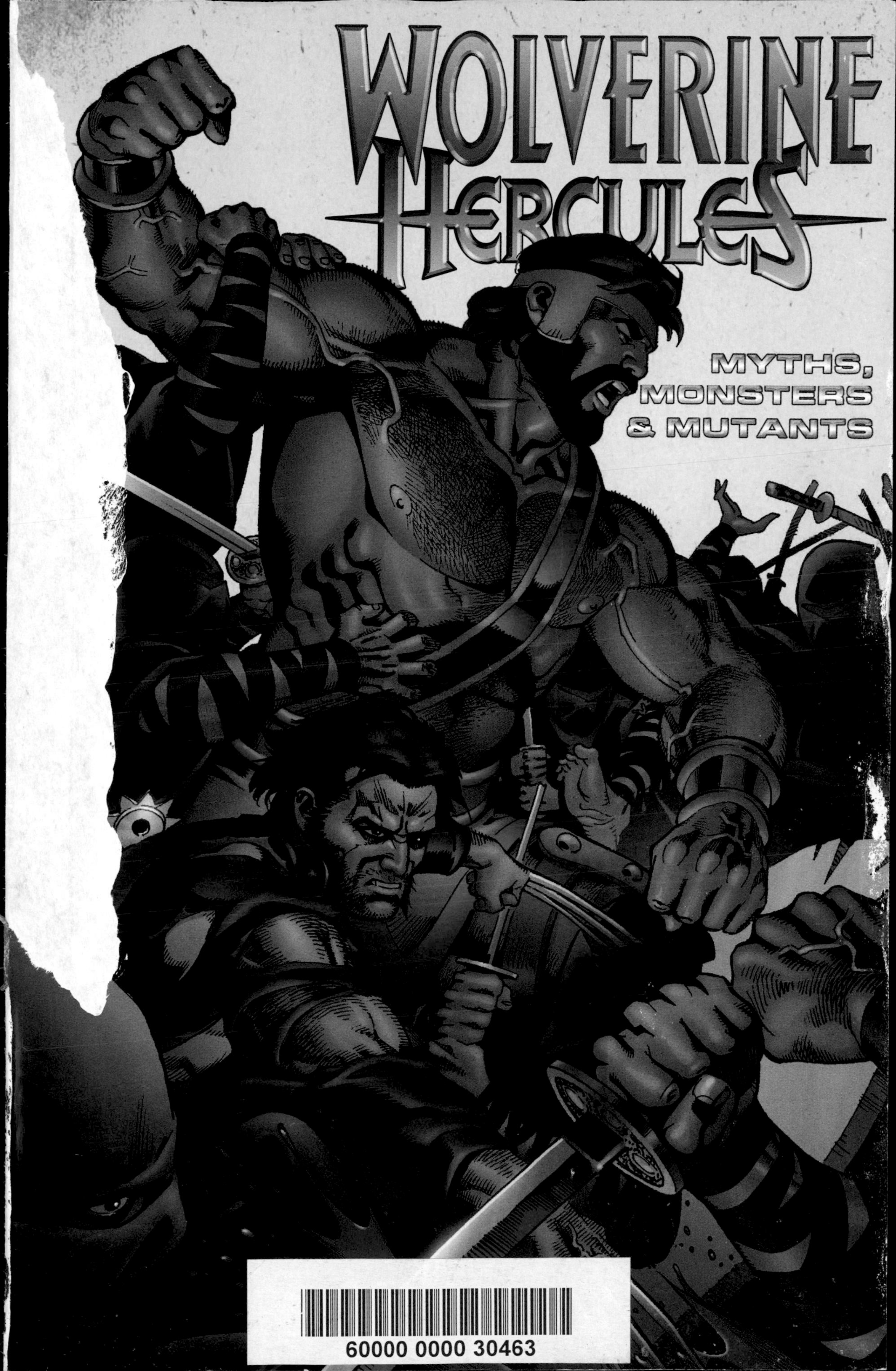
WOLVERINE
HERCULES
MYTHS, MONSTERS & MUTANTS

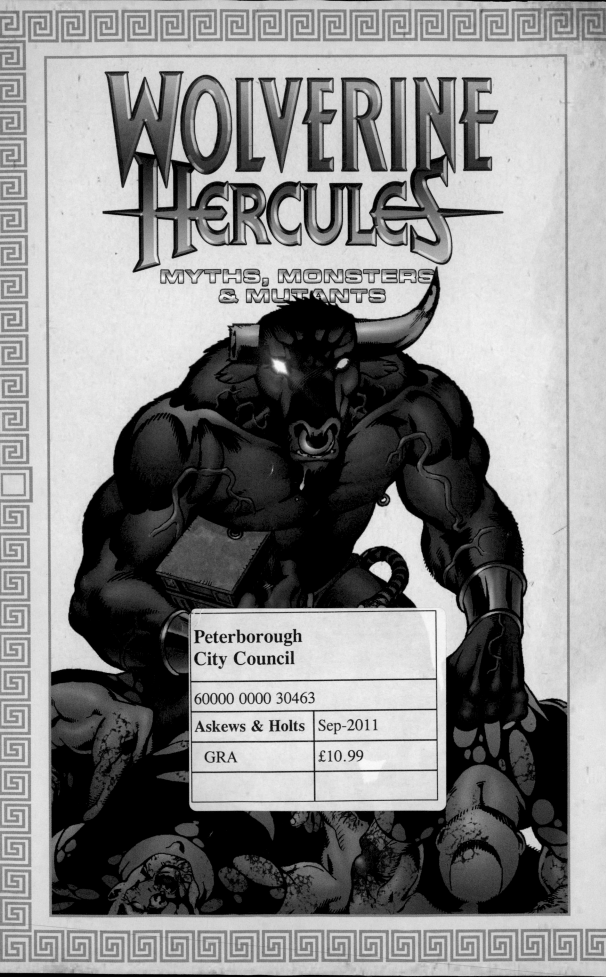

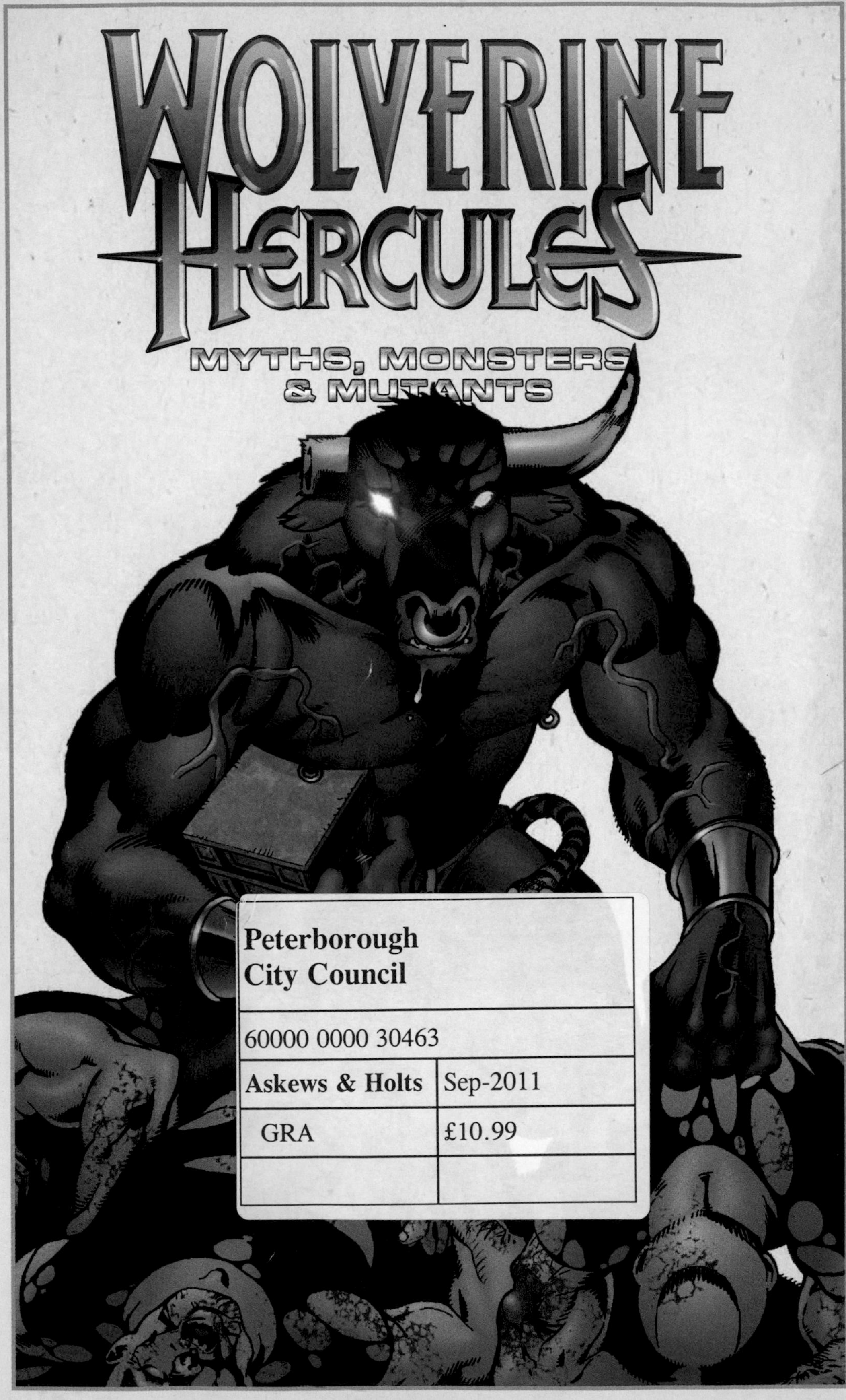
WOLVERINE
HERCULES
MYTHS, MONSTERS
& MUTANTS

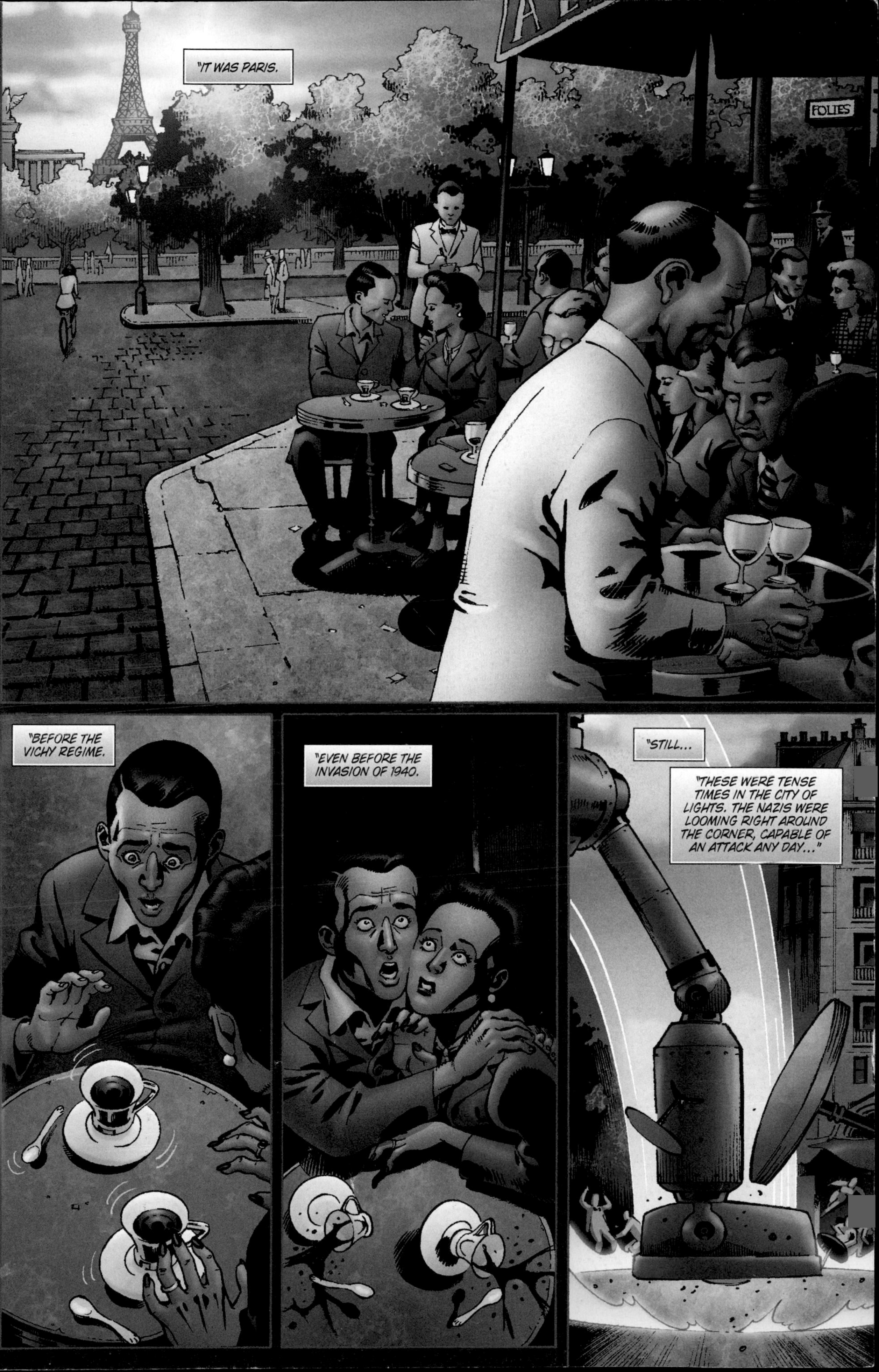

"IT WAS PARIS.
FOLIES
"BEFORE THE VICHY REGIME.
"EVEN BEFORE THE INVASION OF 1940.
"STILL...
"THESE WERE TENSE TIMES IN THE CITY OF LIGHTS. THE NAZIS WERE LOOMING RIGHT AROUND THE CORNER, CAPABLE OF AN ATTACK ANY DAY..."

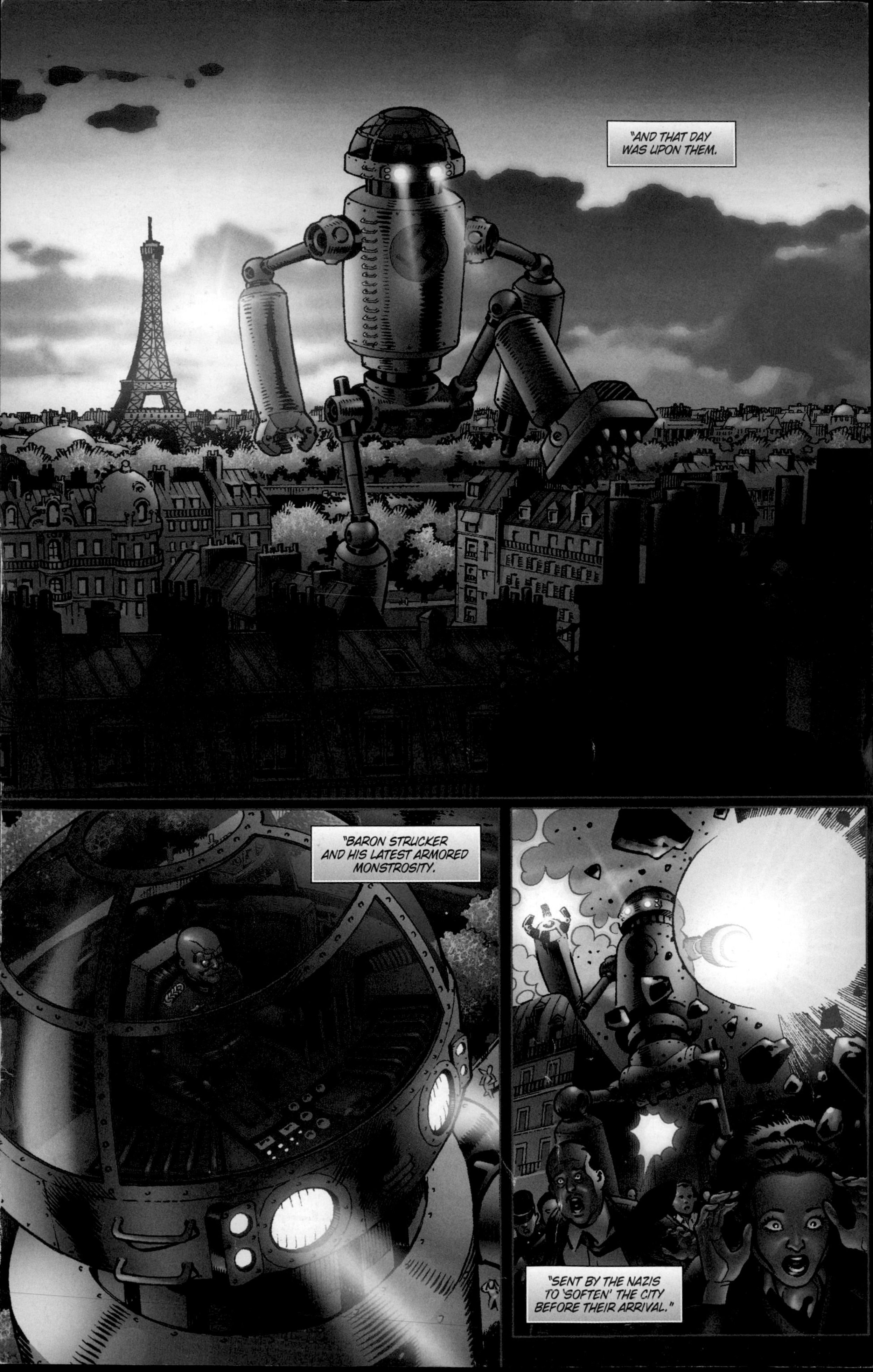
"AND THAT DAY WAS UPON THEM.
"BARON STRUCKER AND HIS LATEST ARMORED MONSTROSITY.
"SENT BY THE NAZIS TO 'SOFTEN' THE CITY BEFORE THEIR ARRIVAL."

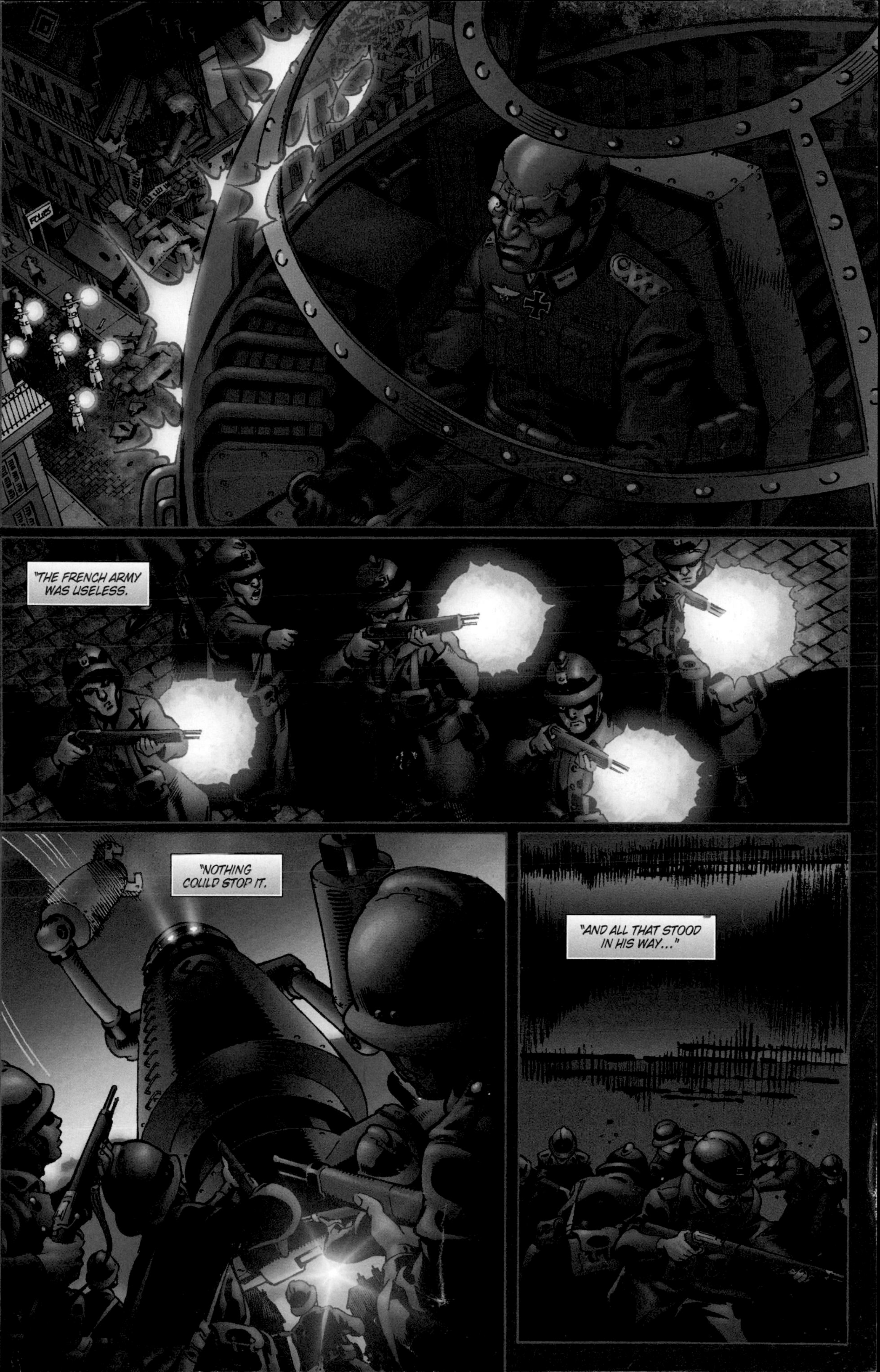
"THE FRENCH ARMY WAS USELESS.
"NOTHING COULD STOP IT.
"AND ALL THAT STOOD IN HIS WAY..."

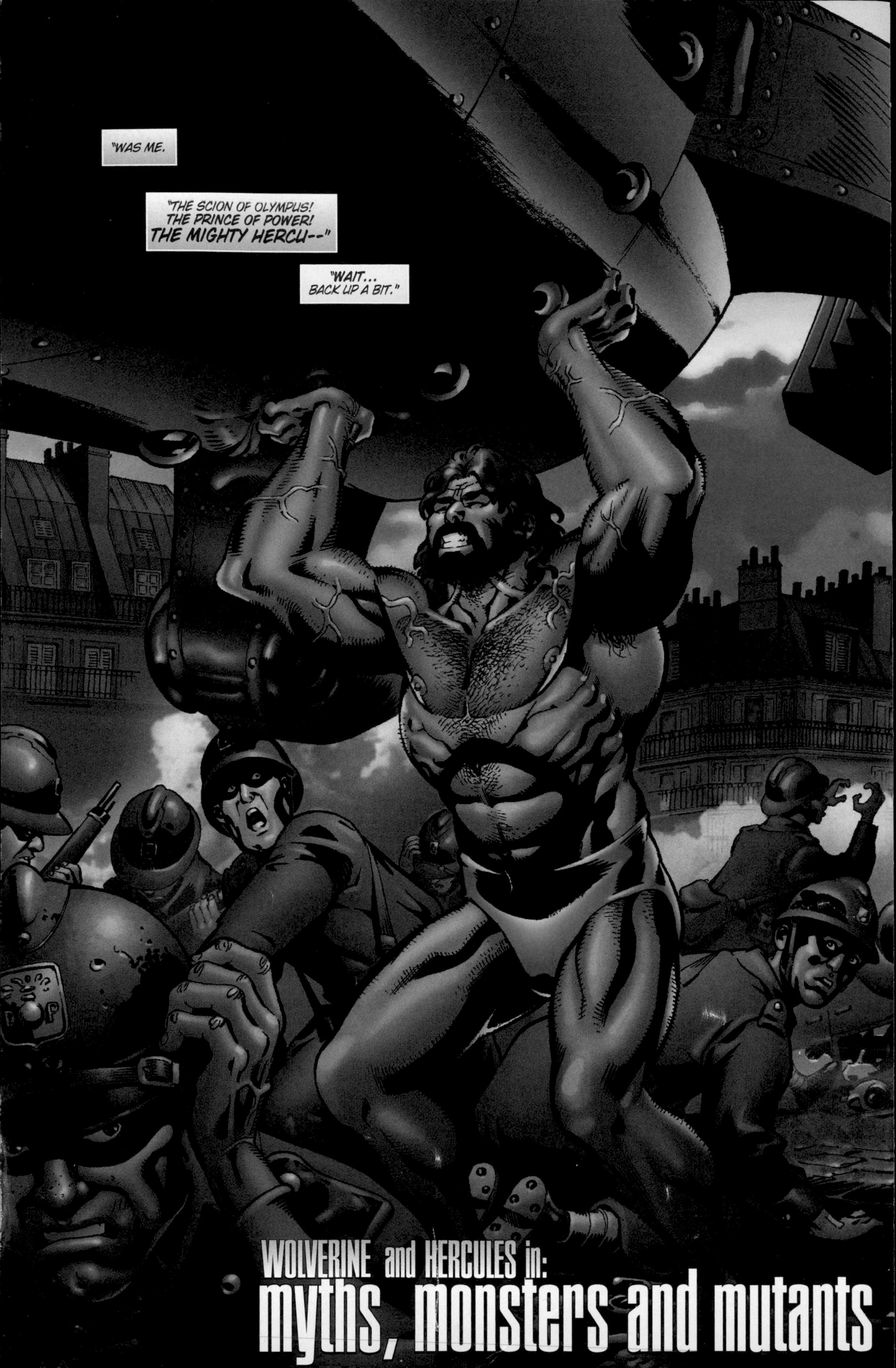
"WAS ME.
"THE SCION OF OLYMPUS! THE PRINCE OF POWER! THE MIGHTY HERCU--"
"WAIT... BACK UP A BIT."
WOLVERINE and HERCULES in:
myths, monsters and mutants

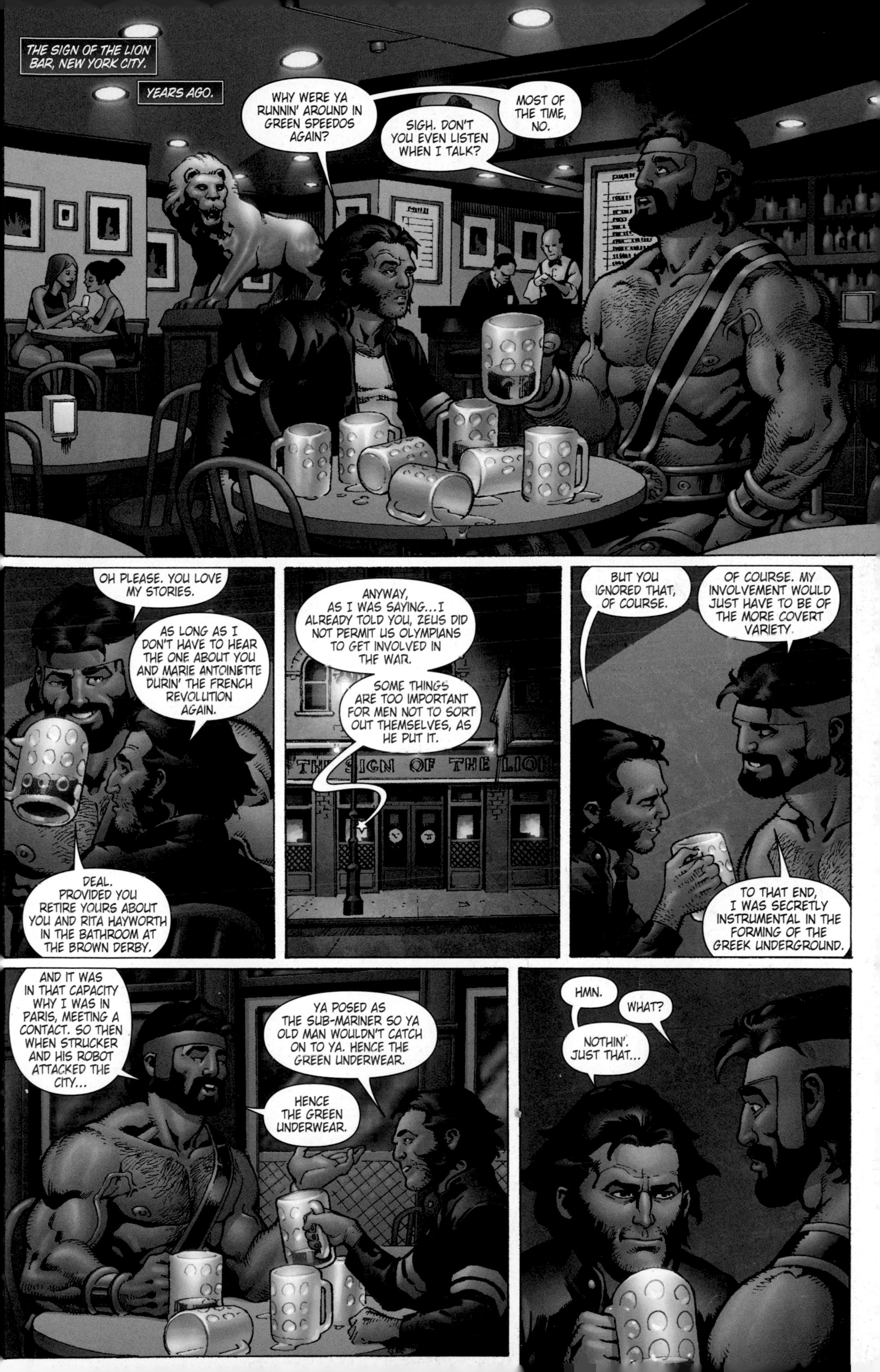
THE SIGN OF THE LION BAR, NEW YORK CITY.
YEARS AGO.
WHY WERE YA RUNNIN' AROUND IN GREEN SPEEDOS AGAIN?
SIGH. DON'T YOU EVEN LISTEN WHEN I TALK?
MOST OF THE TIME, NO.
OH PLEASE. YOU LOVE MY STORIES.
AS LONG AS I DON'T HAVE TO HEAR THE ONE ABOUT YOU AND MARIE ANTOINETTE DURIN' THE FRENCH REVOLUTION AGAIN.
DEAL. PROVIDED YOU RETIRE YOURS ABOUT YOU AND RITA HAYWORTH IN THE BATHROOM AT THE BROWN DERBY.
ANYWAY, AS I WAS SAYING... I ALREADY TOLD YOU, ZEUS DID NOT PERMIT US OLYMPIANS TO GET INVOLVED IN THE WAR.
SOME THINGS ARE TOO IMPORTANT FOR MEN NOT TO SORT OUT THEMSELVES, AS HE PUT IT.
THE SIGN OF THE LION
BUT YOU IGNORED THAT, OF COURSE.
OF COURSE. MY INVOLVEMENT WOULD JUST HAVE TO BE OF THE MORE COVERT VARIETY.
TO THAT END, I WAS SECRETLY INSTRUMENTAL IN THE FORMING OF THE GREEK UNDERGROUND.
AND IT WAS IN THAT CAPACITY WHY I WAS IN PARIS, MEETING A CONTACT. SO THEN WHEN STRUCKER AND HIS ROBOT ATTACKED THE CITY...
YA POSED AS THE SUB-MARINER SO YA OLD MAN WOULDN'T CATCH ON TO YA. HENCE THE GREEN UNDERWEAR.
HENCE THE GREEN UNDERWEAR.
HMN.
WHAT?
NOTHIN'. JUST THAT...

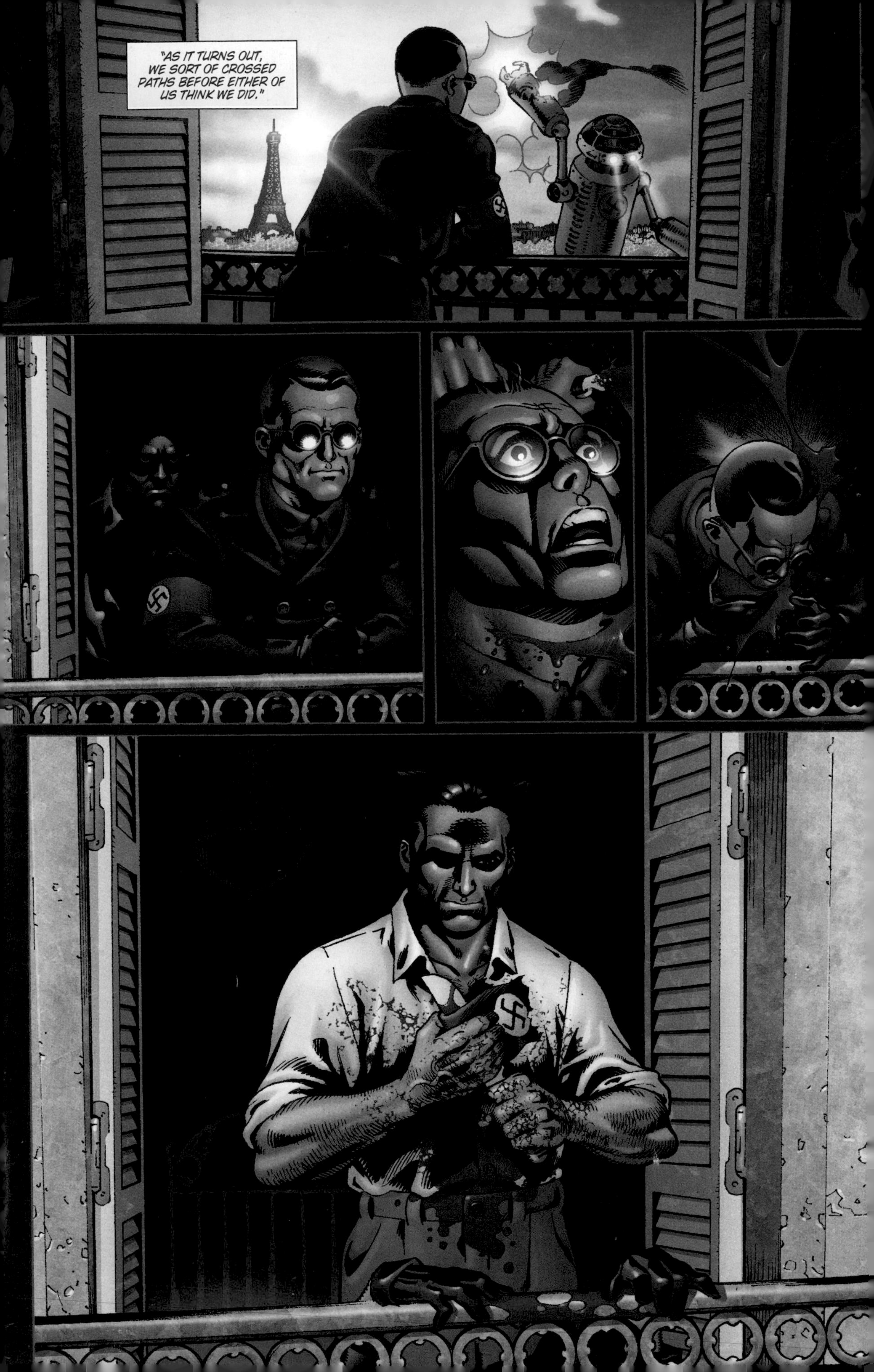
"AS IT TURNS OUT, WE SORT OF CROSSED PATHS BEFORE EITHER OF US THINK WE DID."

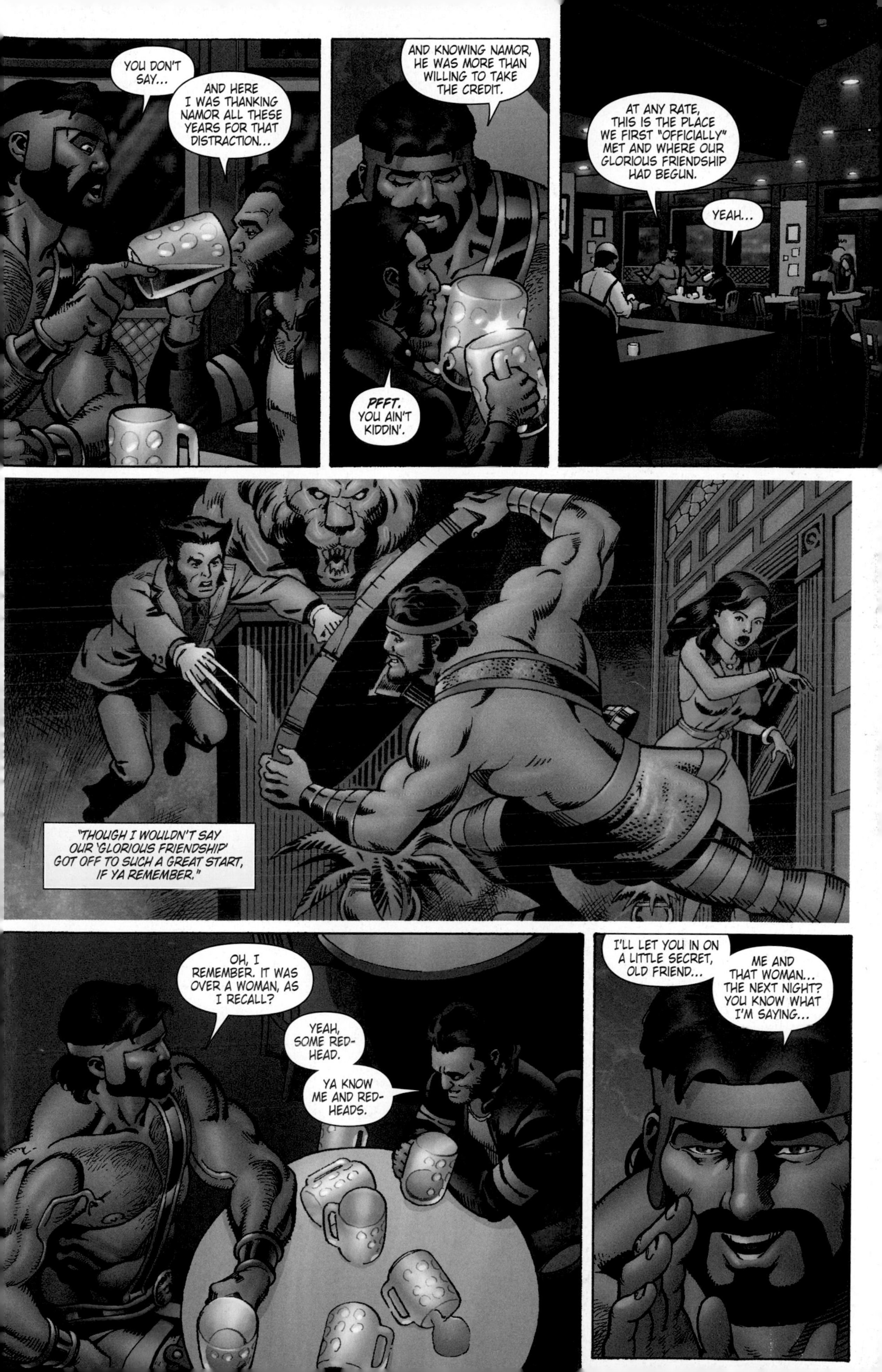
YOU DON'T SAY...
AND HERE I WAS THANKING NAMOR ALL THESE YEARS FOR THAT DISTRACTION...
AND KNOWING NAMOR, HE WAS MORE THAN WILLING TO TAKE THE CREDIT.
PFFT. YOU AIN'T KIDDIN'.
AT ANY RATE, THIS IS THE PLACE WE FIRST "OFFICIALLY" MET AND WHERE OUR GLORIOUS FRIENDSHIP HAD BEGUN.
YEAH...
"THOUGH I WOULDN'T SAY OUR 'GLORIOUS FRIENDSHIP' GOT OFF TO SUCH A GREAT START, IF YA REMEMBER."
OH, I REMEMBER. IT WAS OVER A WOMAN, AS I RECALL?
YEAH, SOME RED-HEAD.
YA KNOW ME AND RED-HEADS.
I'LL LET YOU IN ON A LITTLE SECRET, OLD FRIEND...
ME AND THAT WOMAN... THE NEXT NIGHT? YOU KNOW WHAT I'M SAYING...

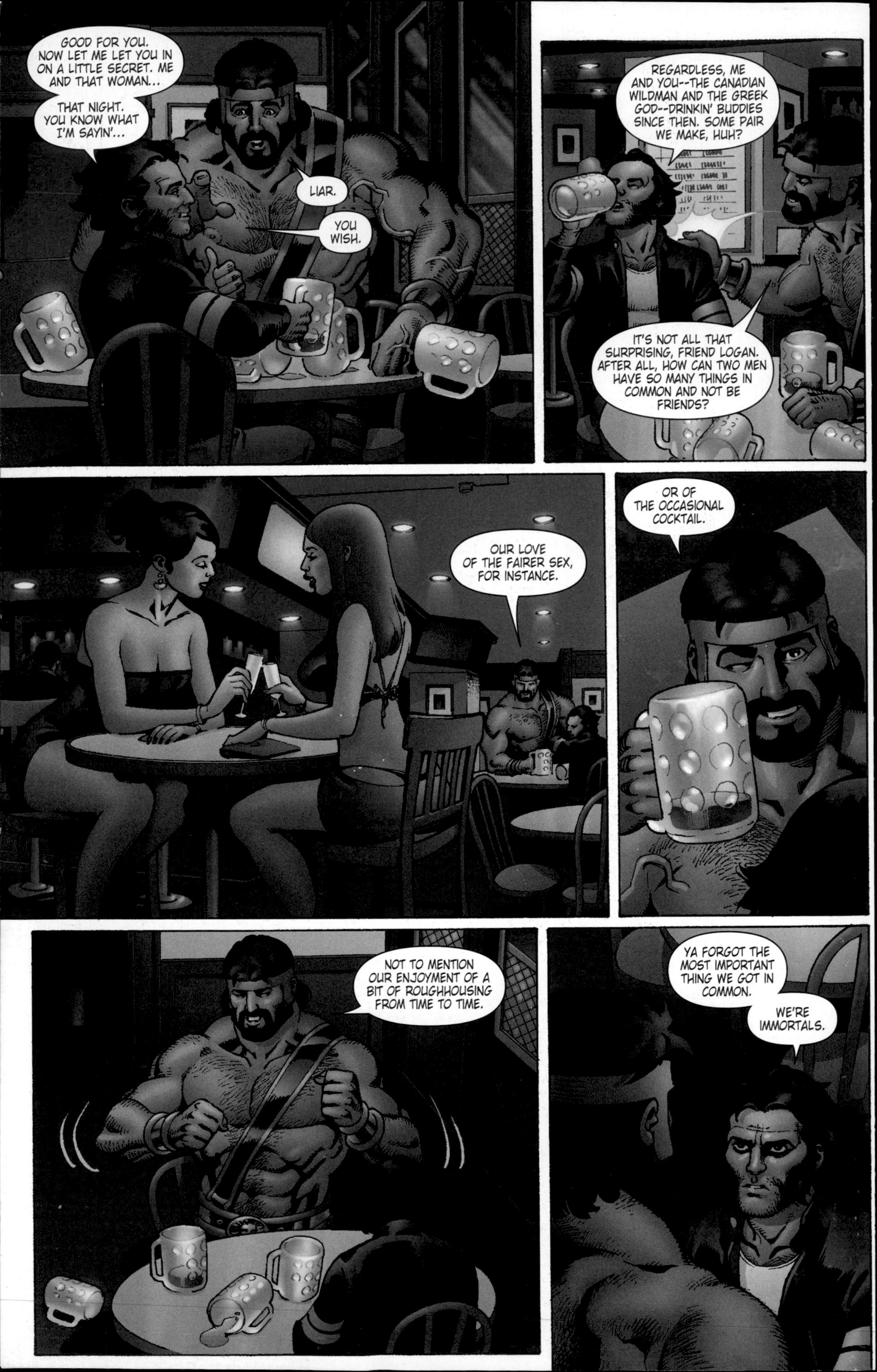
GOOD FOR YOU. NOW LET ME LET YOU IN ON A LITTLE SECRET. ME AND THAT WOMAN...
THAT NIGHT. YOU KNOW WHAT I'M SAYIN'...
LIAR.
YOU WISH.
REGARDLESS, ME AND YOU--THE CANADIAN WILDMAN AND THE GREEK GOD--DRINKIN' BUDDIES SINCE THEN. SOME PAIR WE MAKE, HUH?
IT'S NOT ALL THAT SURPRISING, FRIEND LOGAN. AFTER ALL, HOW CAN TWO MEN HAVE SO MANY THINGS IN COMMON AND NOT BE FRIENDS?
OUR LOVE OF THE FAIRER SEX, FOR INSTANCE.
OR OF THE OCCASIONAL COCKTAIL.
NOT TO MENTION OUR ENJOYMENT OF A BIT OF ROUGHHOUSING FROM TIME TO TIME.
YA FORGOT THE MOST IMPORTANT THING WE GOT IN COMMON.
WE'RE IMMORTALS.

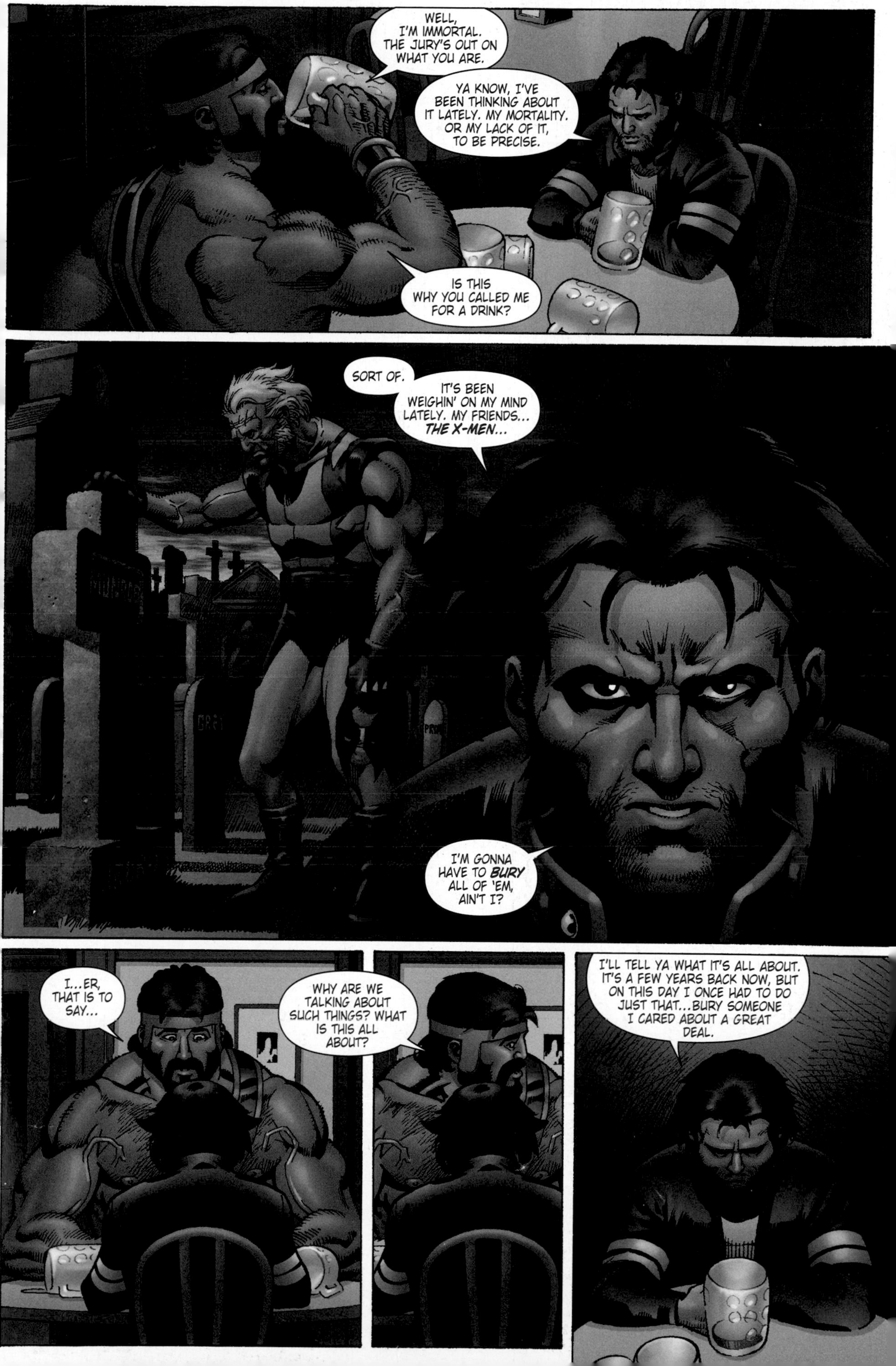
WELL, I'M IMMORTAL. THE JURY'S OUT ON WHAT YOU ARE.
YA KNOW, I'VE BEEN THINKING ABOUT IT LATELY. MY MORTALITY. OR MY LACK OF IT, TO BE PRECISE.
IS THIS WHY YOU CALLED ME FOR A DRINK?
SORT OF.
IT'S BEEN WEIGHIN' ON MY MIND LATELY. MY FRIENDS... THE X-MEN...
I'M GONNA HAVE TO BURY ALL OF 'EM, AIN'T I?
I...ER, THAT IS TO SAY...
WHY ARE WE TALKING ABOUT SUCH THINGS? WHAT IS THIS ALL ABOUT?
I'LL TELL YA WHAT IT'S ALL ABOUT. IT'S A FEW YEARS BACK NOW, BUT ON THIS DAY I ONCE HAD TO DO JUST THAT...BURY SOMEONE I CARED ABOUT A GREAT DEAL.

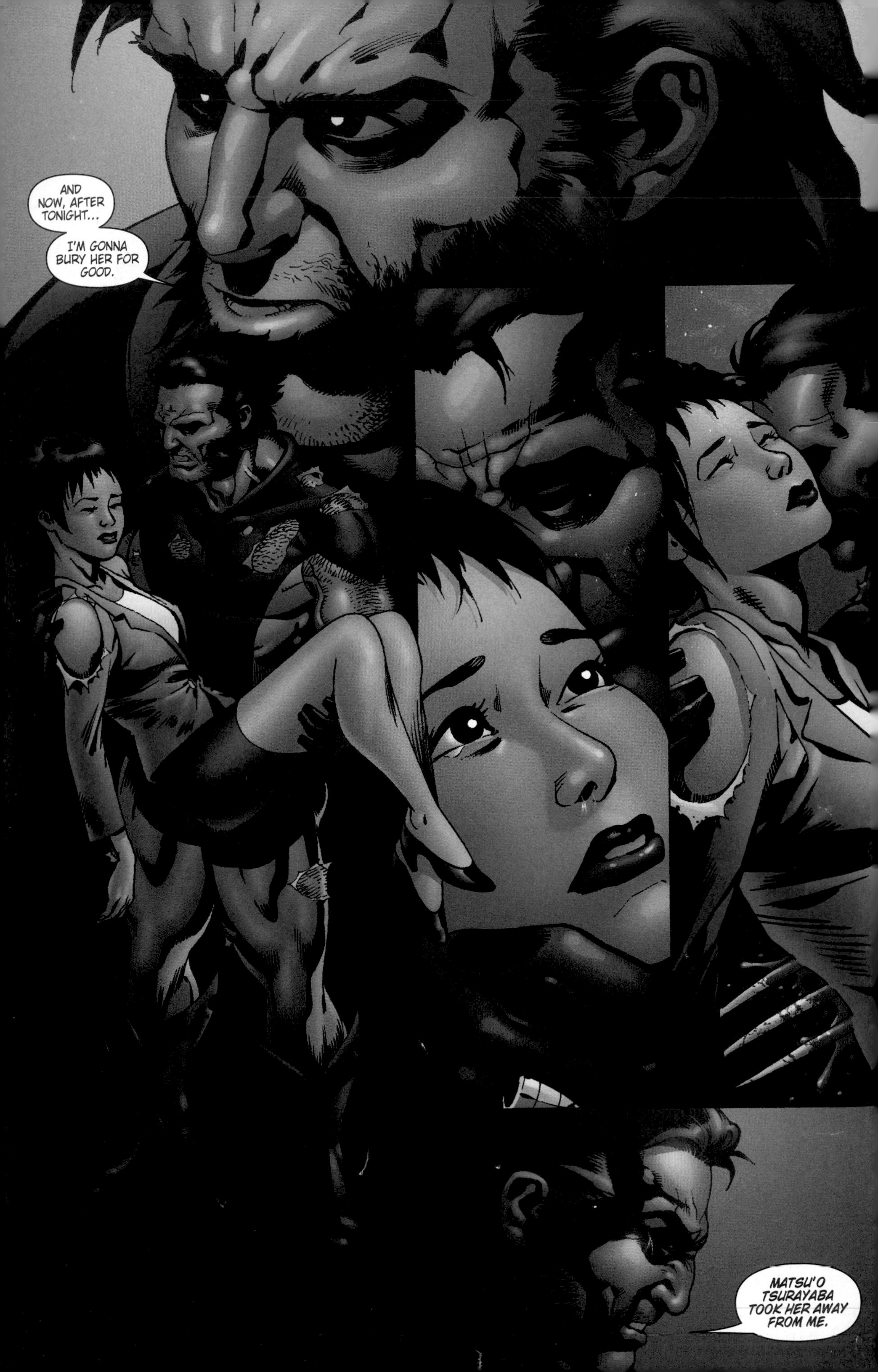
AND NOW, AFTER TONIGHT...
I'M GONNA BURY HER FOR GOOD.
MATSU'O TSURAYABA TOOK HER AWAY FROM ME.

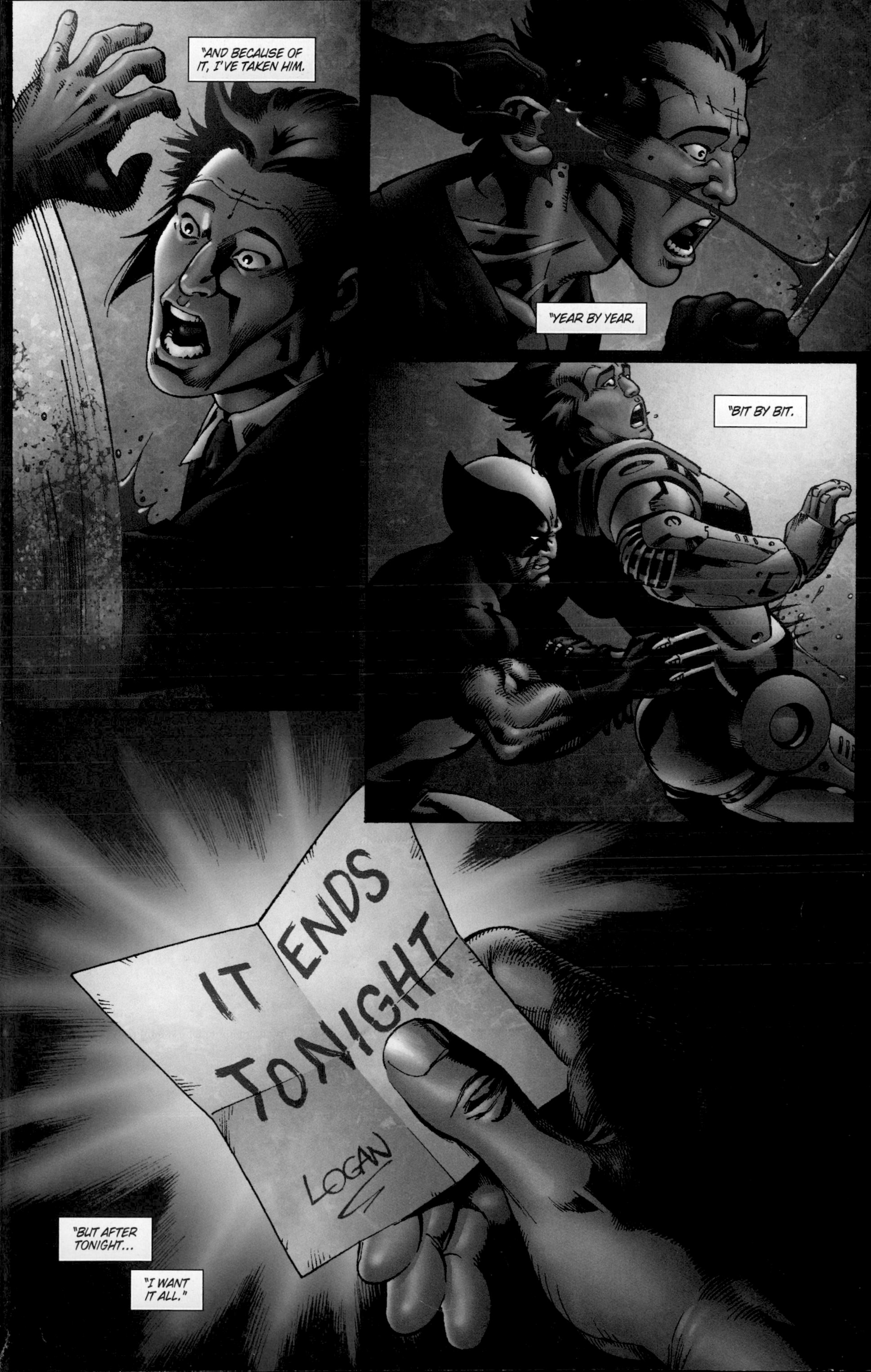
"AND BECAUSE OF IT, I'VE TAKEN HIM.
"YEAR BY YEAR.
"BIT BY BIT.
IT ENDS TONIGHT
LOGAN
"BUT AFTER TONIGHT...
"I WANT IT ALL."

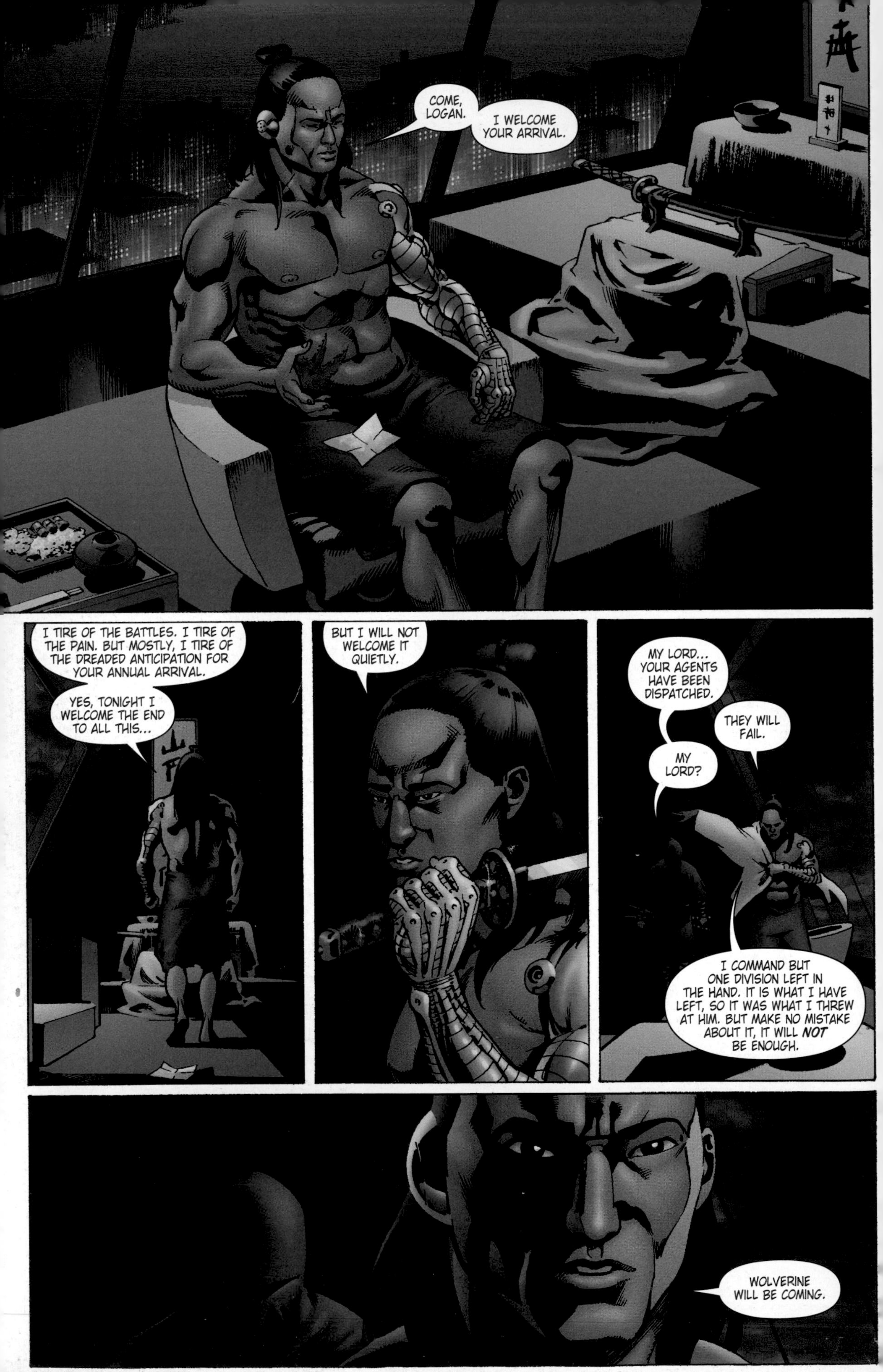
COME, LOGAN.
I WELCOME YOUR ARRIVAL.
I TIRE OF THE BATTLES. I TIRE OF THE PAIN. BUT MOSTLY, I TIRE OF THE DREADED ANTICIPATION FOR YOUR ANNUAL ARRIVAL.
YES, TONIGHT I WELCOME THE END TO ALL THIS...
BUT I WILL NOT WELCOME IT QUIETLY.
MY LORD... YOUR AGENTS HAVE BEEN DISPATCHED.
THEY WILL FAIL.
MY LORD?
I COMMAND BUT ONE DIVISION LEFT IN THE HAND. IT IS WHAT I HAVE LEFT, SO IT WAS WHAT I THREW AT HIM. BUT MAKE NO MISTAKE ABOUT IT, IT WILL ***NOT*** BE ENOUGH.
WOLVERINE WILL BE COMING.

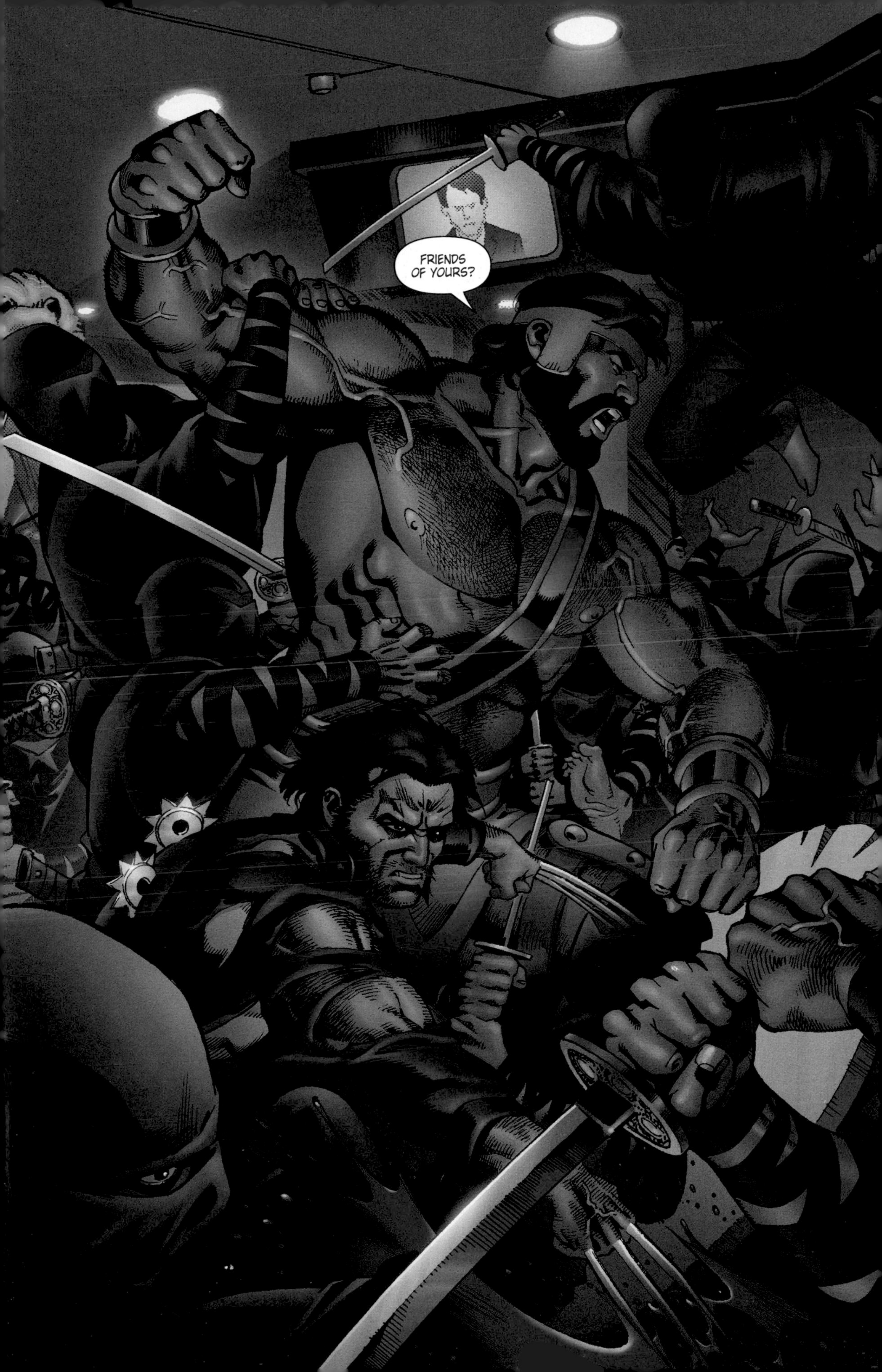
FRIENDS OF YOURS?

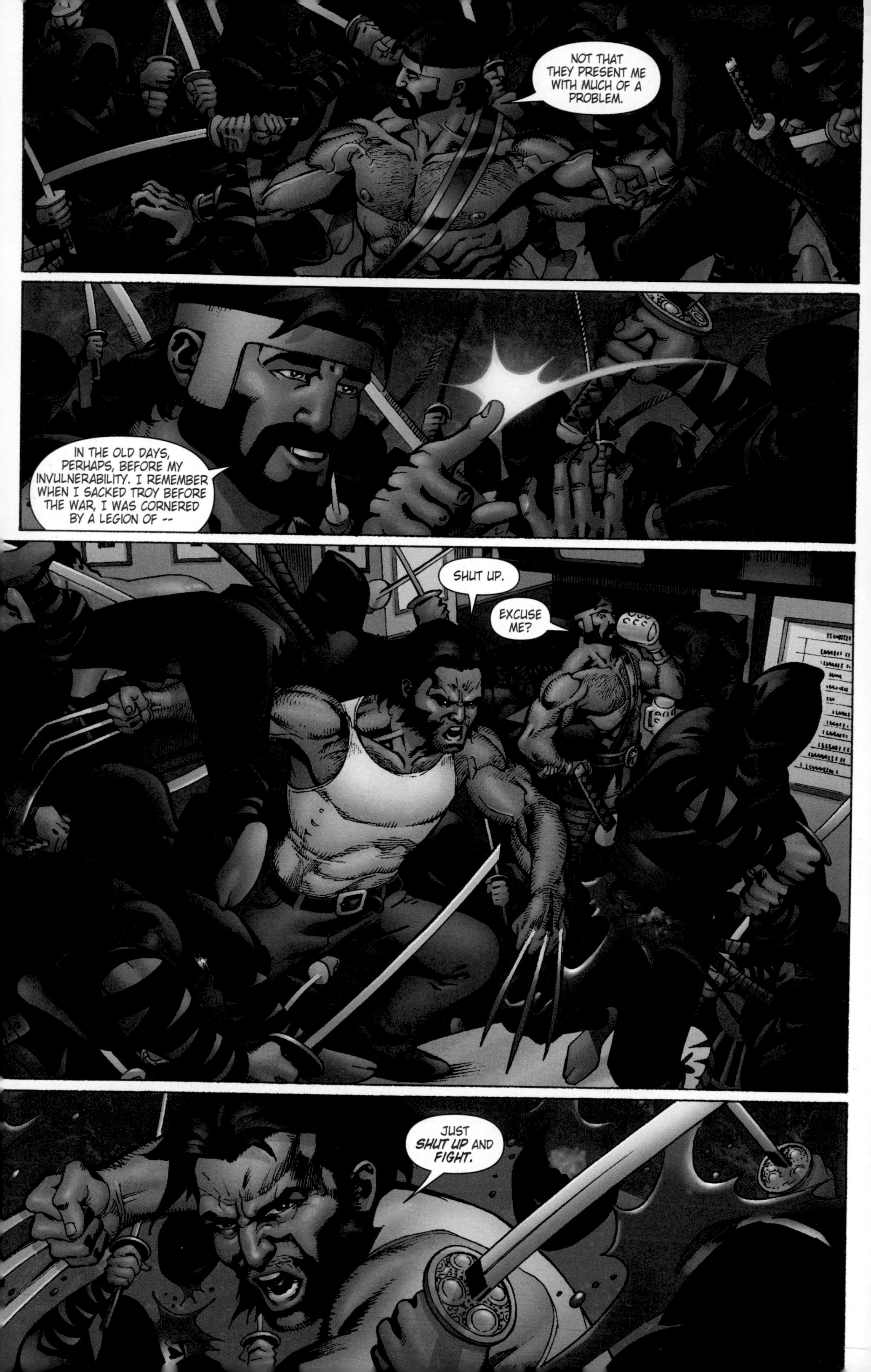
NOT THAT THEY PRESENT ME WITH MUCH OF A PROBLEM.
IN THE OLD DAYS, PERHAPS, BEFORE MY INVULNERABILITY. I REMEMBER WHEN I SACKED TROY BEFORE THE WAR, I WAS CORNERED BY A LEGION OF --
SHUT UP.
EXCUSE ME?
JUST SHUT UP AND FIGHT.

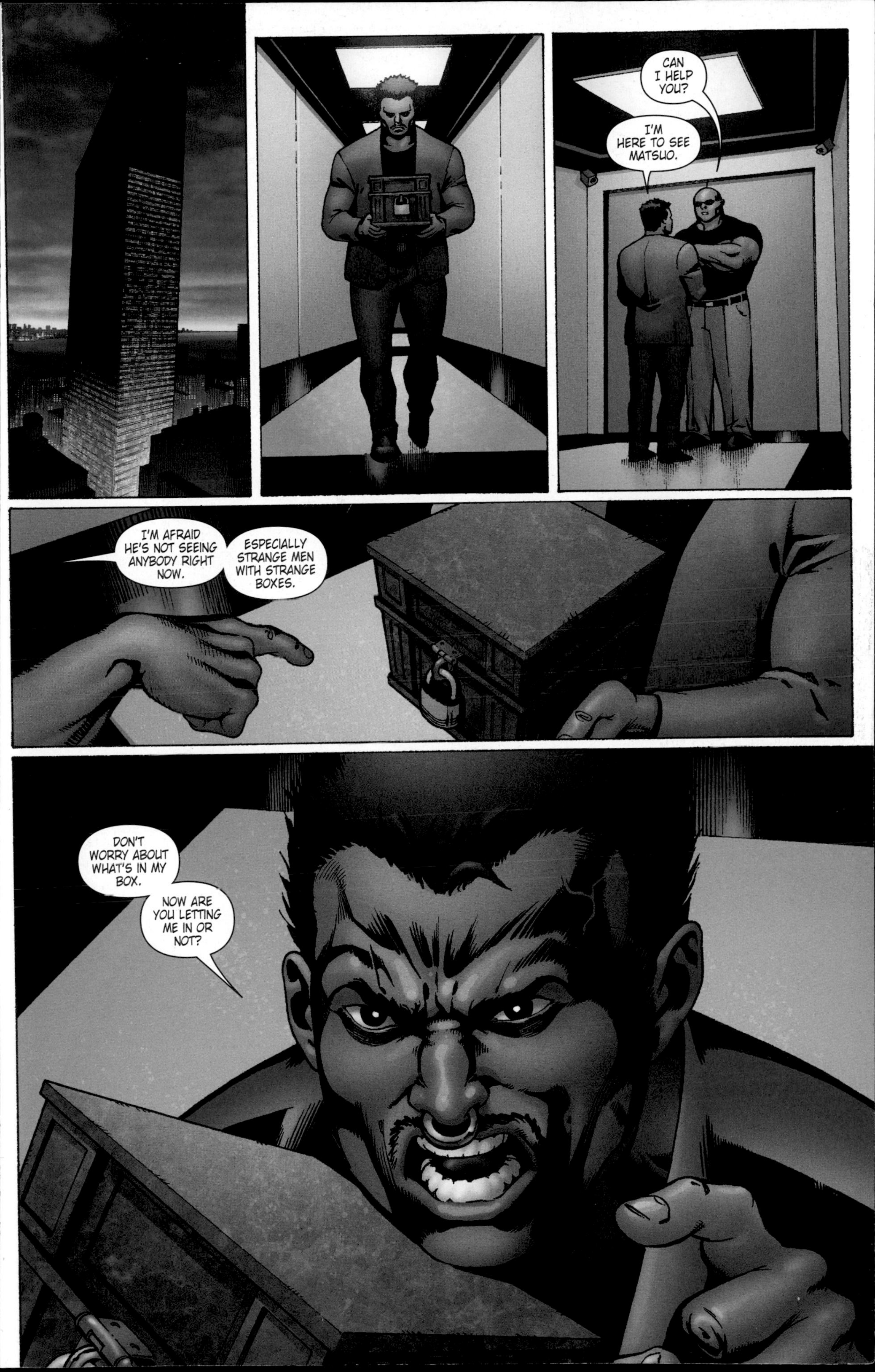
CAN I HELP YOU?
I'M HERE TO SEE MATSUO.
I'M AFRAID HE'S NOT SEEING ANYBODY RIGHT NOW.
ESPECIALLY STRANGE MEN WITH STRANGE BOXES.
DON'T WORRY ABOUT WHAT'S IN MY BOX.
NOW ARE YOU LETTING ME IN OR NOT?

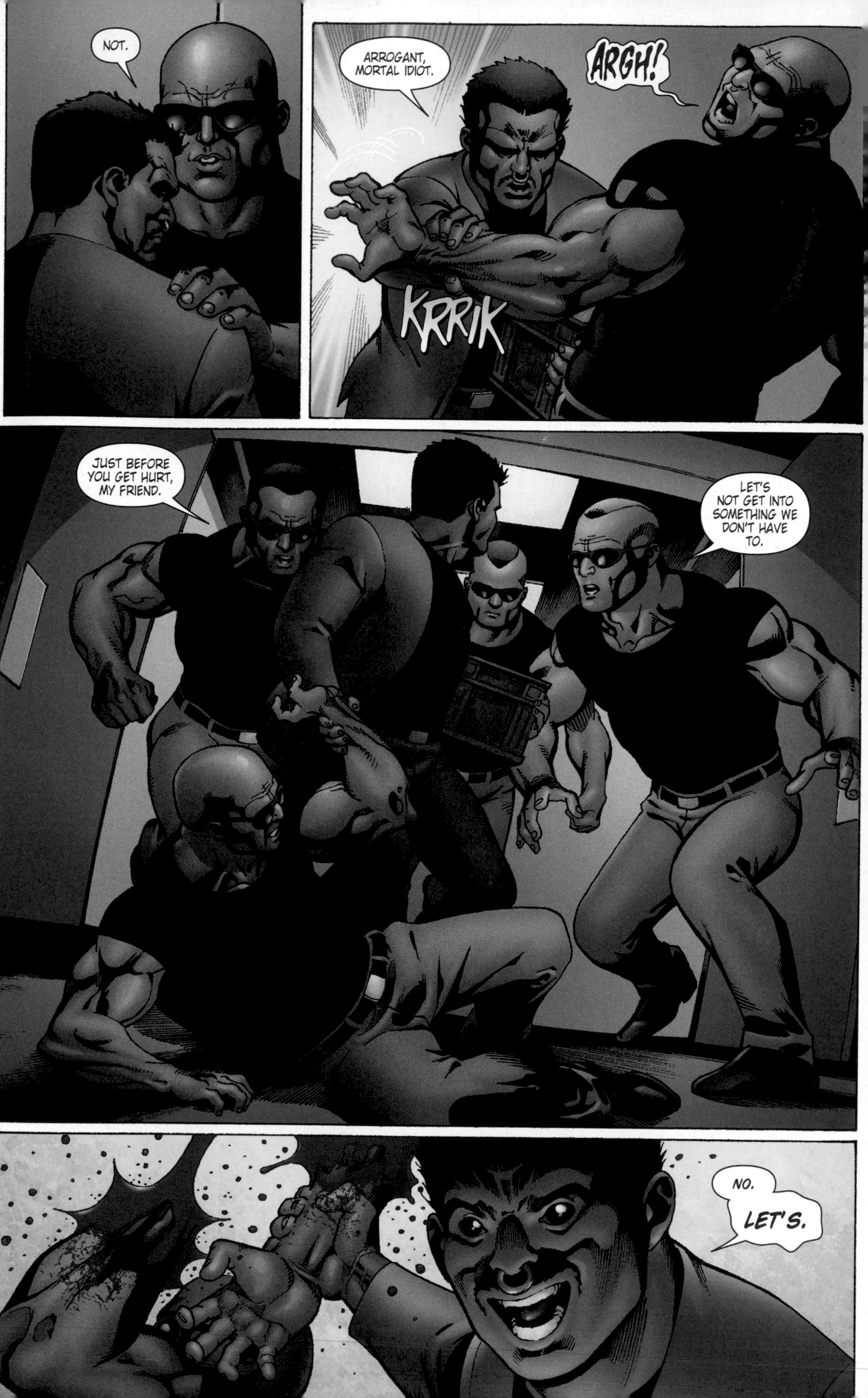
NOT.
ARROGANT, MORTAL IDIOT.
ARGH!
KRRIK
JUST BEFORE YOU GET HURT, MY FRIEND.
LET'S NOT GET INTO SOMETHING WE DON'T HAVE TO.
NO.
LET'S.

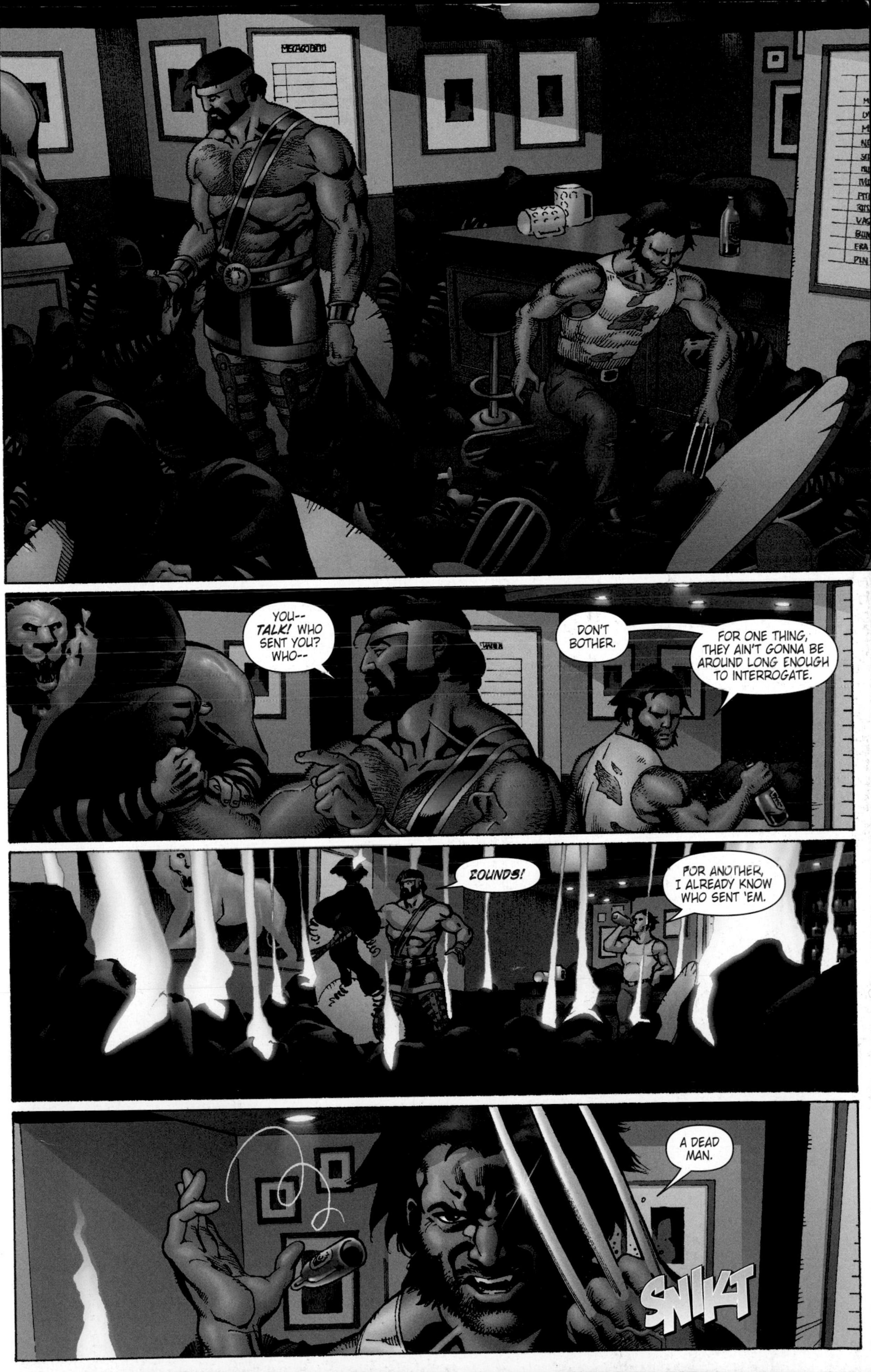

YOU-- TALK! WHO SENT YOU? WHO--
DON'T BOTHER.
FOR ONE THING, THEY AIN'T GONNA BE AROUND LONG ENOUGH TO INTERROGATE.
ZOUNDS!
FOR ANOTHER, I ALREADY KNOW WHO SENT 'EM.
A DEAD MAN.
SNIKT

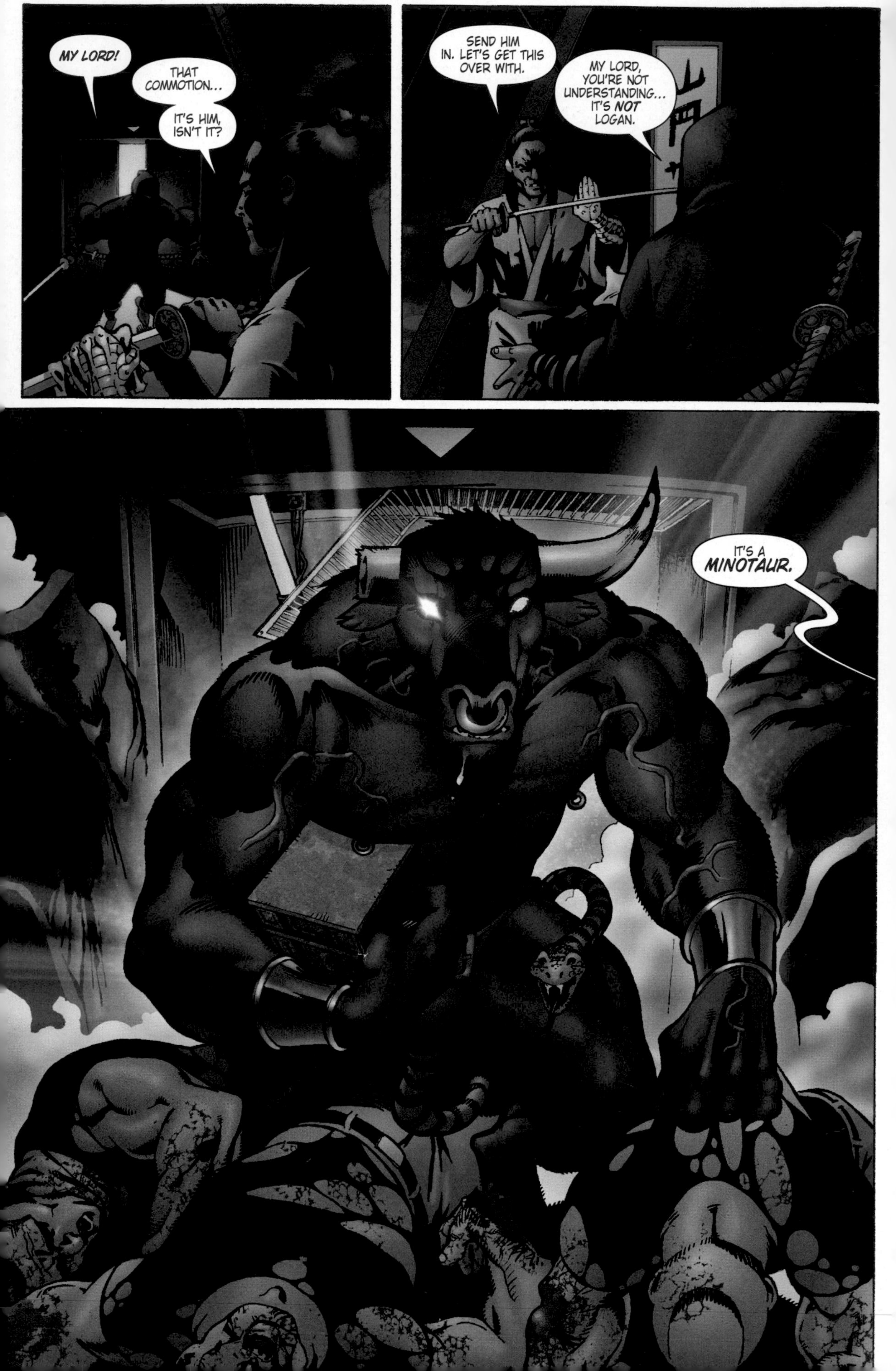
MY LORD!
THAT COMMOTION...
IT'S HIM, ISN'T IT?
SEND HIM IN. LET'S GET THIS OVER WITH.
MY LORD, YOU'RE NOT UNDERSTANDING... IT'S NOT LOGAN.
IT'S A MINOTAUR.

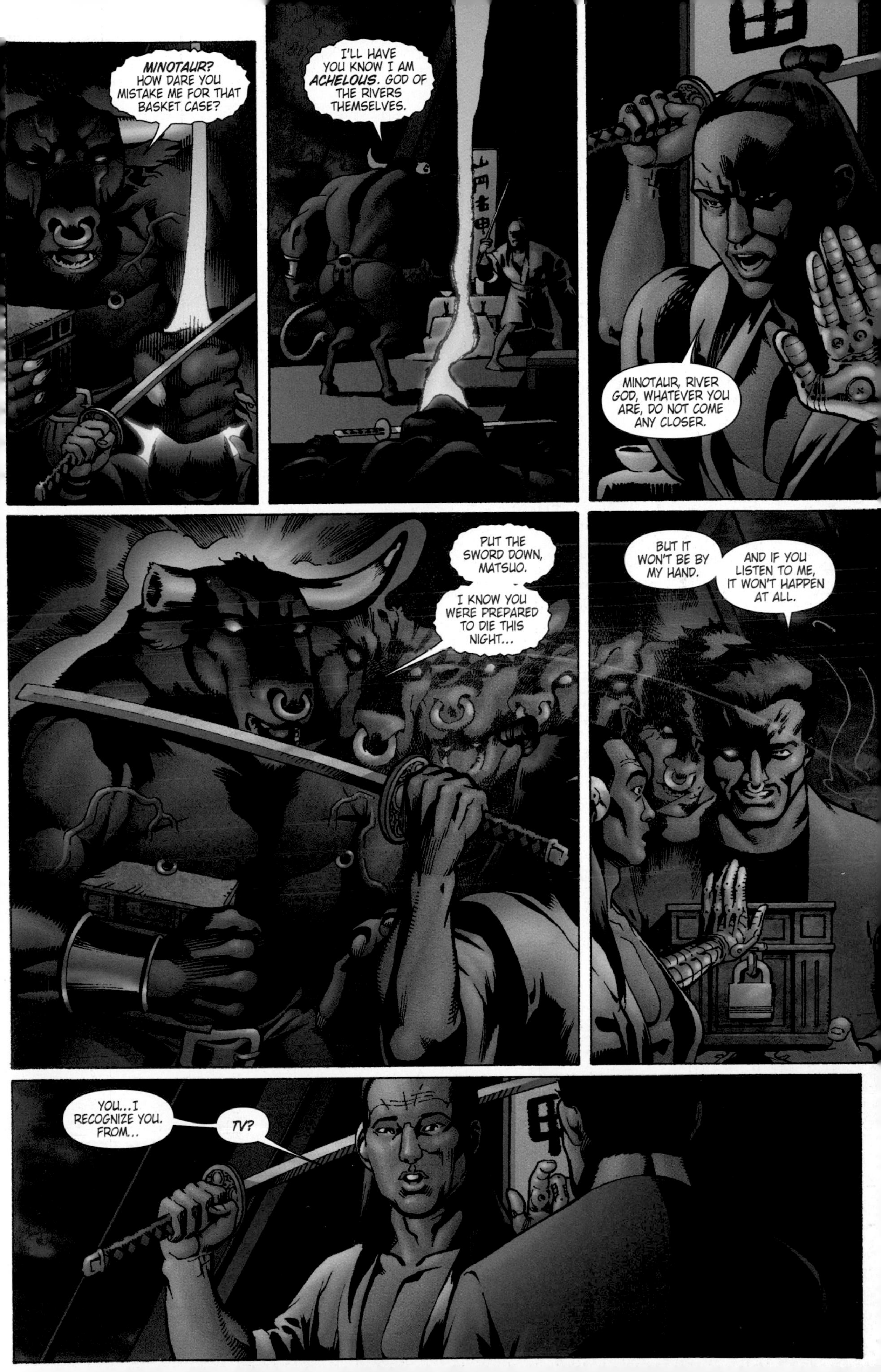
MINOTAUR? HOW DARE YOU MISTAKE ME FOR THAT BASKET CASE?
I'LL HAVE YOU KNOW I AM ACHELOUS. GOD OF THE RIVERS THEMSELVES.
MINOTAUR, RIVER GOD, WHATEVER YOU ARE, DO NOT COME ANY CLOSER.
PUT THE SWORD DOWN, MATSUO.
I KNOW YOU WERE PREPARED TO DIE THIS NIGHT...
BUT IT WON'T BE BY MY HAND.
AND IF YOU LISTEN TO ME, IT WON'T HAPPEN AT ALL.
YOU...I RECOGNIZE YOU. FROM...
TV?

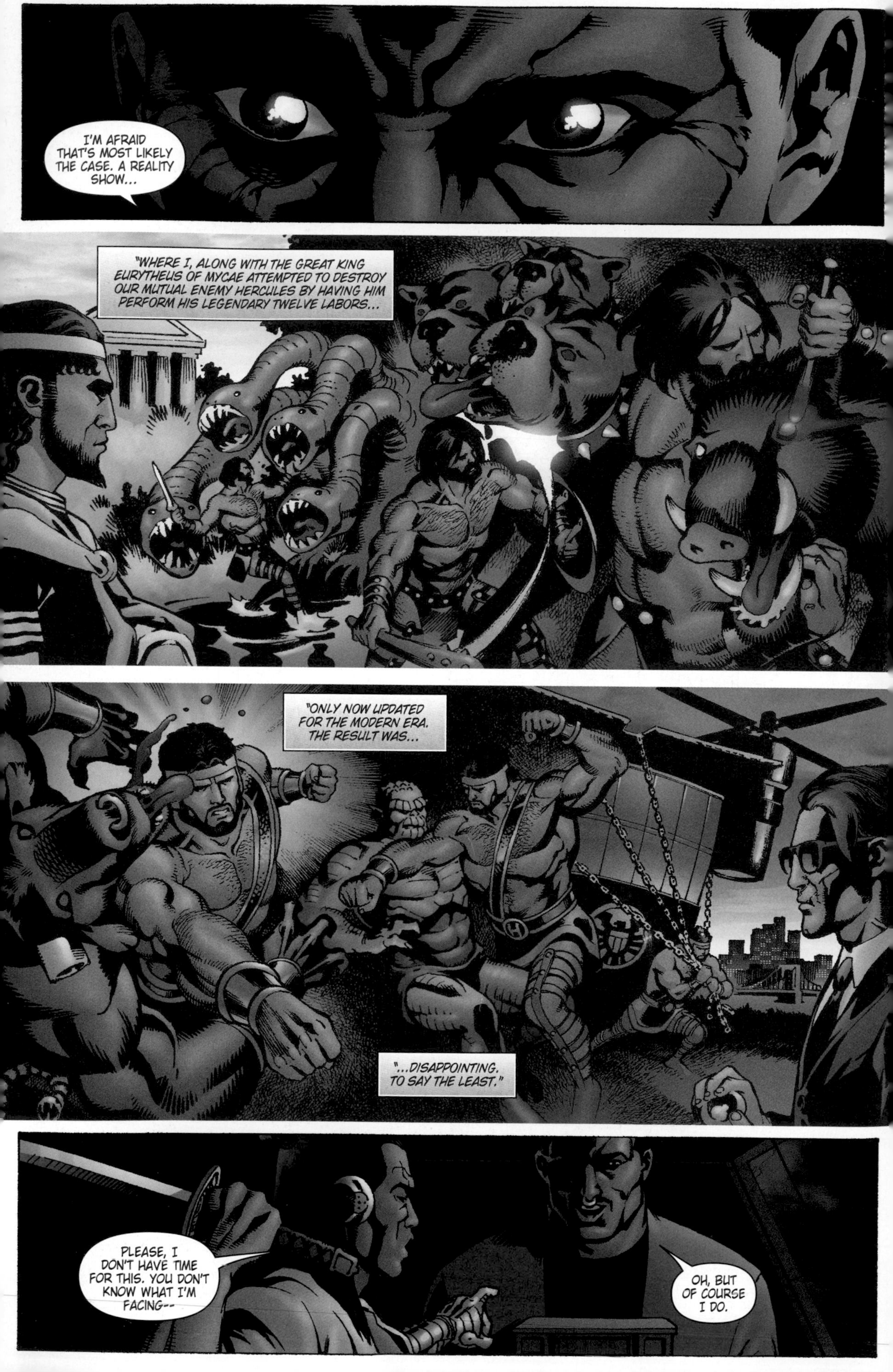
I'M AFRAID THAT'S MOST LIKELY THE CASE. A REALITY SHOW...
"WHERE I, ALONG WITH THE GREAT KING EURYTHEUS OF MYCAE ATTEMPTED TO DESTROY OUR MUTUAL ENEMY HERCULES BY HAVING HIM PERFORM HIS LEGENDARY TWELVE LABORS...
"ONLY NOW UPDATED FOR THE MODERN ERA. THE RESULT WAS...
"...DISAPPOINTING. TO SAY THE LEAST."
PLEASE, I DON'T HAVE TIME FOR THIS. YOU DON'T KNOW WHAT I'M FACING--
OH, BUT OF COURSE I DO.

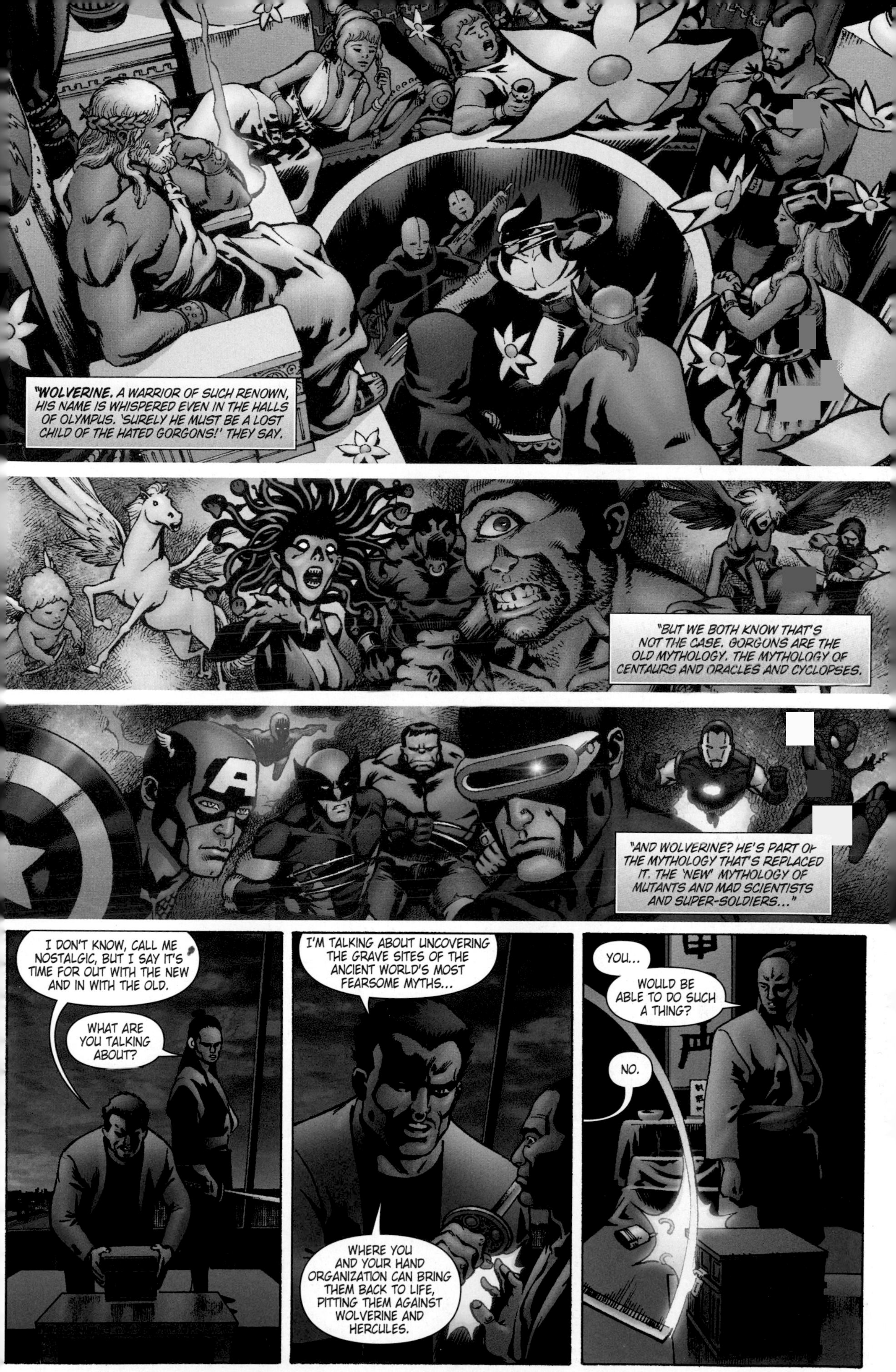
"WOLVERINE. A WARRIOR OF SUCH RENOWN, HIS NAME IS WHISPERED EVEN IN THE HALLS OF OLYMPUS. 'SURELY HE MUST BE A LOST CHILD OF THE HATED GORGONS!' THEY SAY.
"BUT WE BOTH KNOW THAT'S NOT THE CASE. GORGONS ARE THE OLD MYTHOLOGY. THE MYTHOLOGY OF CENTAURS AND ORACLES AND CYCLOPSES.
"AND WOLVERINE? HE'S PART OF THE MYTHOLOGY THAT'S REPLACED IT. THE 'NEW' MYTHOLOGY OF MUTANTS AND MAD SCIENTISTS AND SUPER-SOLDIERS..."
I DON'T KNOW, CALL ME NOSTALGIC, BUT I SAY IT'S TIME FOR OUT WITH THE NEW AND IN WITH THE OLD.
WHAT ARE YOU TALKING ABOUT?
I'M TALKING ABOUT UNCOVERING THE GRAVE SITES OF THE ANCIENT WORLD'S MOST FEARSOME MYTHS...
WHERE YOU AND YOUR HAND ORGANIZATION CAN BRING THEM BACK TO LIFE, PITTING THEM AGAINST WOLVERINE AND HERCULES.
YOU...
WOULD BE ABLE TO DO SUCH A THING?
NO.

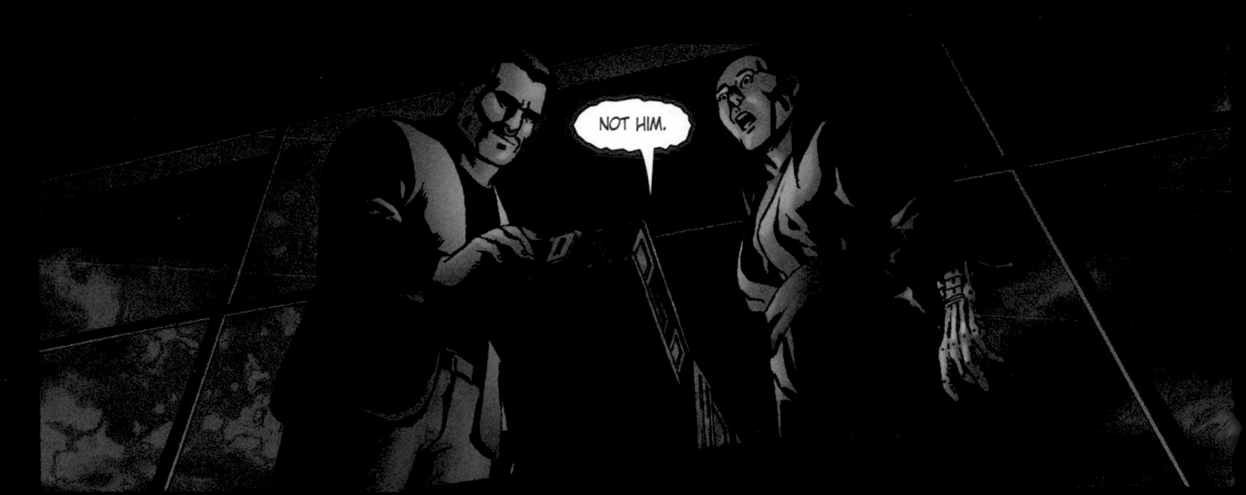
NOT HIM.

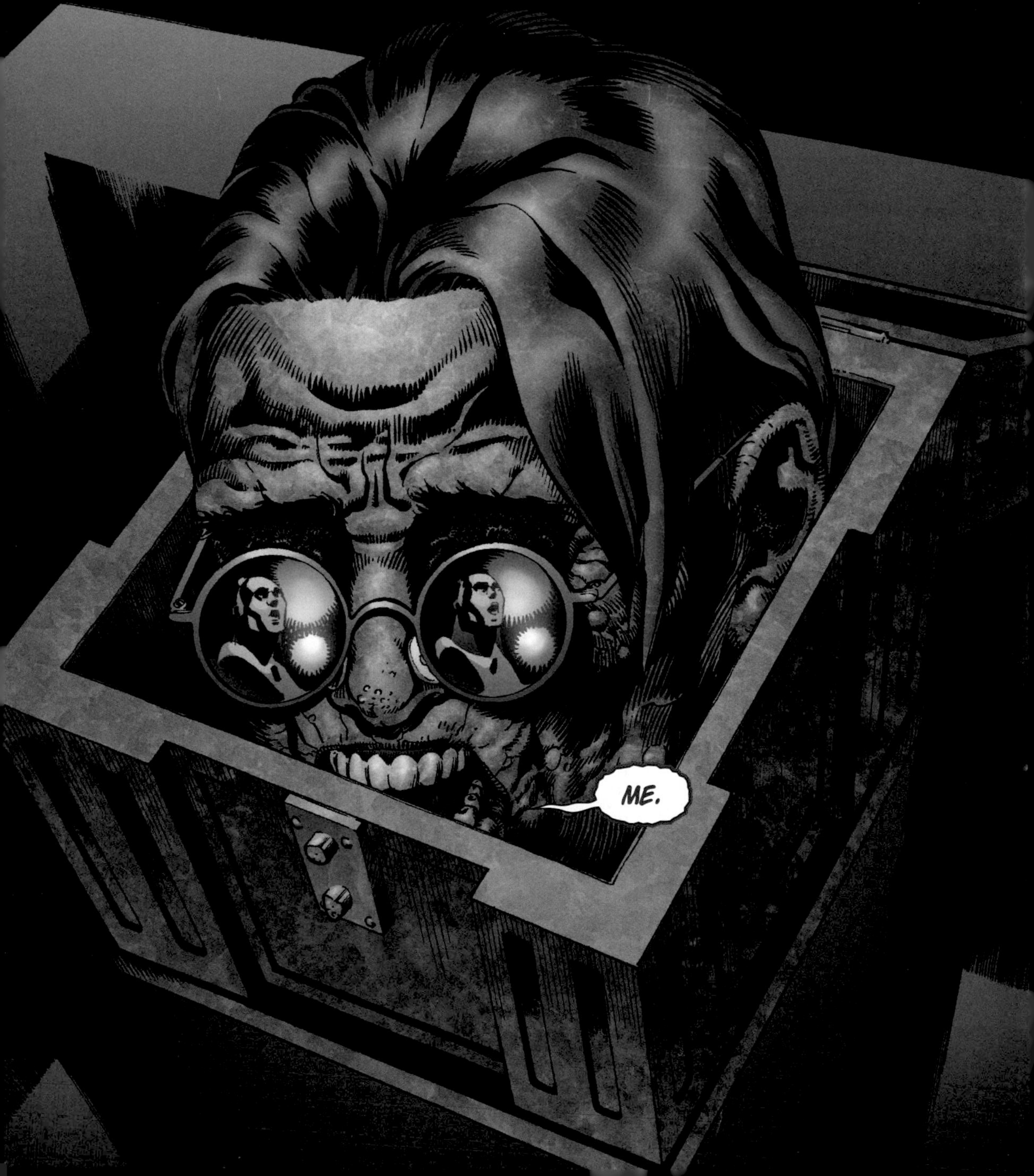
ME.

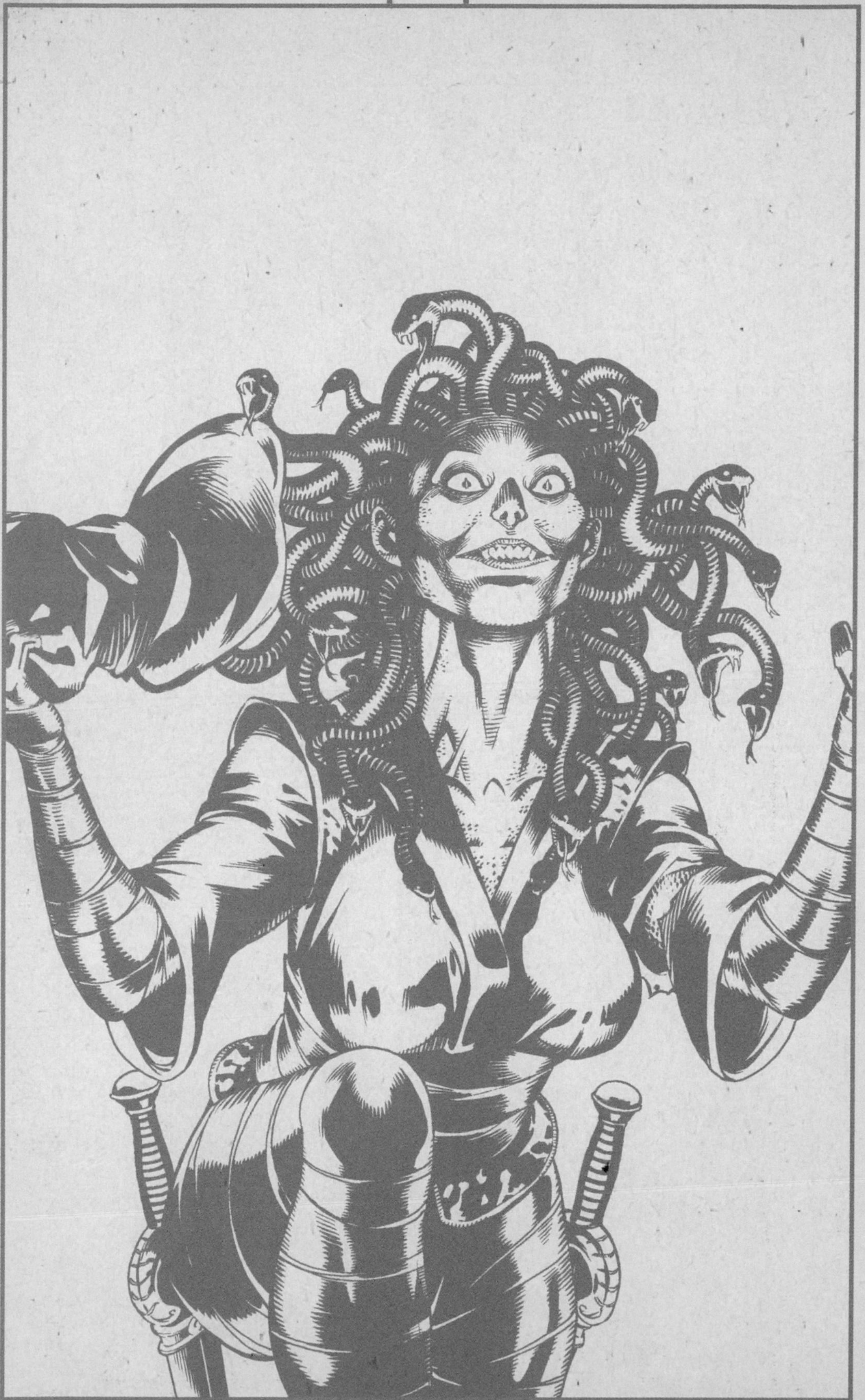

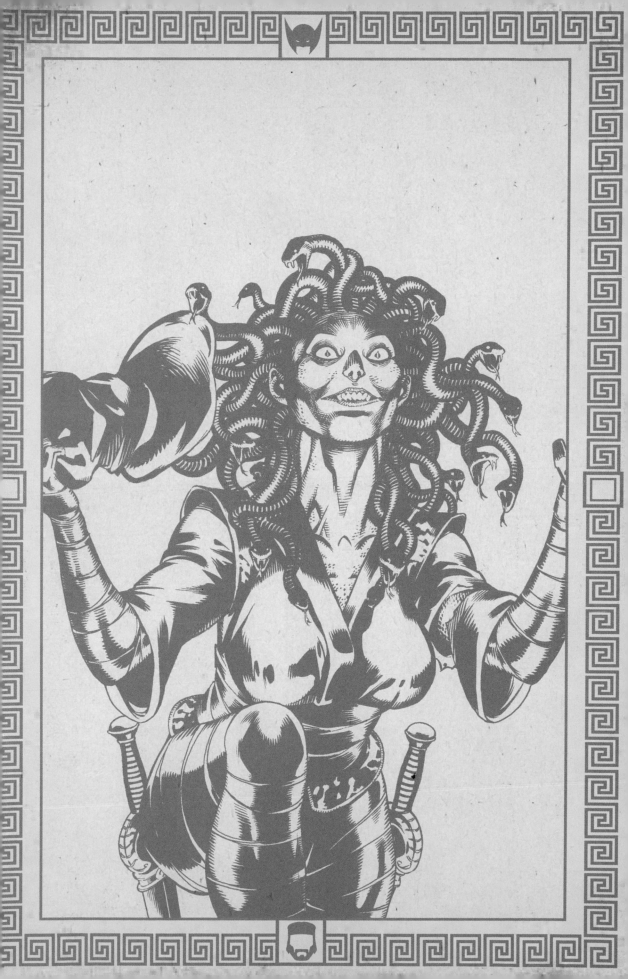

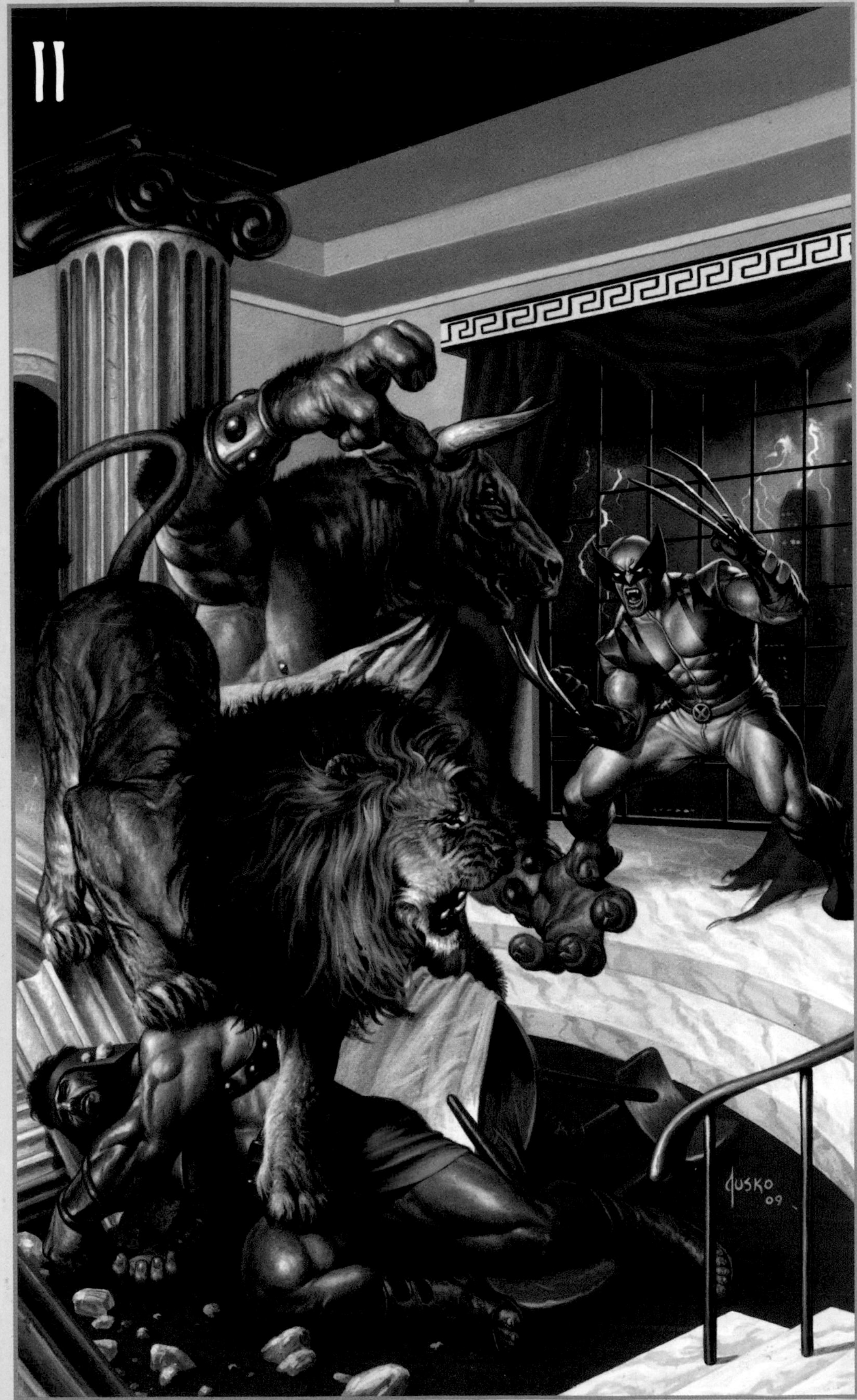
II

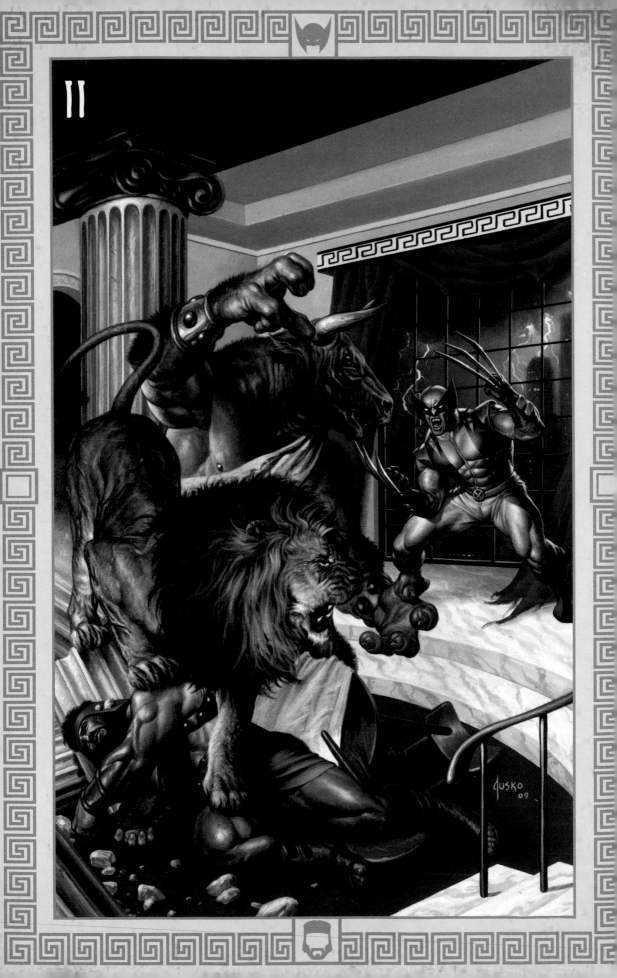

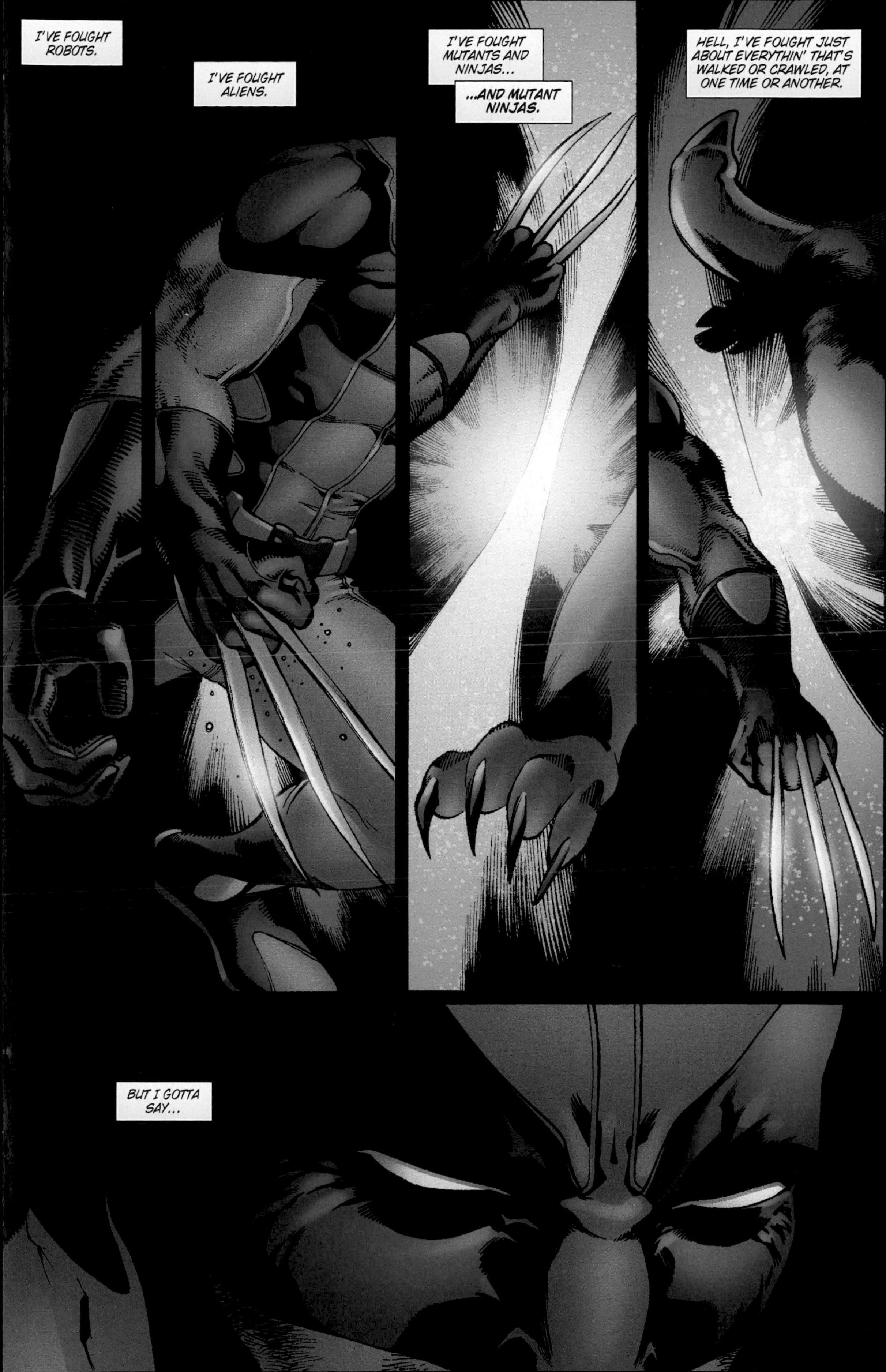
I'VE FOUGHT ROBOTS.
I'VE FOUGHT ALIENS.
I'VE FOUGHT MUTANTS AND NINJAS...
...AND MUTANT NINJAS.
HELL, I'VE FOUGHT JUST ABOUT EVERYTHIN' THAT'S WALKED OR CRAWLED, AT ONE TIME OR ANOTHER.
BUT I GOTTA SAY...

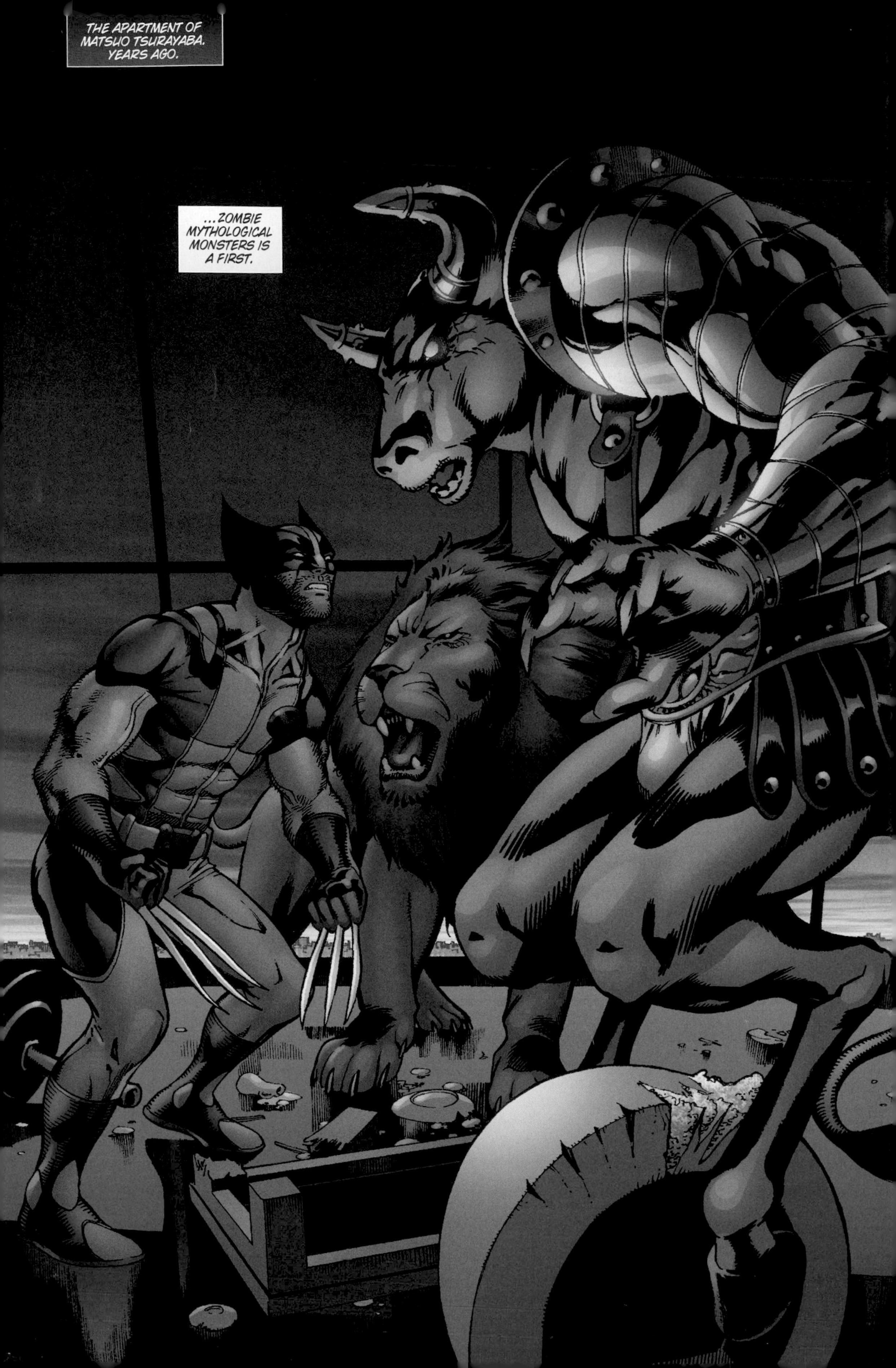
THE APARTMENT OF MATSUO TSURAYABA. YEARS AGO.
...ZOMBIE MYTHOLOGICAL MONSTERS IS A FIRST.

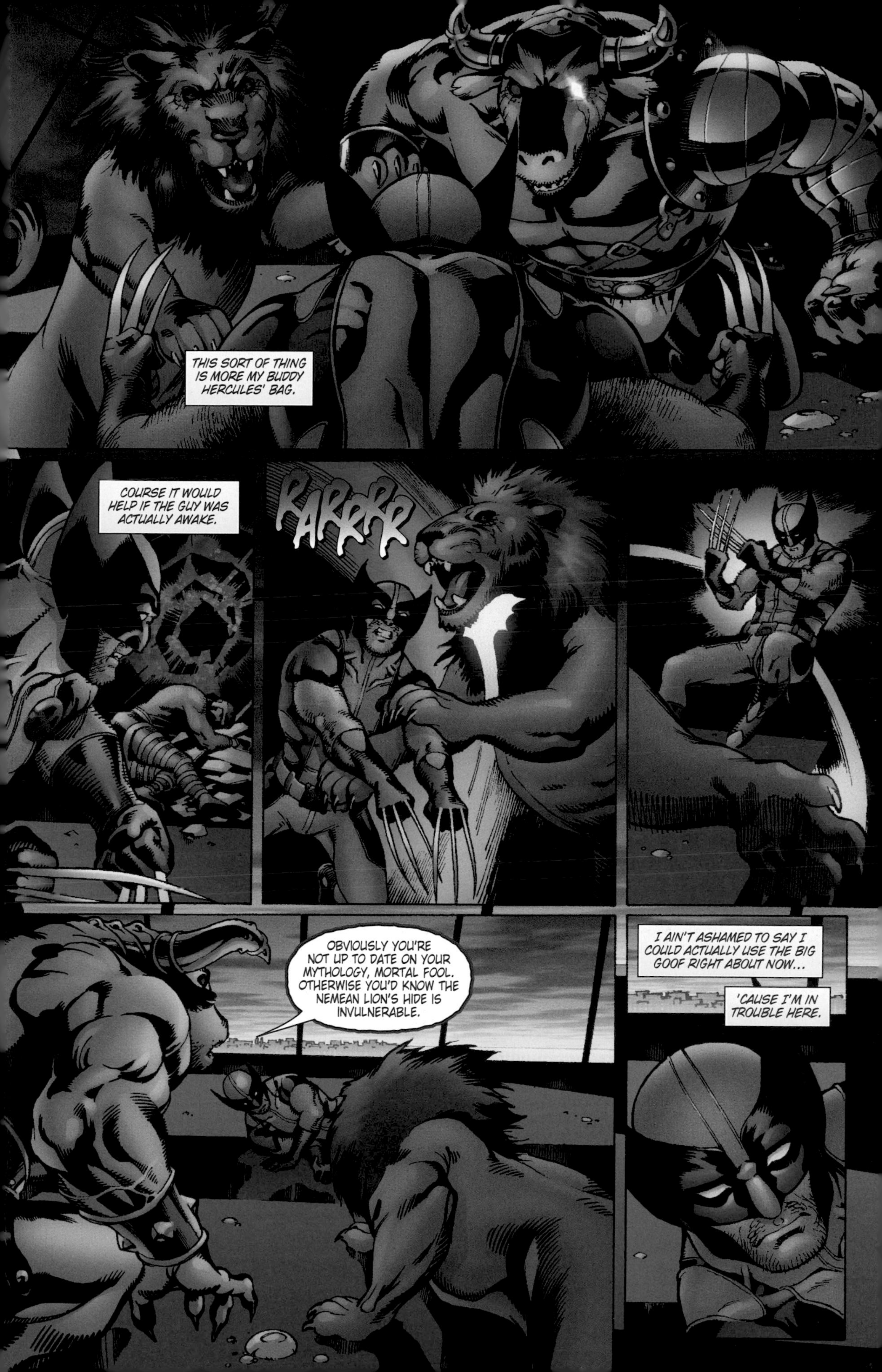
THIS SORT OF THING IS MORE MY BUDDY HERCULES' BAG.
COURSE IT WOULD HELP IF THE GUY WAS ACTUALLY AWAKE.
RARRRR
OBVIOUSLY YOU'RE NOT UP TO DATE ON YOUR MYTHOLOGY, MORTAL FOOL. OTHERWISE YOU'D KNOW THE NEMEAN LION'S HIDE IS INVULNERABLE.
I AIN'T ASHAMED TO SAY I COULD ACTUALLY USE THE BIG GOOF RIGHT ABOUT NOW...
'CAUSE I'M IN TROUBLE HERE.

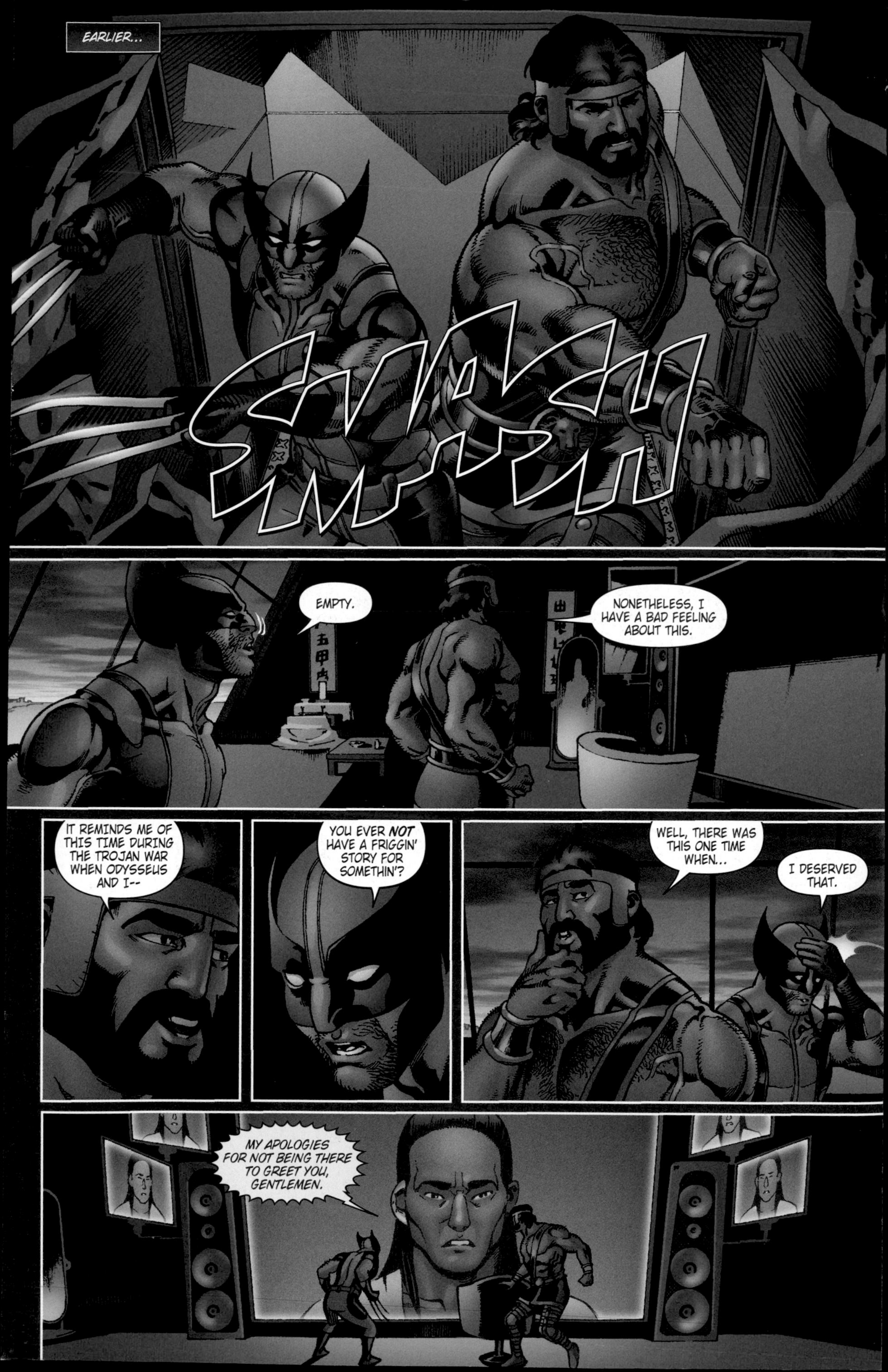
EARLIER...
SMASH
EMPTY.
NONETHELESS, I HAVE A BAD FEELING ABOUT THIS.
IT REMINDS ME OF THIS TIME DURING THE TROJAN WAR WHEN ODYSSEUS AND I--
YOU EVER NOT HAVE A FRIGGIN' STORY FOR SOMETHIN'?
WELL, THERE WAS THIS ONE TIME WHEN...
I DESERVED THAT.
MY APOLOGIES FOR NOT BEING THERE TO GREET YOU, GENTLEMEN.

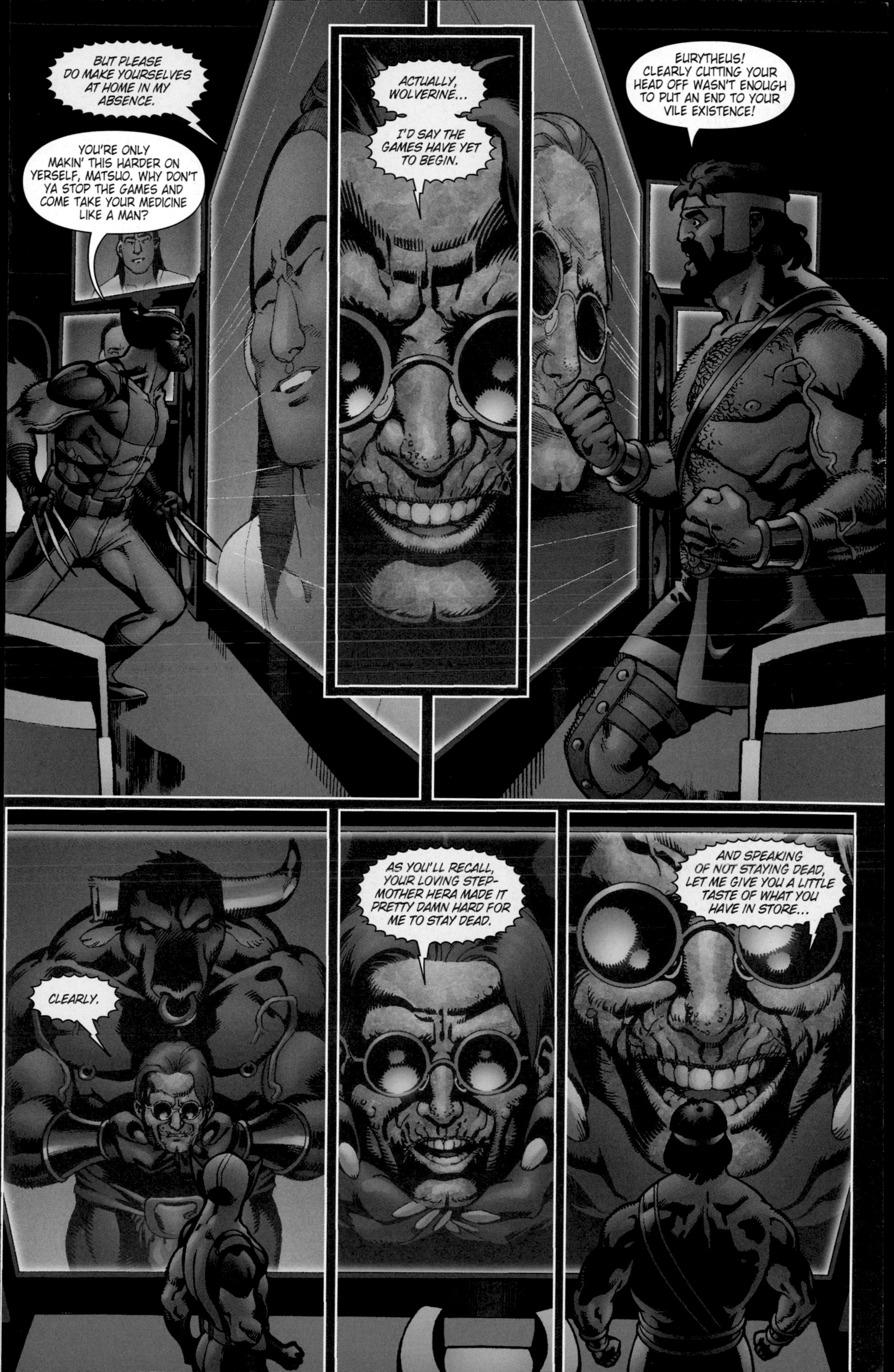
BUT PLEASE DO MAKE YOURSELVES AT HOME IN MY ABSENCE.
YOU'RE ONLY MAKIN' THIS HARDER ON YERSELF, MATSUO. WHY DON'T YA STOP THE GAMES AND COME TAKE YOUR MEDICINE LIKE A MAN?
ACTUALLY, WOLVERINE...
I'D SAY THE GAMES HAVE YET TO BEGIN.
EURYTHEUS! CLEARLY CUTTING YOUR HEAD OFF WASN'T ENOUGH TO PUT AN END TO YOUR VILE EXISTENCE!
CLEARLY.
AS YOU'LL RECALL, YOUR LOVING STEP-MOTHER HERA MADE IT PRETTY DAMN HARD FOR ME TO STAY DEAD.
AND SPEAKING OF NOT STAYING DEAD, LET ME GIVE YOU A LITTLE TASTE OF WHAT YOU HAVE IN STORE...

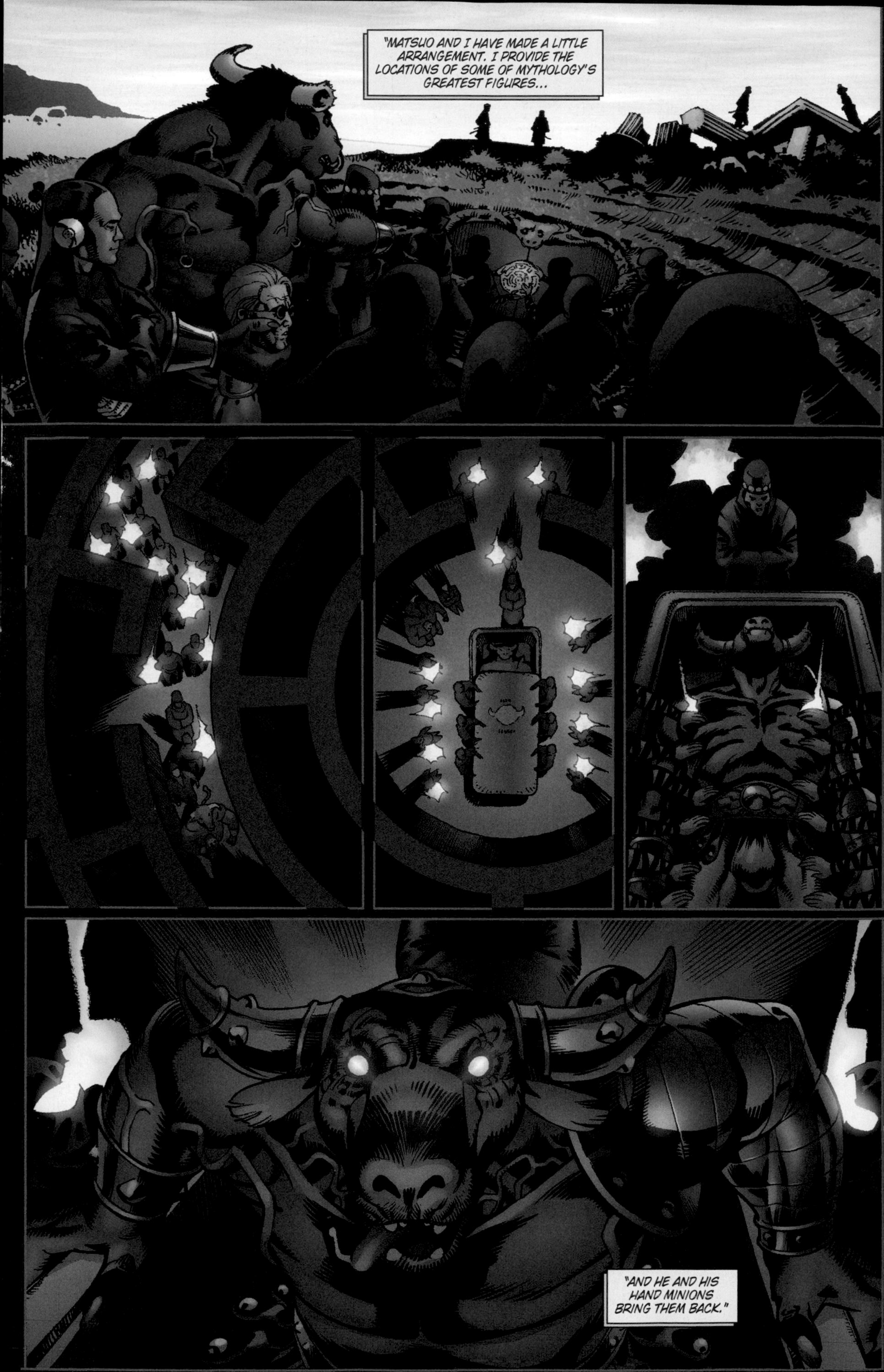
"MATSUO AND I HAVE MADE A LITTLE ARRANGEMENT. I PROVIDE THE LOCATIONS OF SOME OF MYTHOLOGY'S GREATEST FIGURES...
"AND HE AND HIS HAND MINIONS BRING THEM BACK."

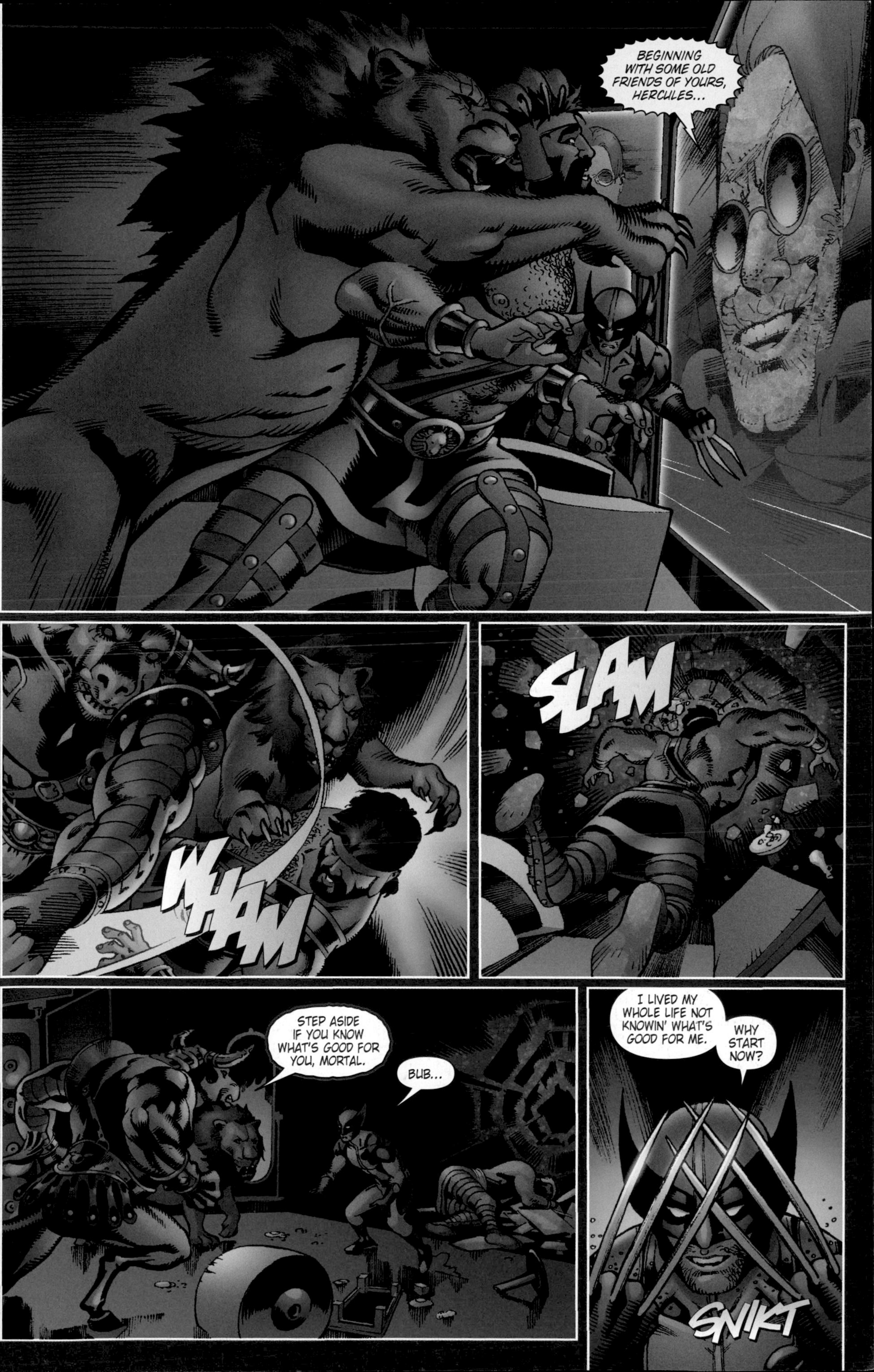
BEGINNING WITH SOME OLD FRIENDS OF YOURS, HERCULES...
WHAM
SLAM
STEP ASIDE IF YOU KNOW WHAT'S GOOD FOR YOU, MORTAL.
BUB...
I LIVED MY WHOLE LIFE NOT KNOWIN' WHAT'S GOOD FOR ME.
WHY START NOW?
SNIKT

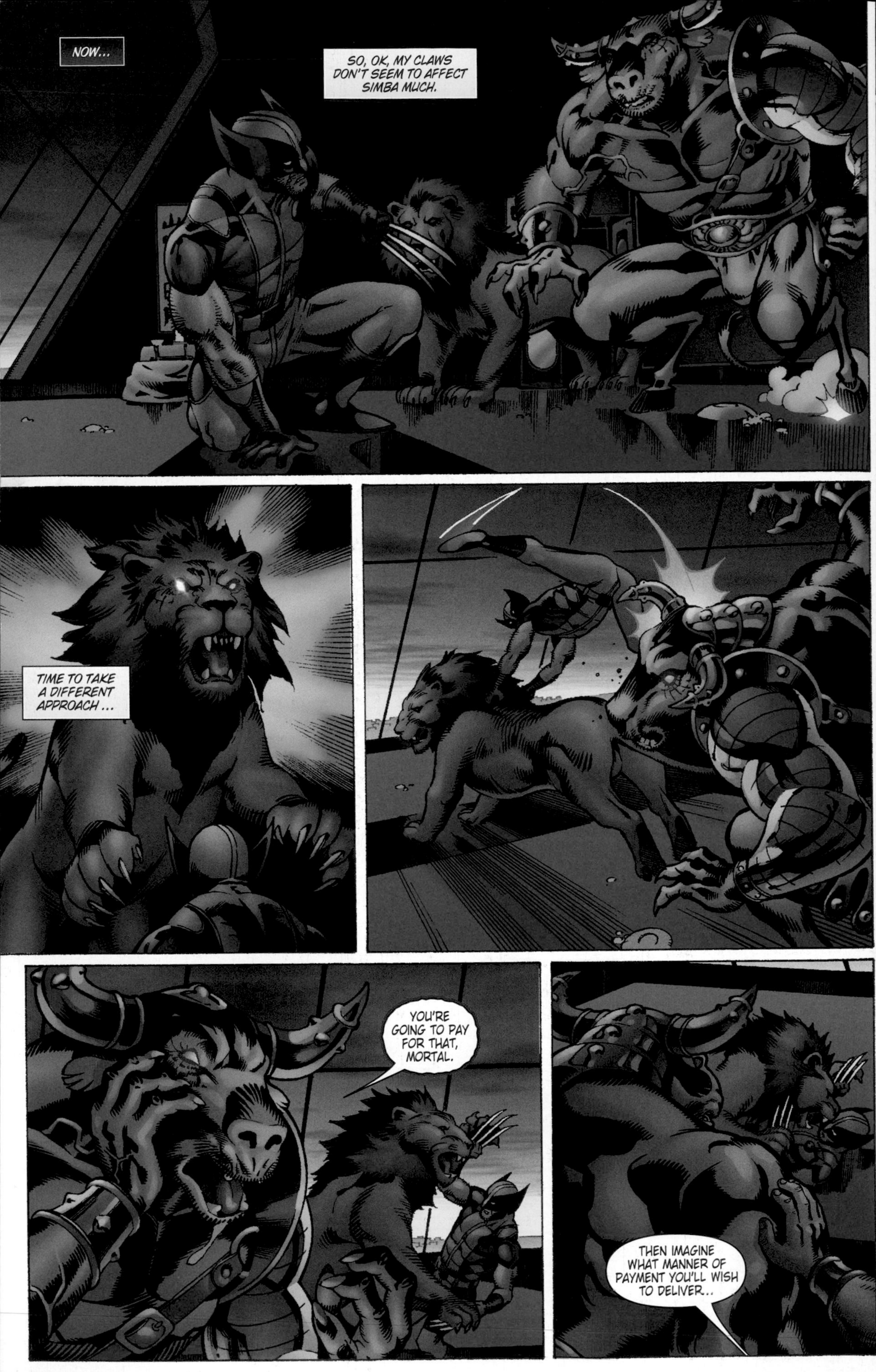
NOW...
SO, OK, MY CLAWS DON'T SEEM TO AFFECT SIMBA MUCH.
TIME TO TAKE A DIFFERENT APPROACH...
YOU'RE GOING TO PAY FOR THAT, MORTAL.
THEN IMAGINE WHAT MANNER OF PAYMENT YOU'LL WISH TO DELIVER..

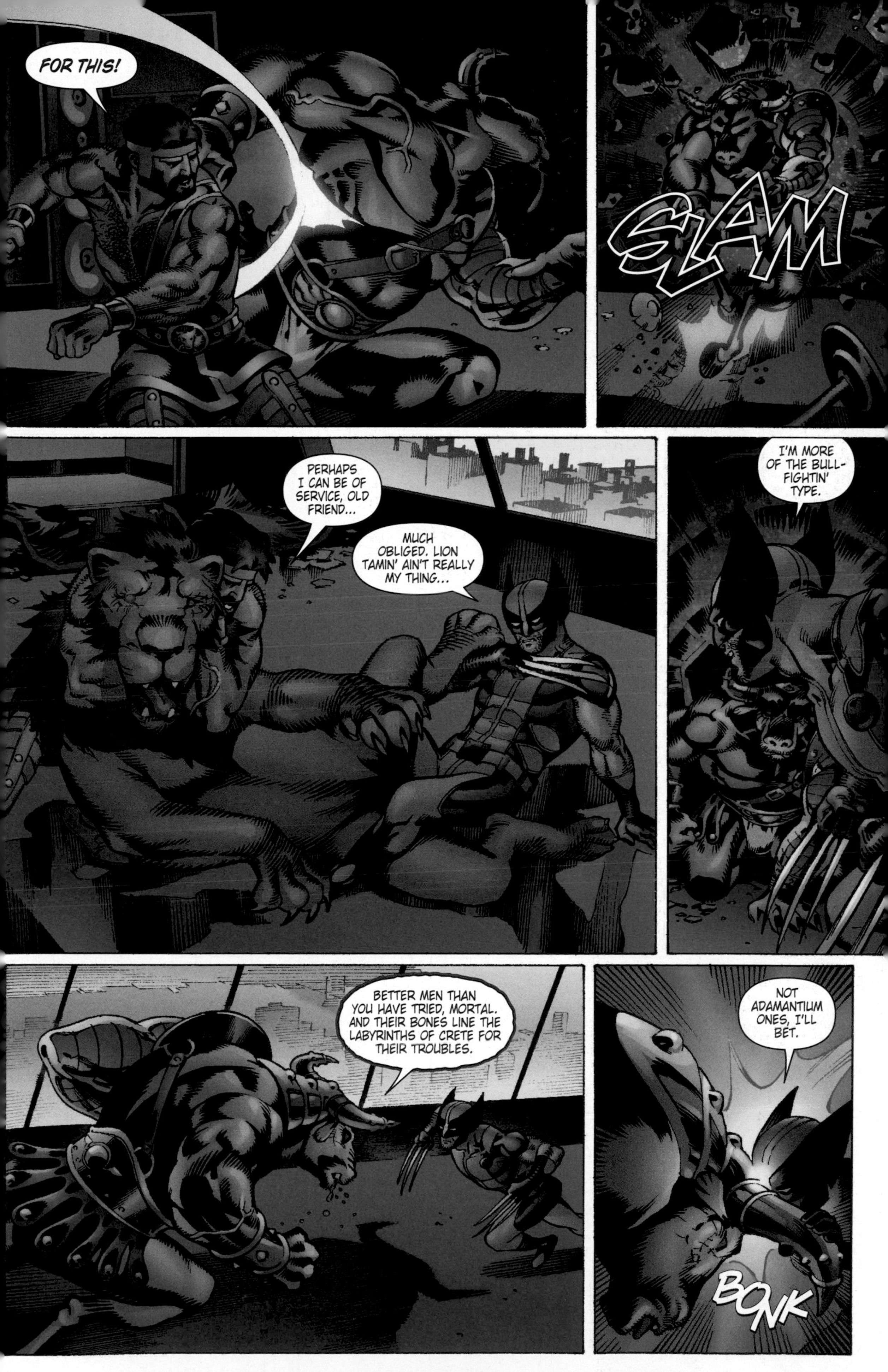
FOR THIS!
SLAM
PERHAPS I CAN BE OF SERVICE, OLD FRIEND...
MUCH OBLIGED. LION TAMIN' AIN'T REALLY MY THING...
I'M MORE OF THE BULL-FIGHTIN' TYPE.
BETTER MEN THAN YOU HAVE TRIED, MORTAL. AND THEIR BONES LINE THE LABYRINTHS OF CRETE FOR THEIR TROUBLES.
NOT ADAMANTIUM ONES, I'LL BET.
BONK

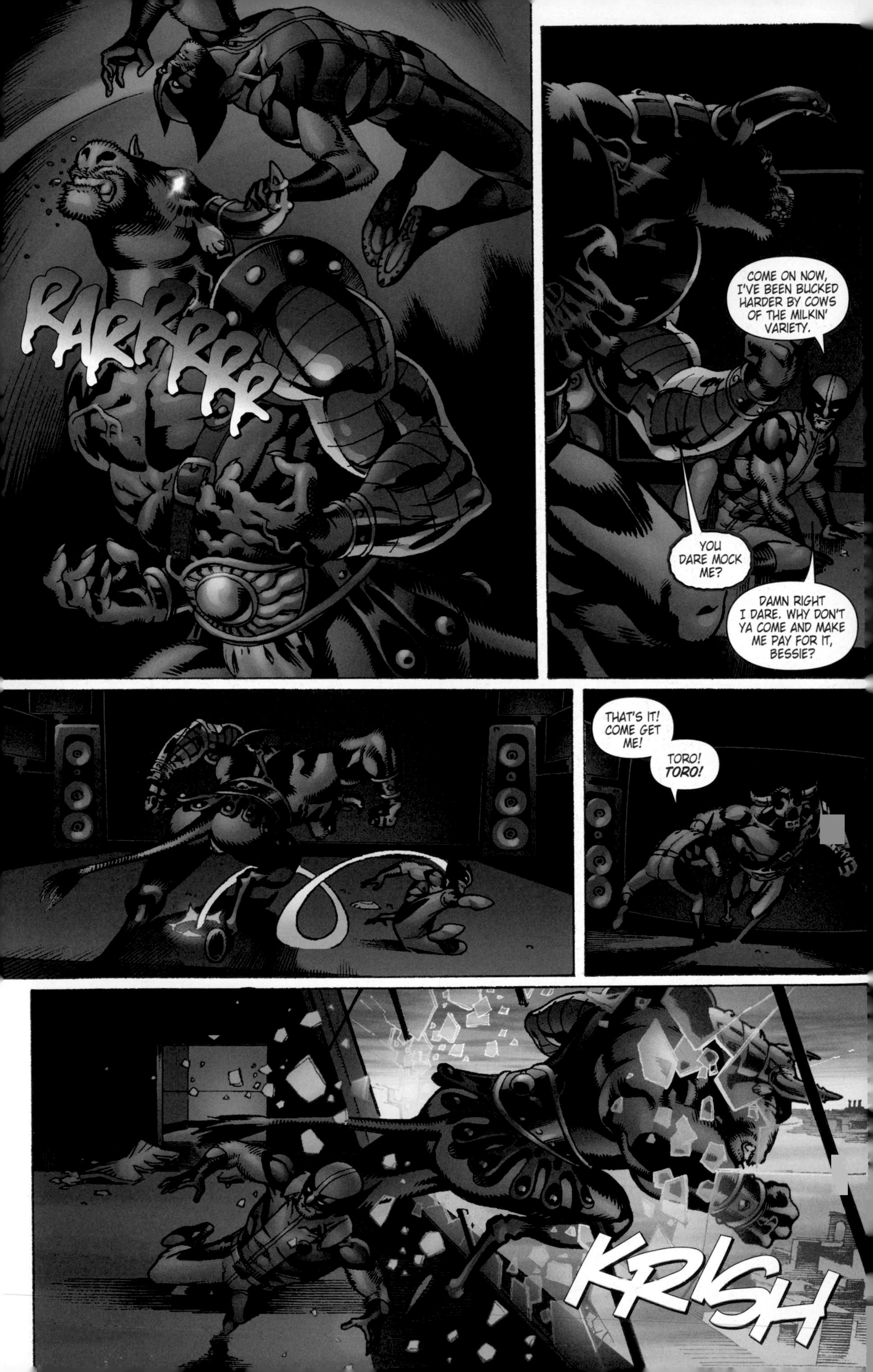
RARRRRR
COME ON NOW, I'VE BEEN BUCKED HARDER BY COWS OF THE MILKIN' VARIETY.
YOU DARE MOCK ME?
DAMN RIGHT I DARE. WHY DON'T YA COME AND MAKE ME PAY FOR IT, BESSIE?
THAT'S IT! COME GET ME!
TORO! TORO!
KRISH

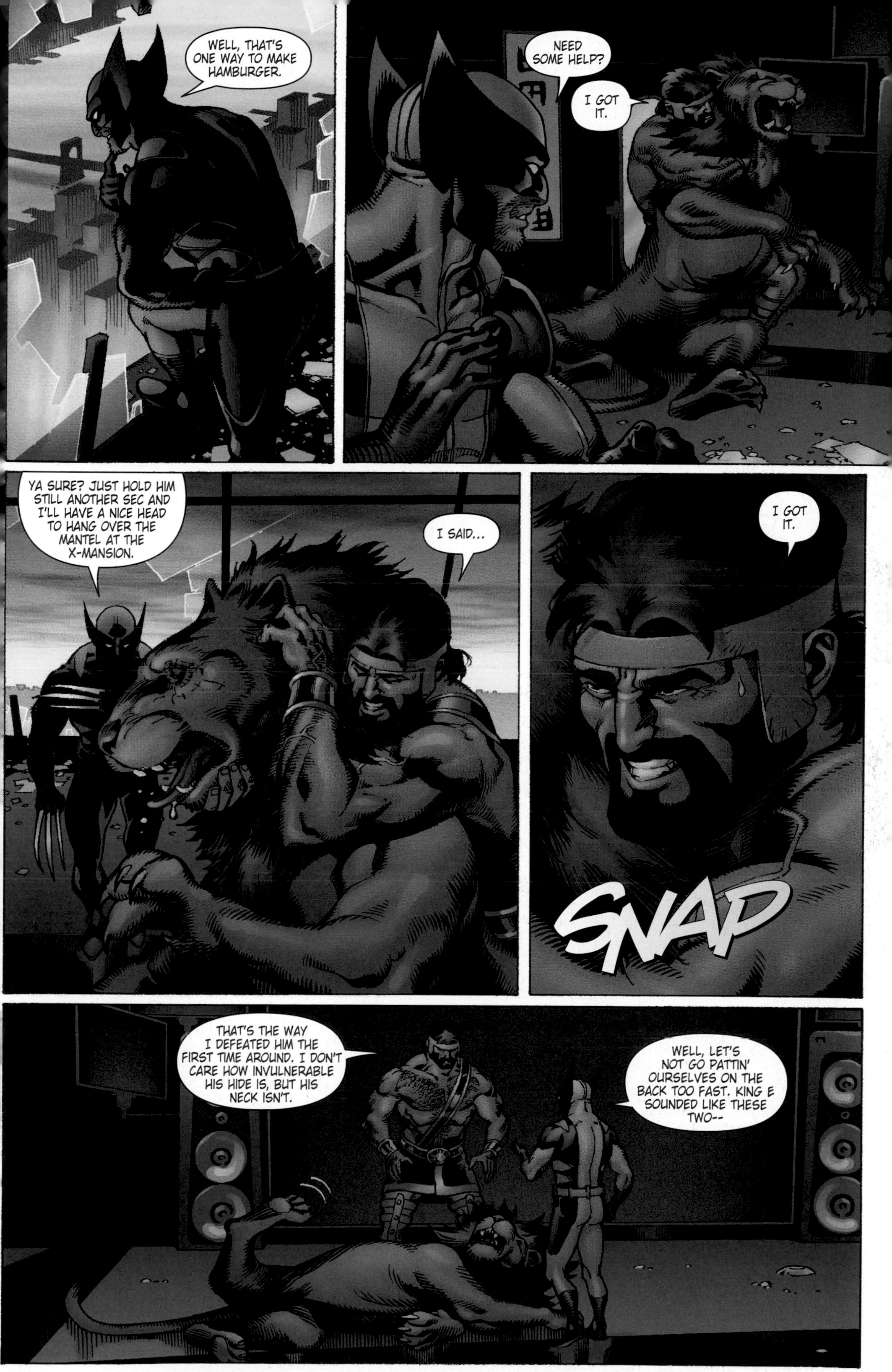
WELL, THAT'S ONE WAY TO MAKE HAMBURGER.
NEED SOME HELP?
I GOT IT.
YA SURE? JUST HOLD HIM STILL ANOTHER SEC AND I'LL HAVE A NICE HEAD TO HANG OVER THE MANTEL AT THE X-MANSION.
I SAID...
I GOT IT.
SNAP
THAT'S THE WAY I DEFEATED HIM THE FIRST TIME AROUND. I DON'T CARE HOW INVULNERABLE HIS HIDE IS, BUT HIS NECK ISN'T.
WELL, LET'S NOT GO PATTIN' OURSELVES ON THE BACK TOO FAST. KING E SOUNDED LIKE THESE TWO--

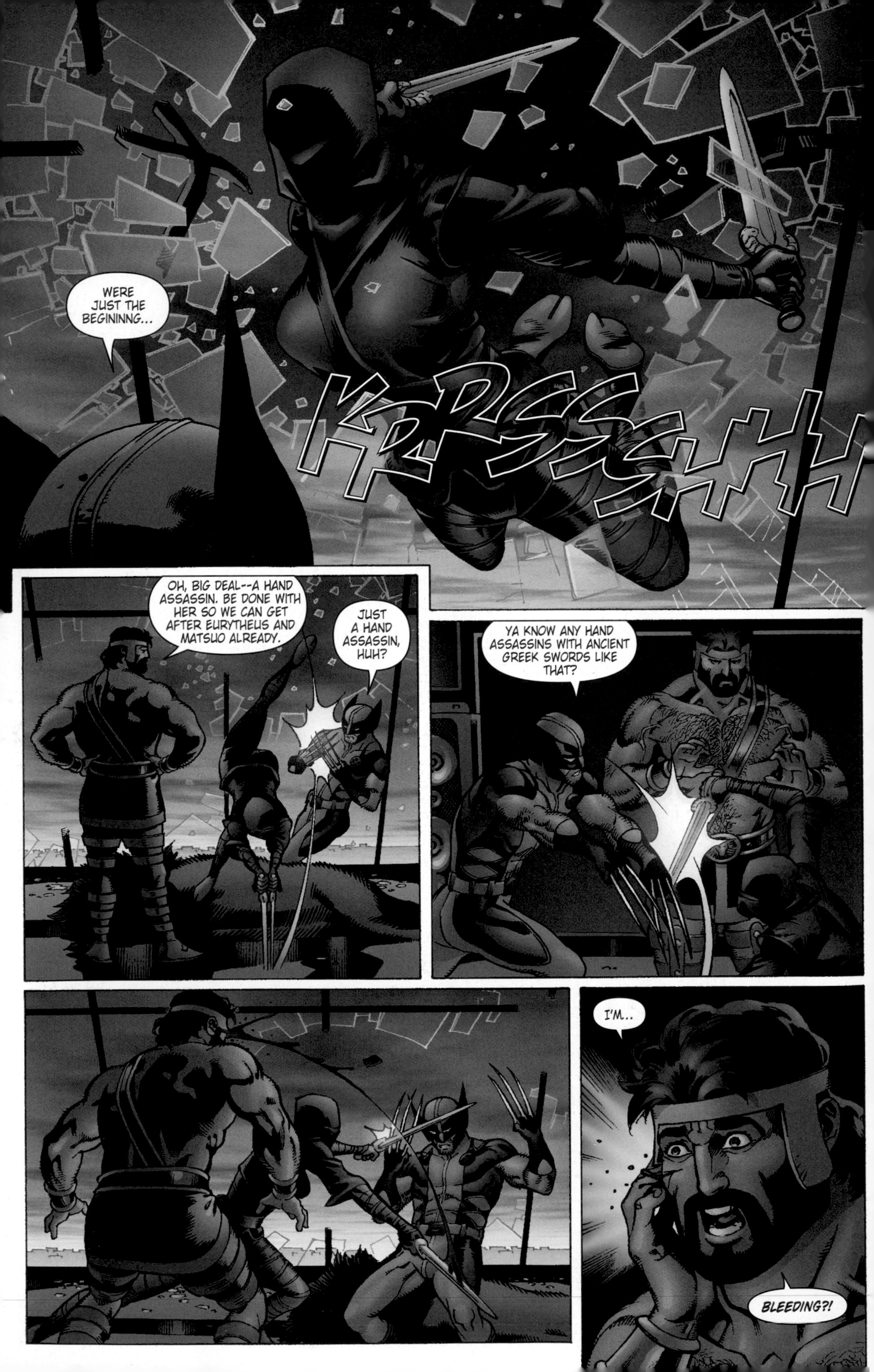
WERE JUST THE BEGININNG...
KRSSSHH
OH, BIG DEAL--A HAND ASSASSIN. BE DONE WITH HER SO WE CAN GET AFTER EURYTHEUS AND MATSUO ALREADY.
JUST A HAND ASSASSIN, HUH?
YA KNOW ANY HAND ASSASSINS WITH ANCIENT GREEK SWORDS LIKE THAT?
I'M...
BLEEDING?!

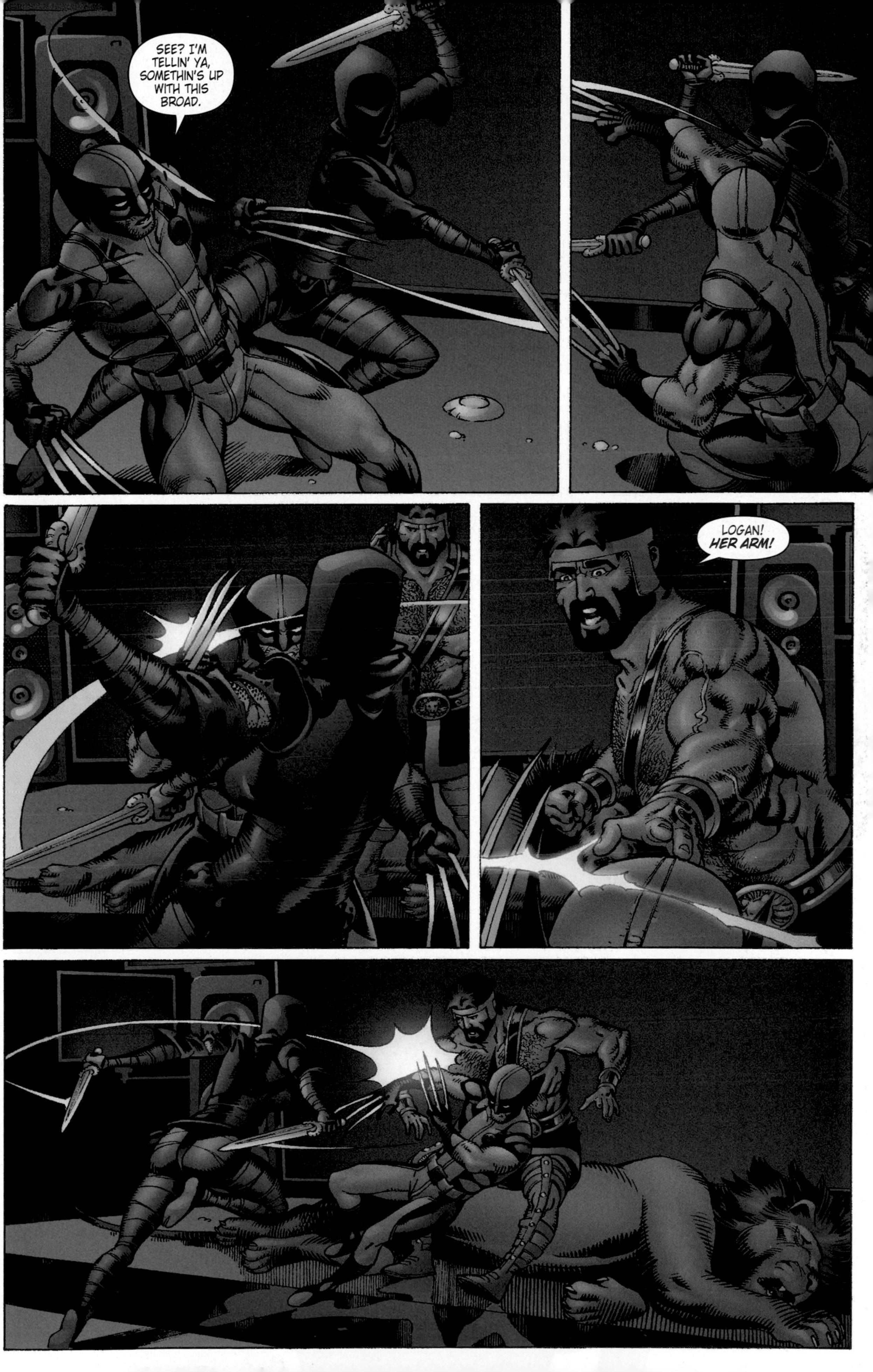
SEE? I'M TELLIN' YA, SOMETHIN'S UP WITH THIS BROAD.
LOGAN! HER ARM!

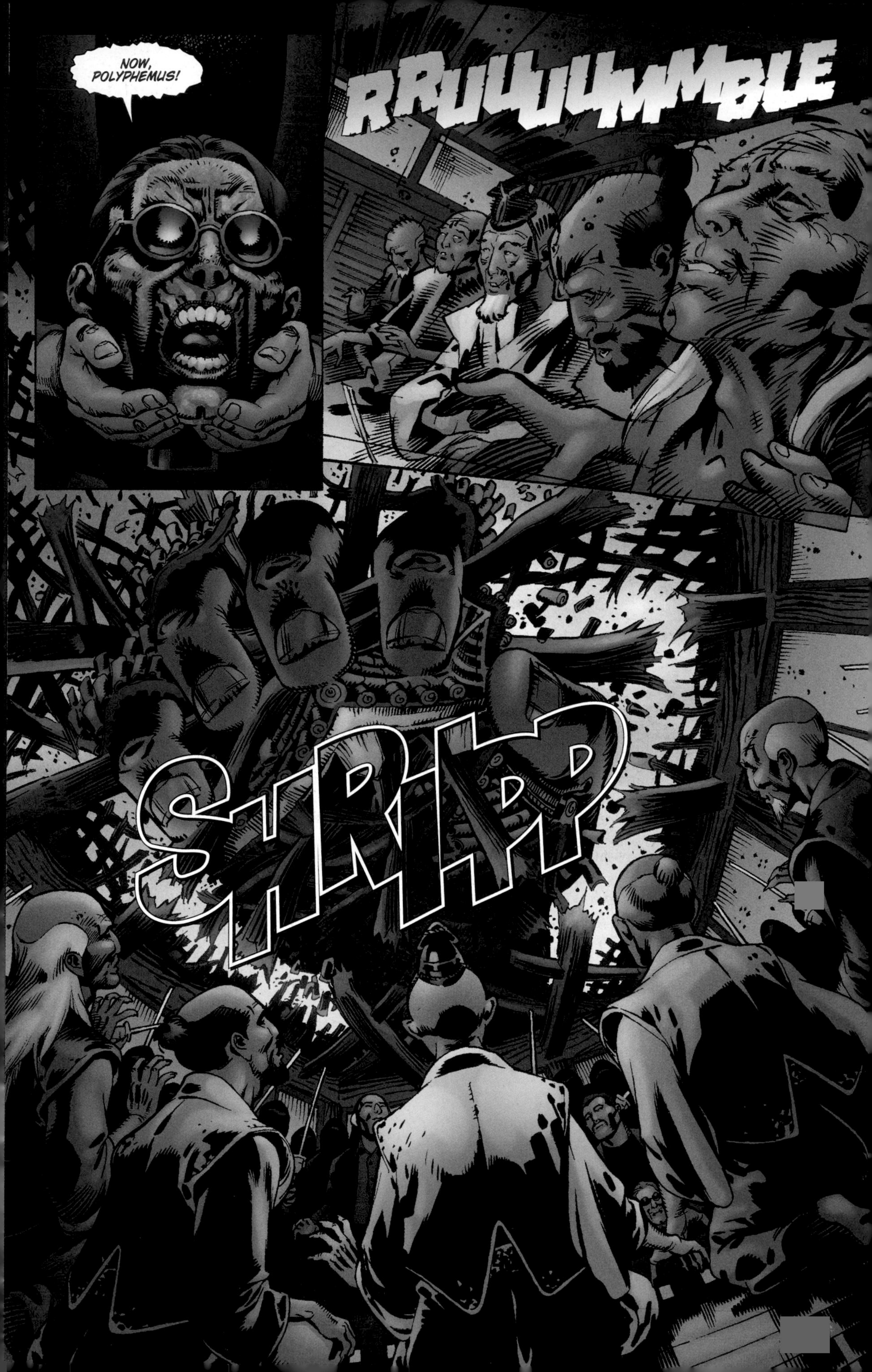
NOW, POLYPHEMUS!
RRUUUUMMBLE
SKRIPP

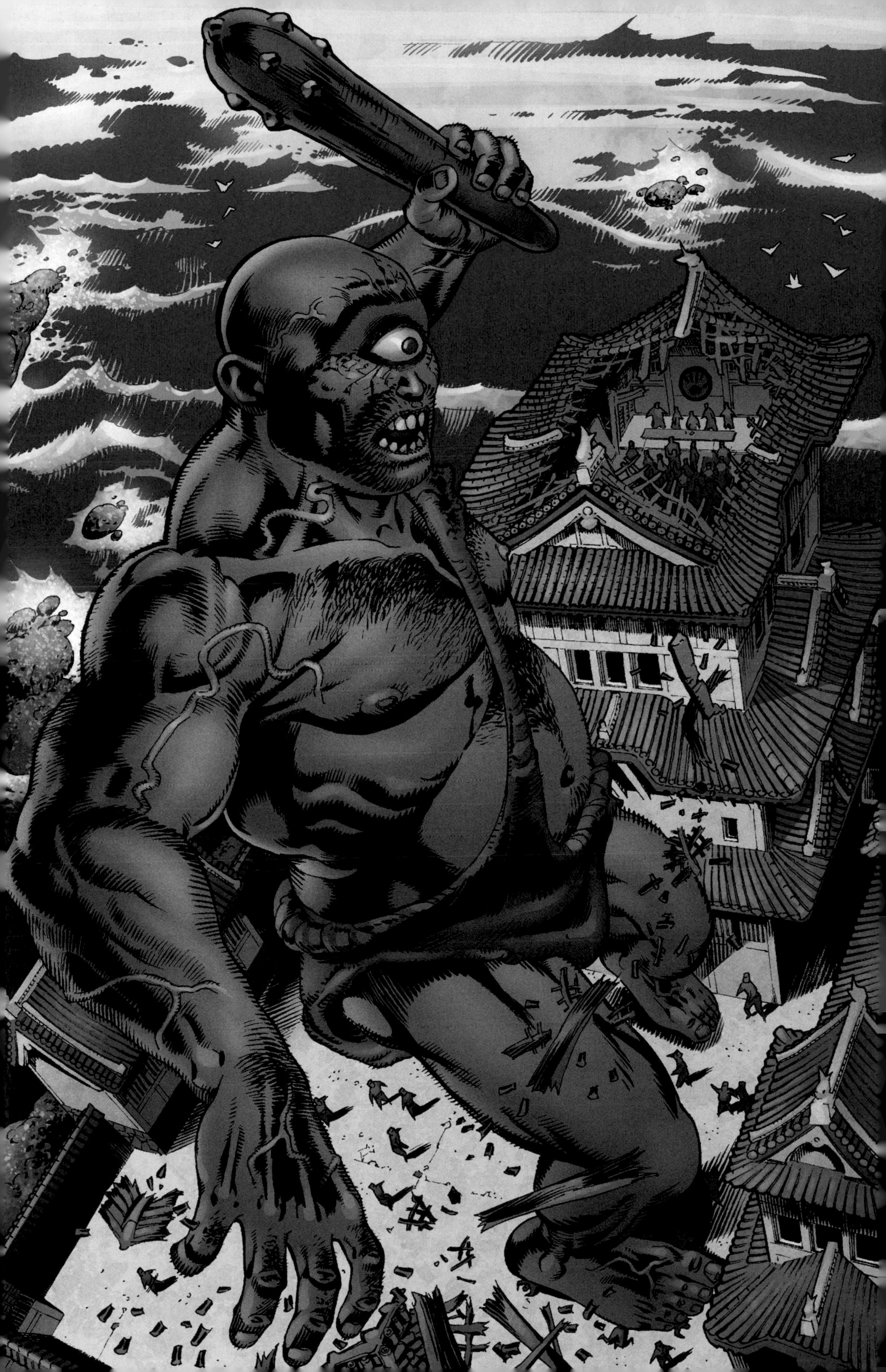

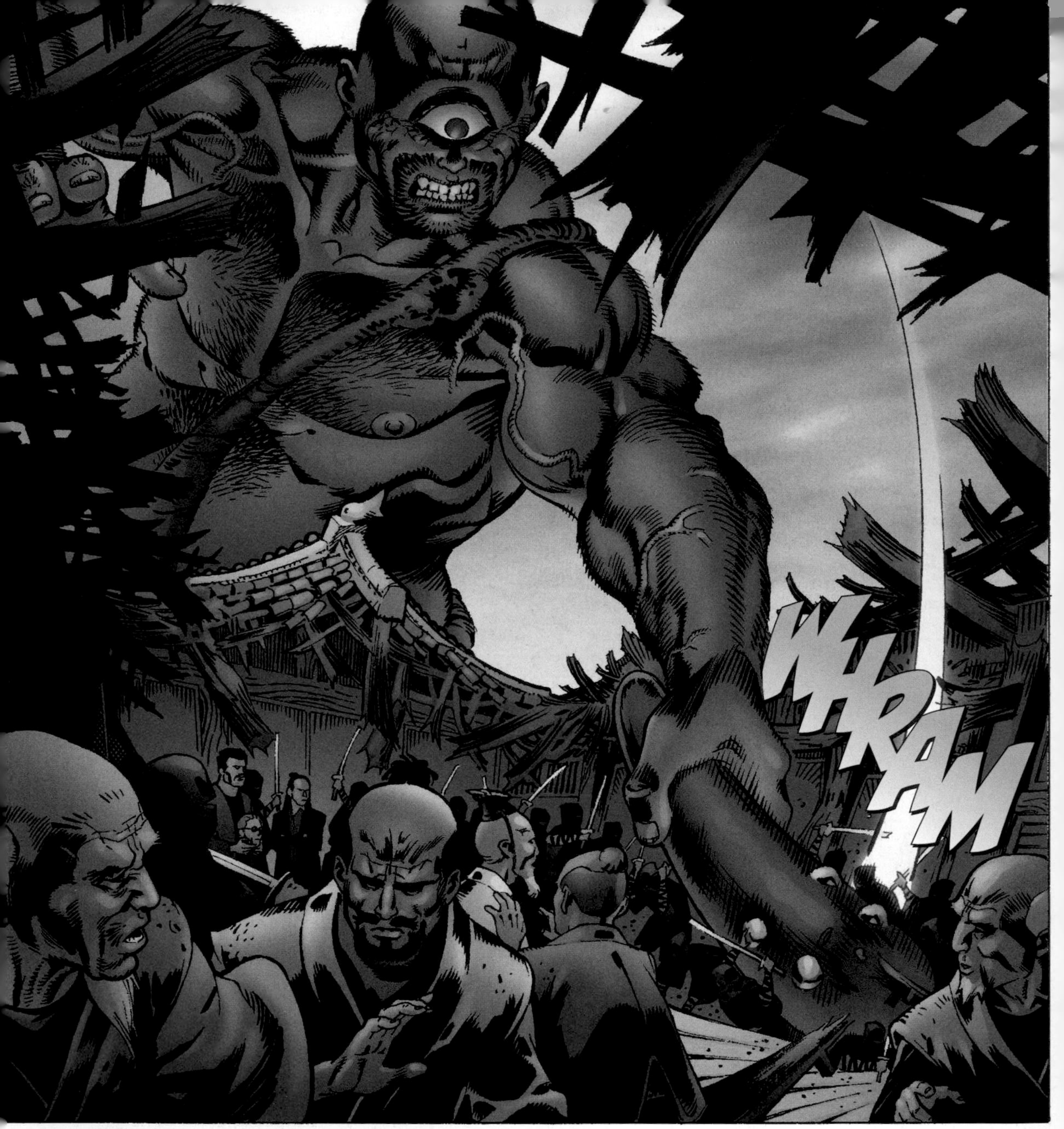
WHRAM

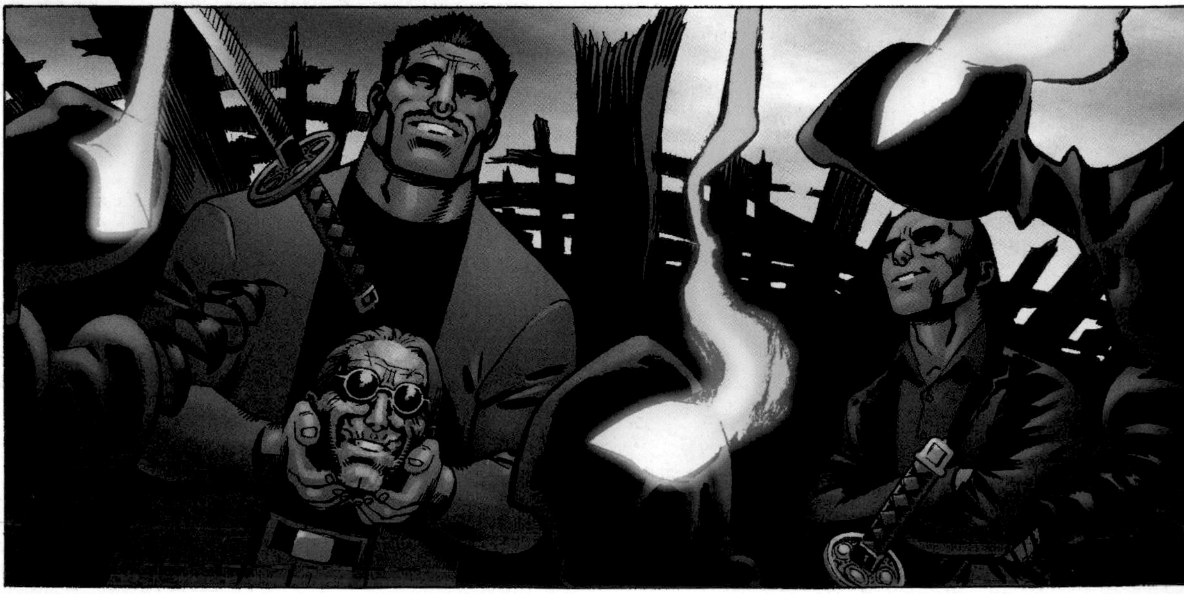

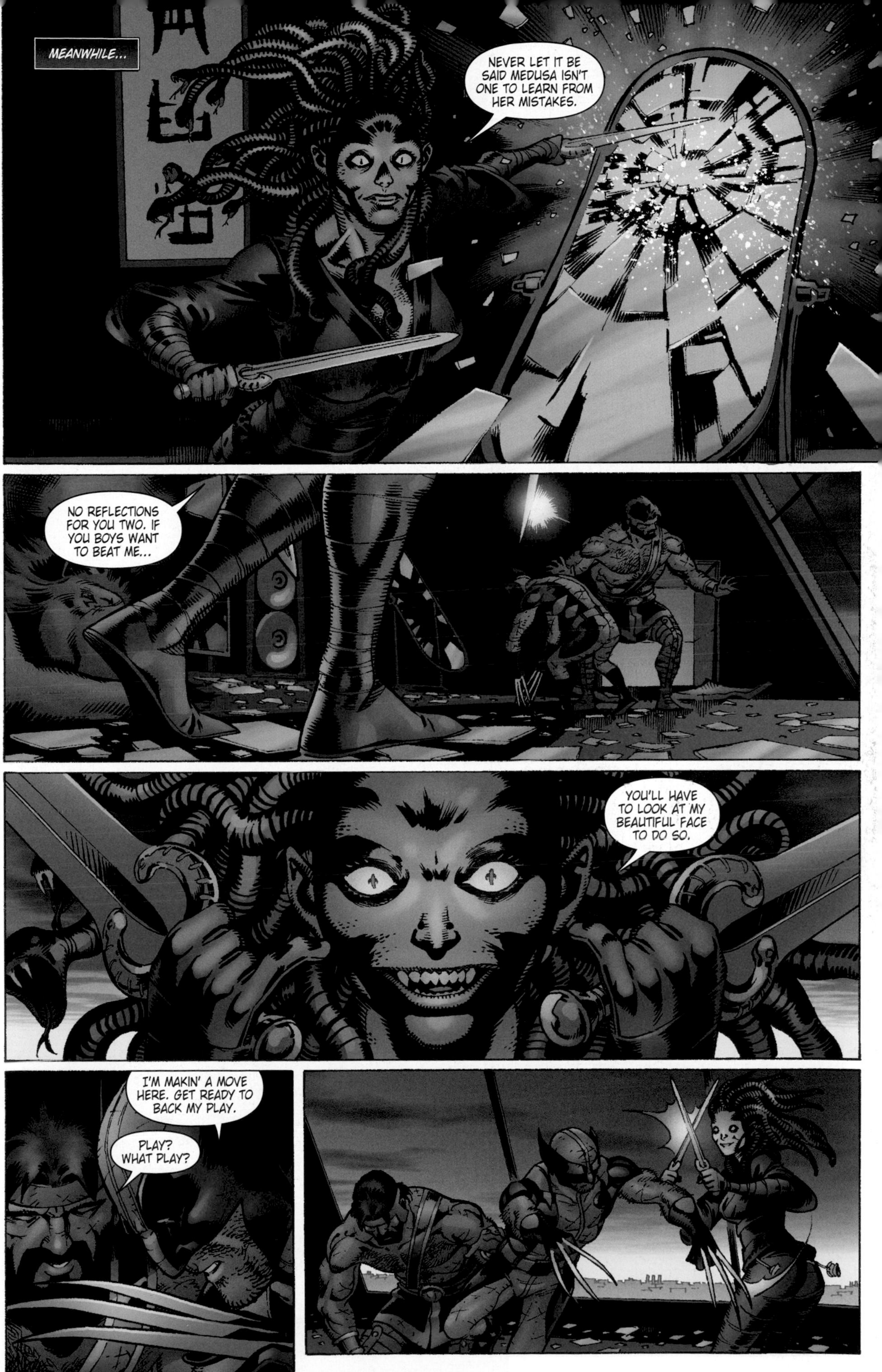
MEANWHILE...
NEVER LET IT BE SAID MEDUSA ISN'T ONE TO LEARN FROM HER MISTAKES.
NO REFLECTIONS FOR YOU TWO. IF YOU BOYS WANT TO BEAT ME...
YOU'LL HAVE TO LOOK AT MY BEAUTIFUL FACE TO DO SO.
I'M MAKIN' A MOVE HERE. GET READY TO BACK MY PLAY.
PLAY? WHAT PLAY?

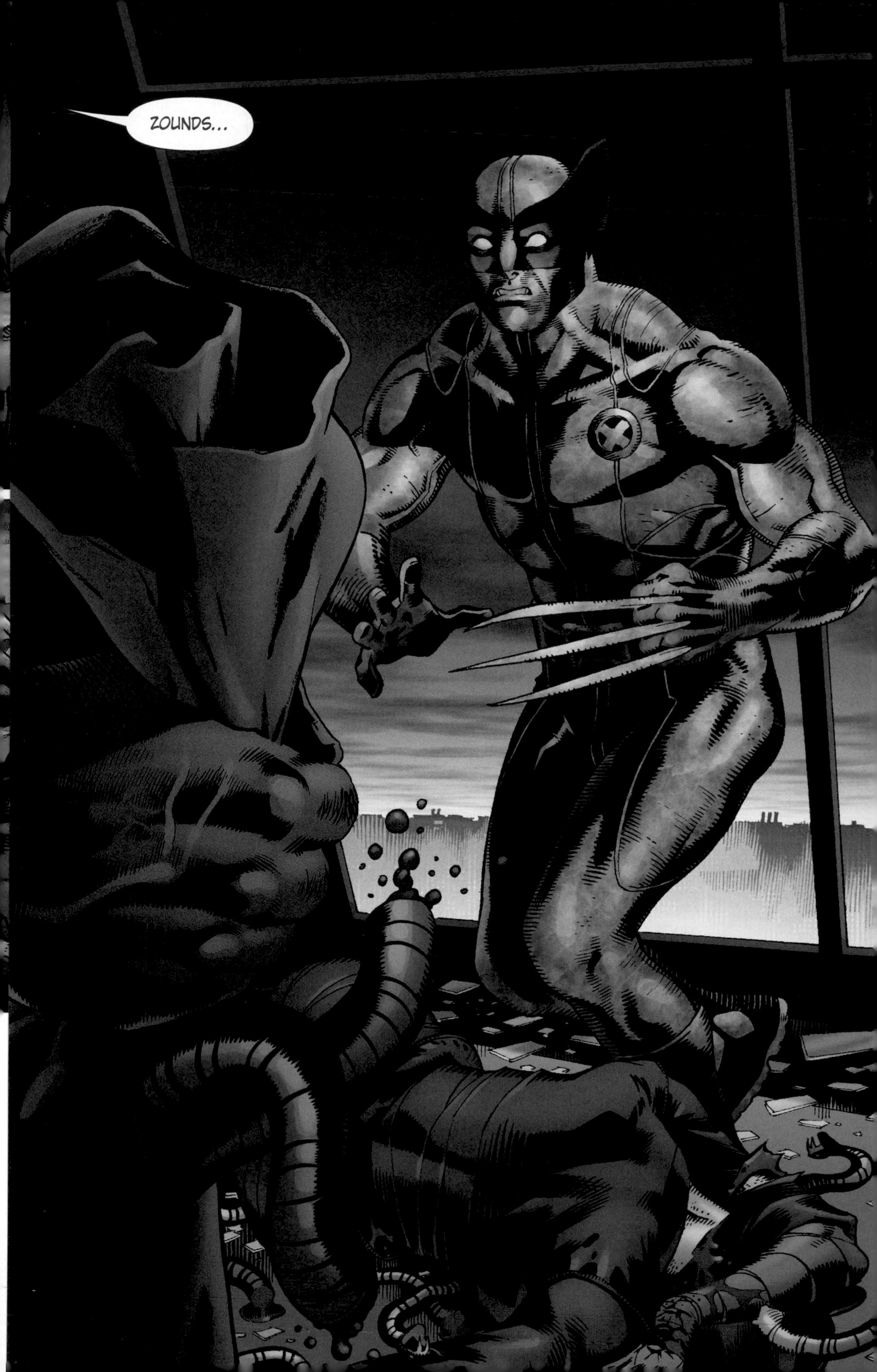
ZOUNDS...

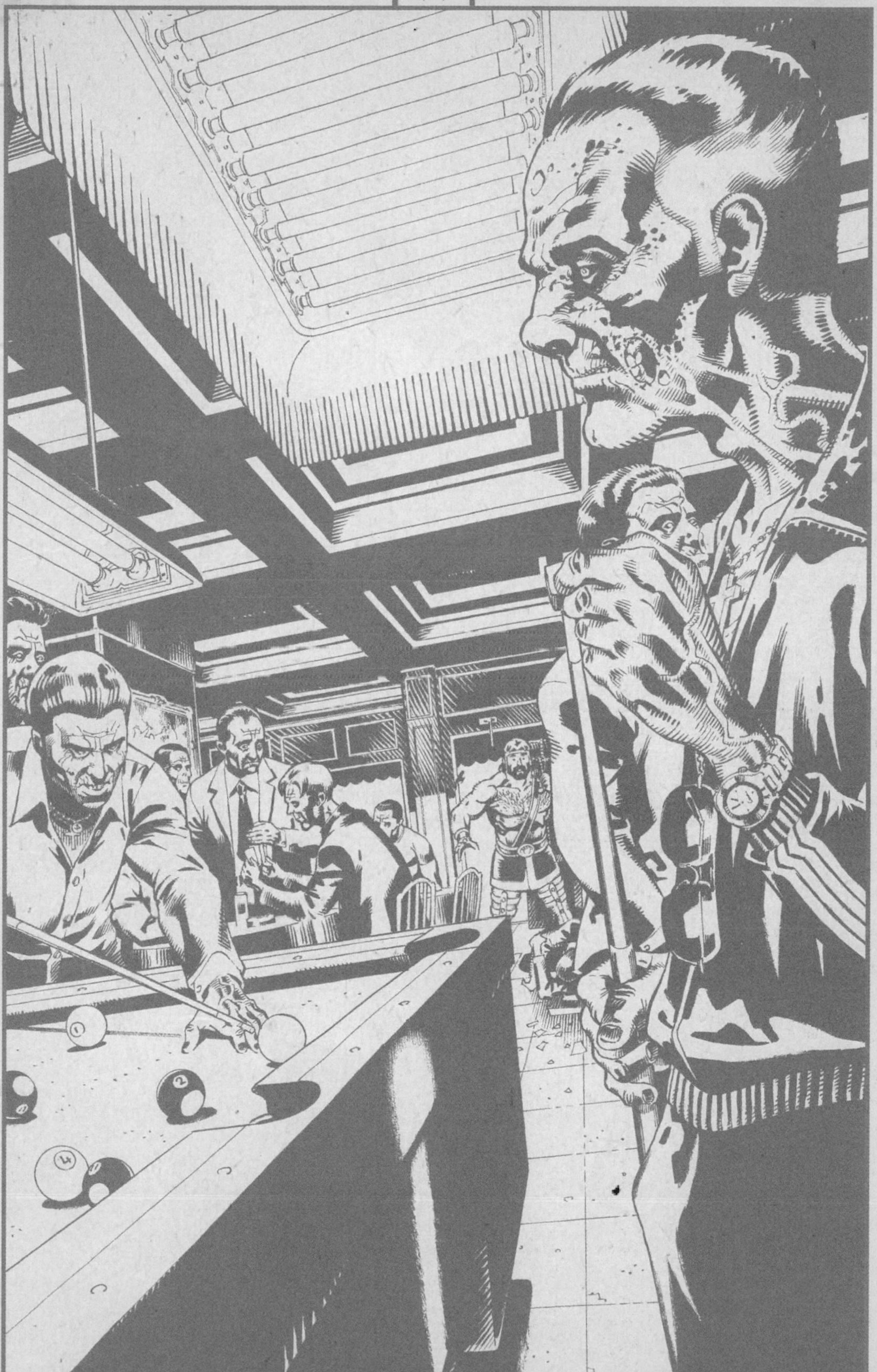

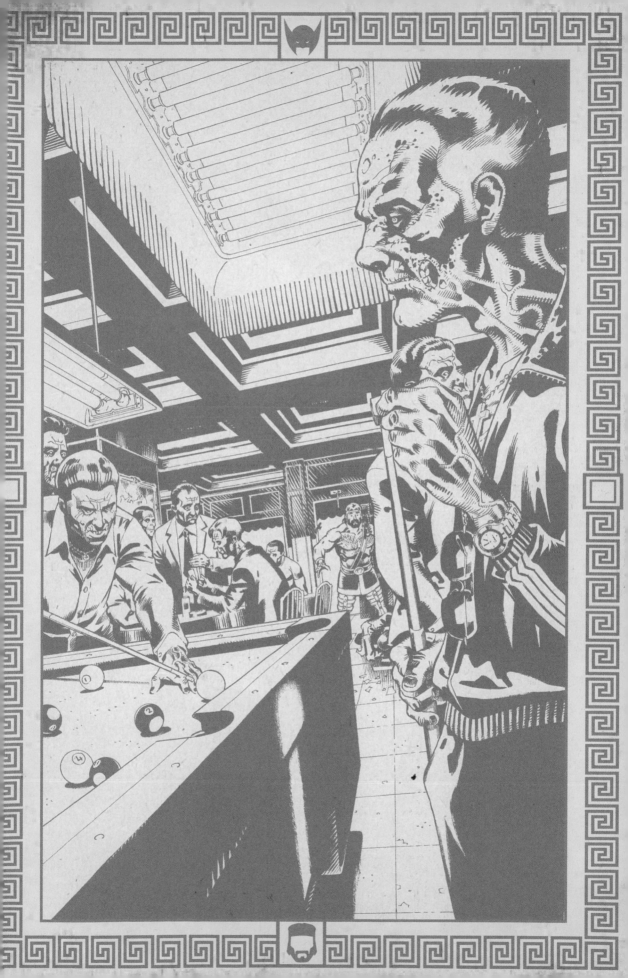

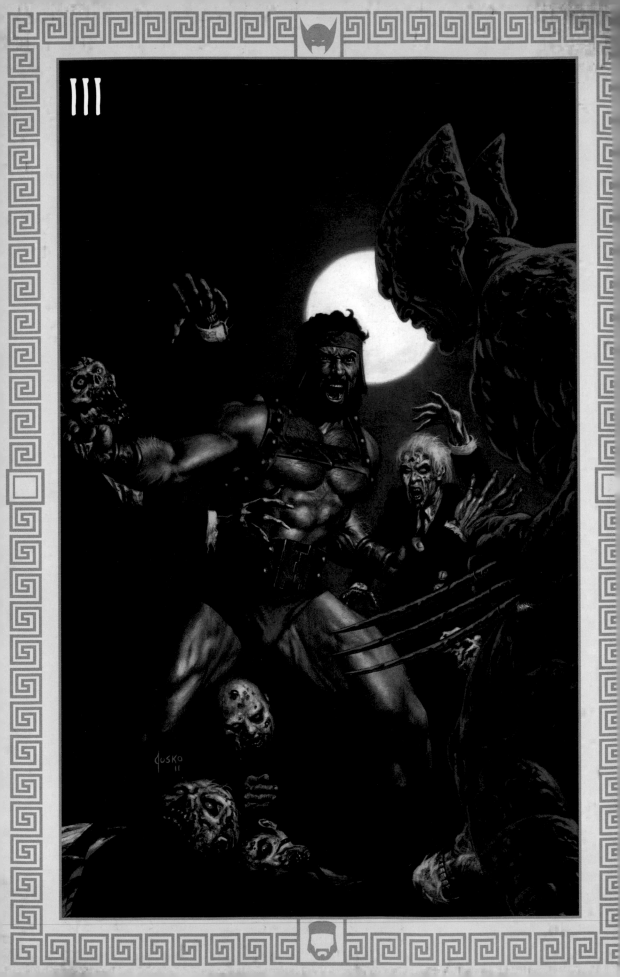

III

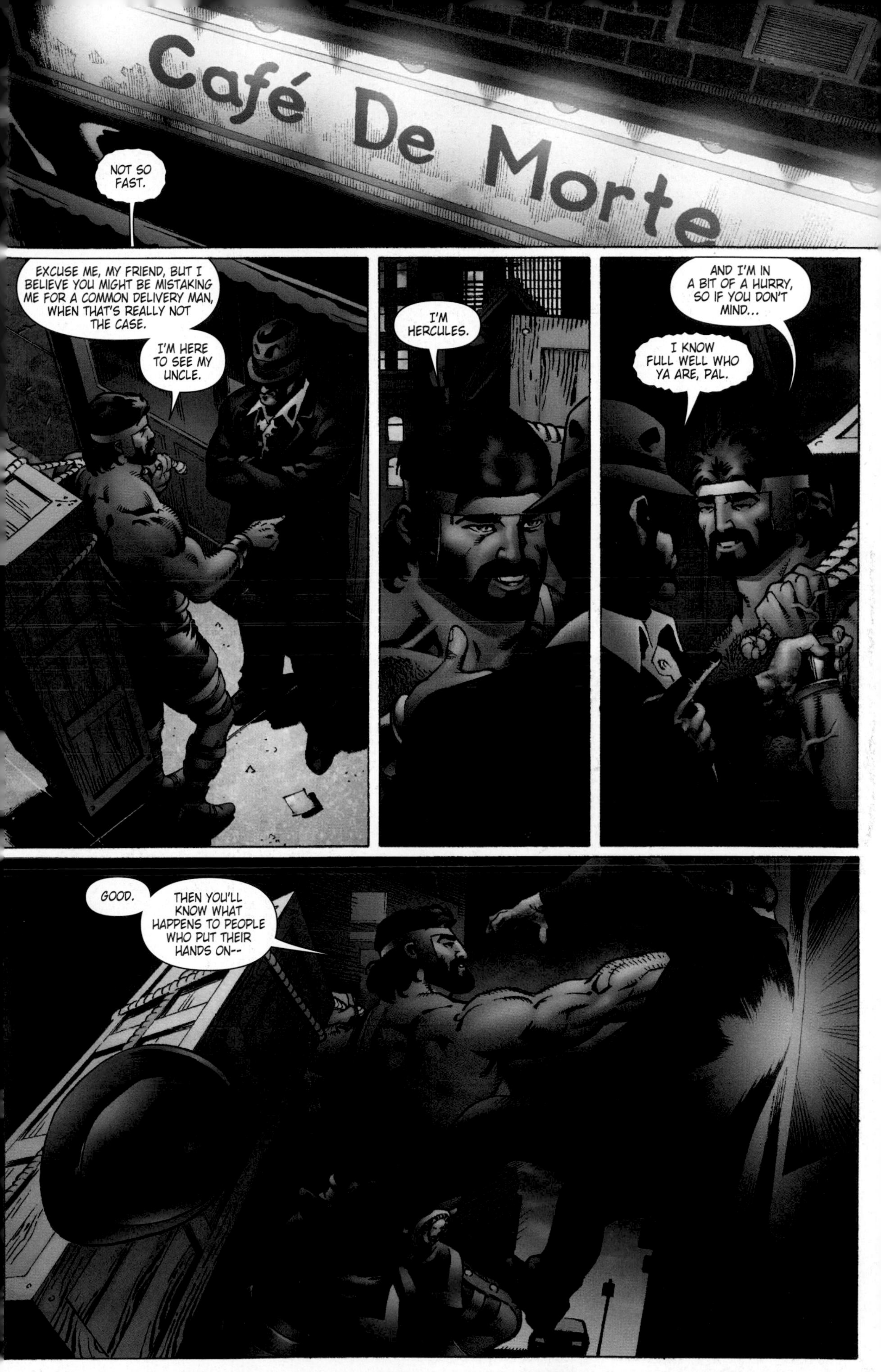
Café De Morte
NOT SO FAST.
EXCUSE ME, MY FRIEND, BUT I BELIEVE YOU MIGHT BE MISTAKING ME FOR A COMMON DELIVERY MAN, WHEN THAT'S REALLY NOT THE CASE.
I'M HERE TO SEE MY UNCLE.
I'M HERCULES.
AND I'M IN A BIT OF A HURRY, SO IF YOU DON'T MIND...
I KNOW FULL WELL WHO YA ARE, PAL.
GOOD.
THEN YOU'LL KNOW WHAT HAPPENS TO PEOPLE WHO PUT THEIR HANDS ON--

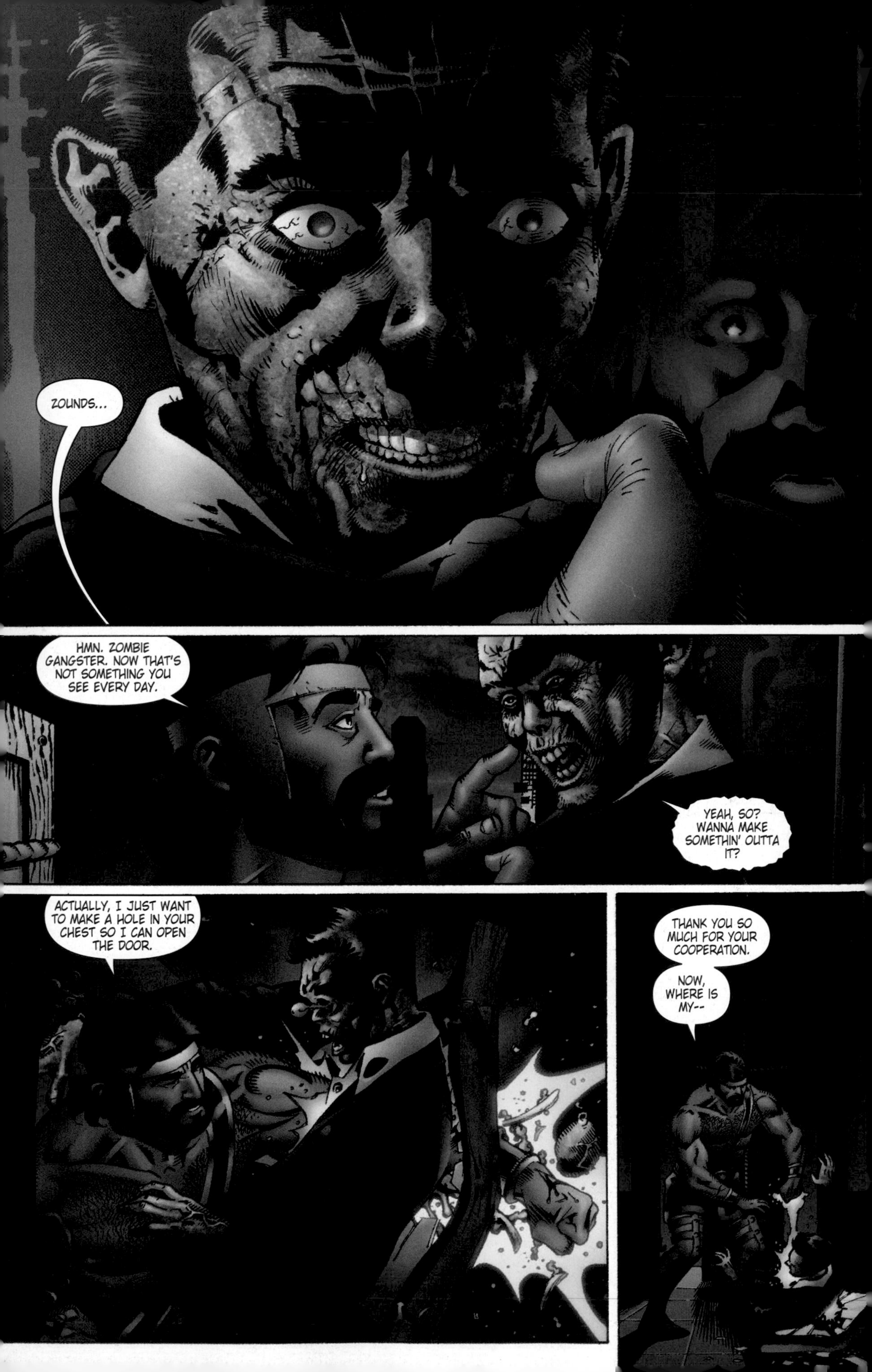
ZOUNDS...
HMN. ZOMBIE GANGSTER. NOW THAT'S NOT SOMETHING YOU SEE EVERY DAY.
YEAH, SO? WANNA MAKE SOMETHIN' OUTTA IT?
ACTUALLY, I JUST WANT TO MAKE A HOLE IN YOUR CHEST SO I CAN OPEN THE DOOR.
THANK YOU SO MUCH FOR YOUR COOPERATION.
NOW, WHERE IS MY--

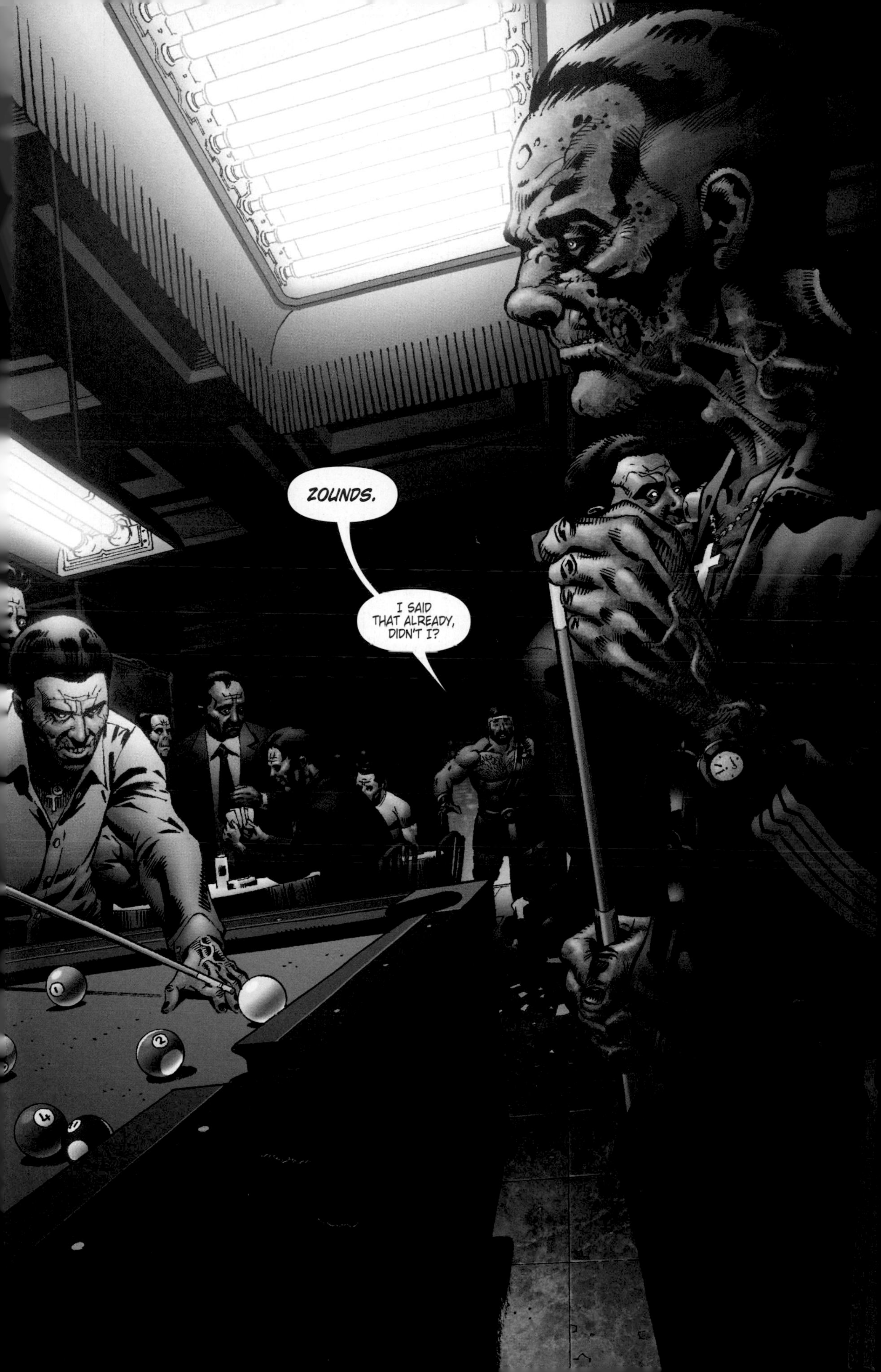
ZOUNDS.
I SAID THAT ALREADY, DIDN'T I?

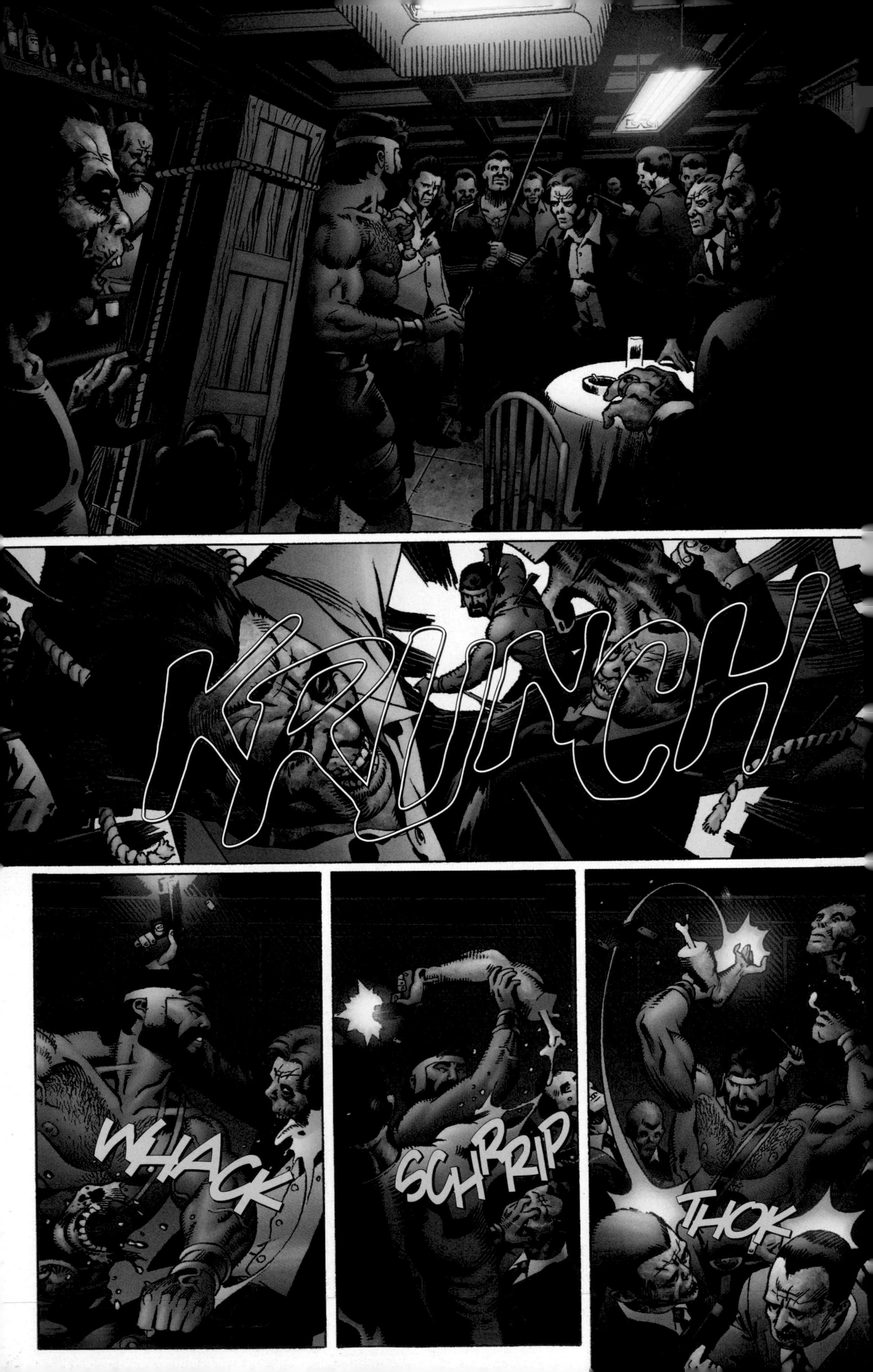
KRUNCH
WHACK
SCHRRIP
THOK

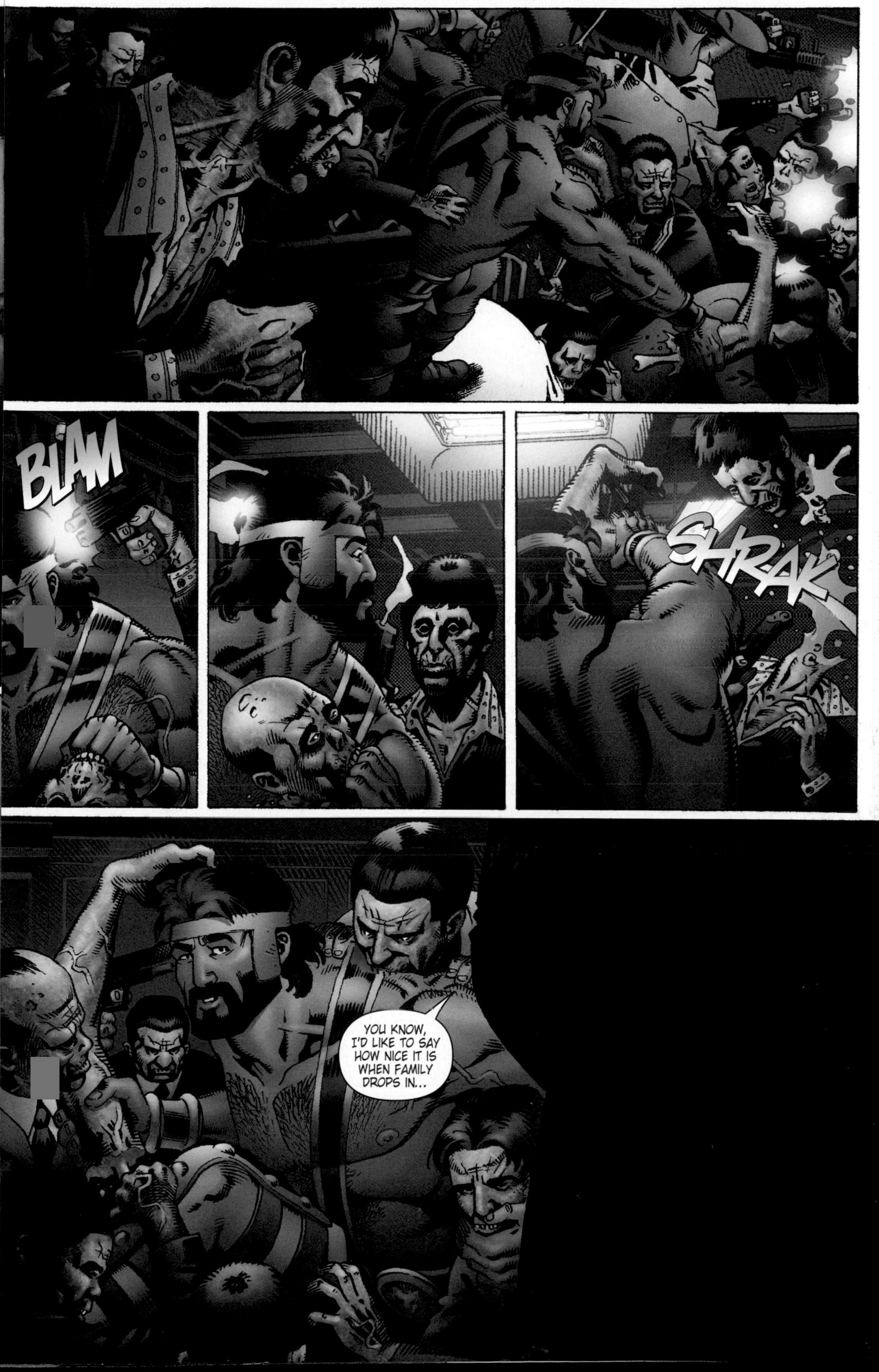
BLAM
SHRAK
YOU KNOW, I'D LIKE TO SAY HOW NICE IT IS WHEN FAMILY DROPS IN...

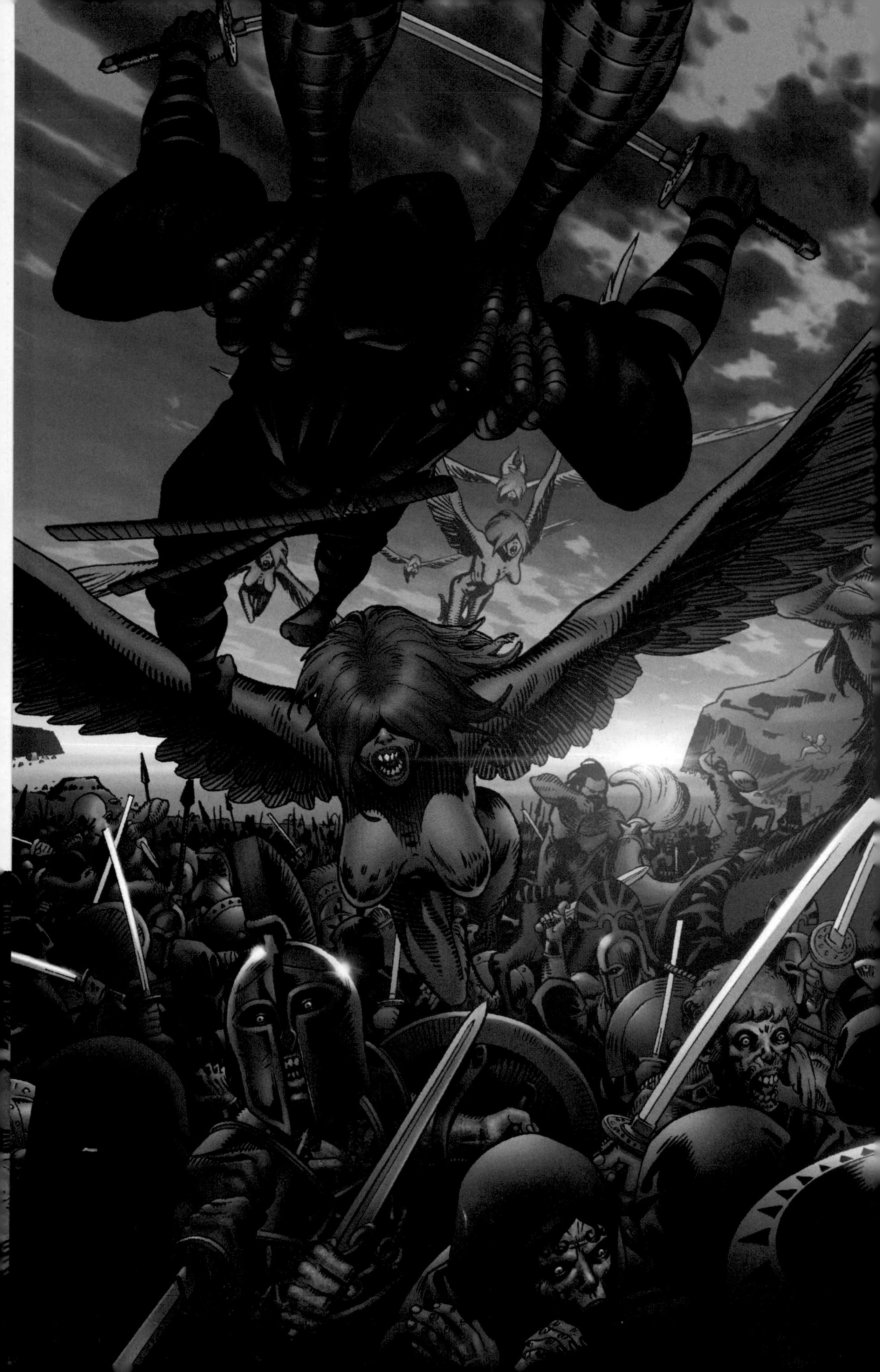

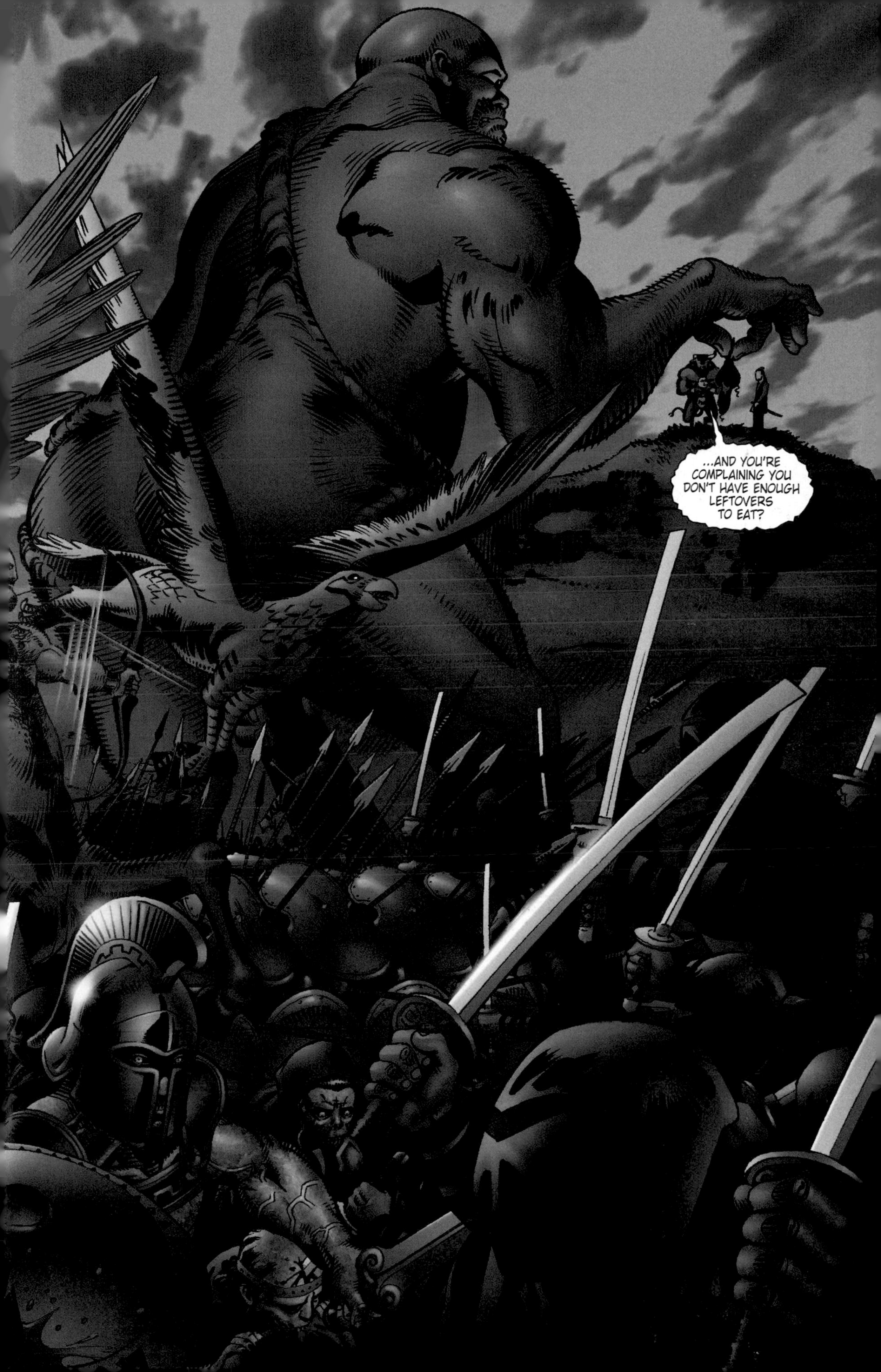
...AND YOU'RE COMPLAINING YOU DON'T HAVE ENOUGH LEFTOVERS TO EAT?

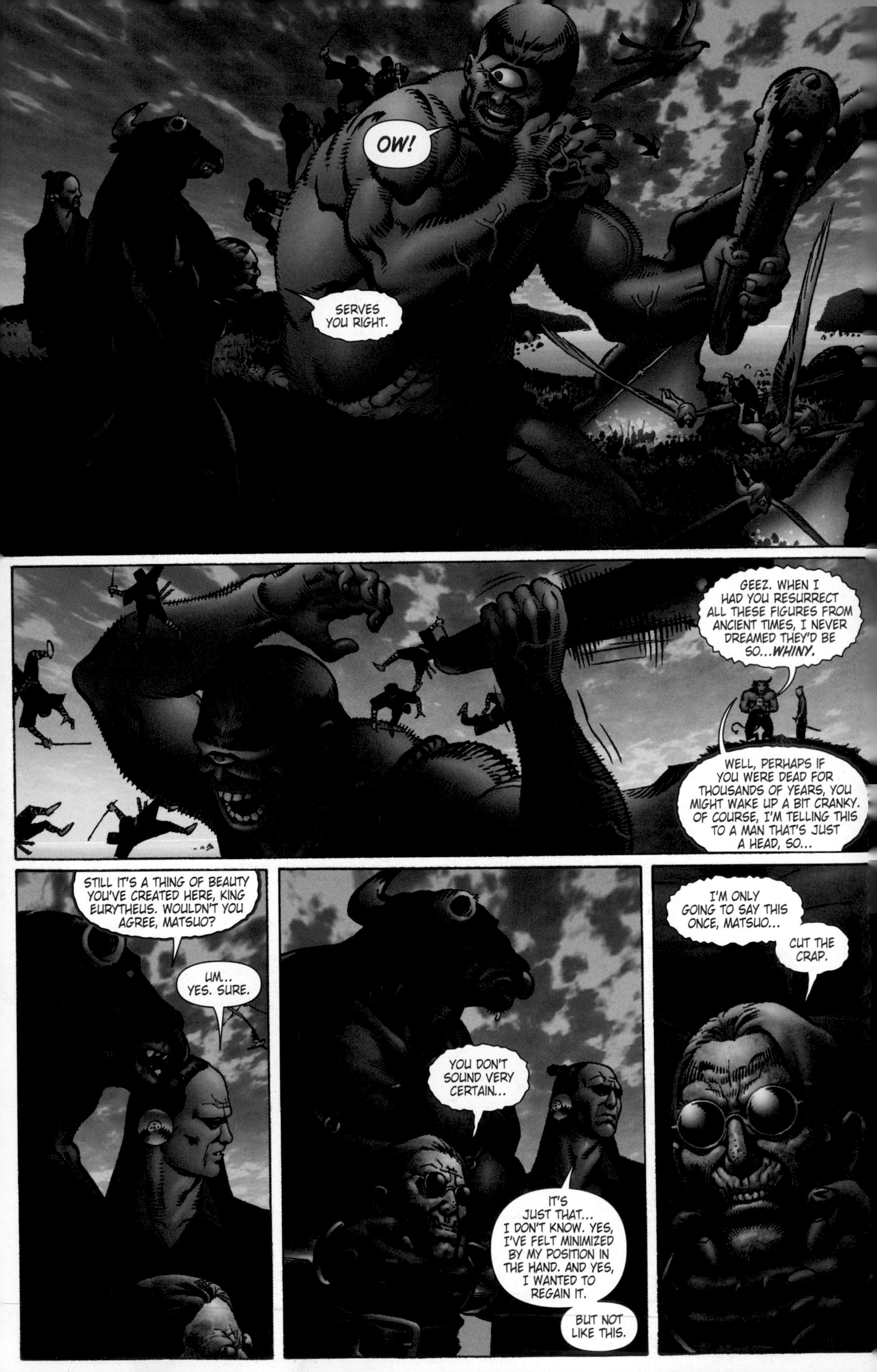
OW!
SERVES YOU RIGHT.
GEEZ. WHEN I HAD YOU RESURRECT ALL THESE FIGURES FROM ANCIENT TIMES, I NEVER DREAMED THEY'D BE SO...*WHINY.*
WELL, PERHAPS IF YOU WERE DEAD FOR THOUSANDS OF YEARS, YOU MIGHT WAKE UP A BIT CRANKY. OF COURSE, I'M TELLING THIS TO A MAN THAT'S JUST A HEAD, SO...
STILL IT'S A THING OF BEAUTY YOU'VE CREATED HERE, KING EURYTHEUS. WOULDN'T YOU AGREE, MATSUO?
UM... YES. SURE.
YOU DON'T SOUND VERY CERTAIN...
IT'S JUST THAT... I DON'T KNOW. YES, I'VE FELT MINIMIZED BY MY POSITION IN THE HAND. AND YES, I WANTED TO REGAIN IT.
BUT NOT LIKE THIS.
I'M ONLY GOING TO SAY THIS ONCE, MATSUO...
CUT THE CRAP.

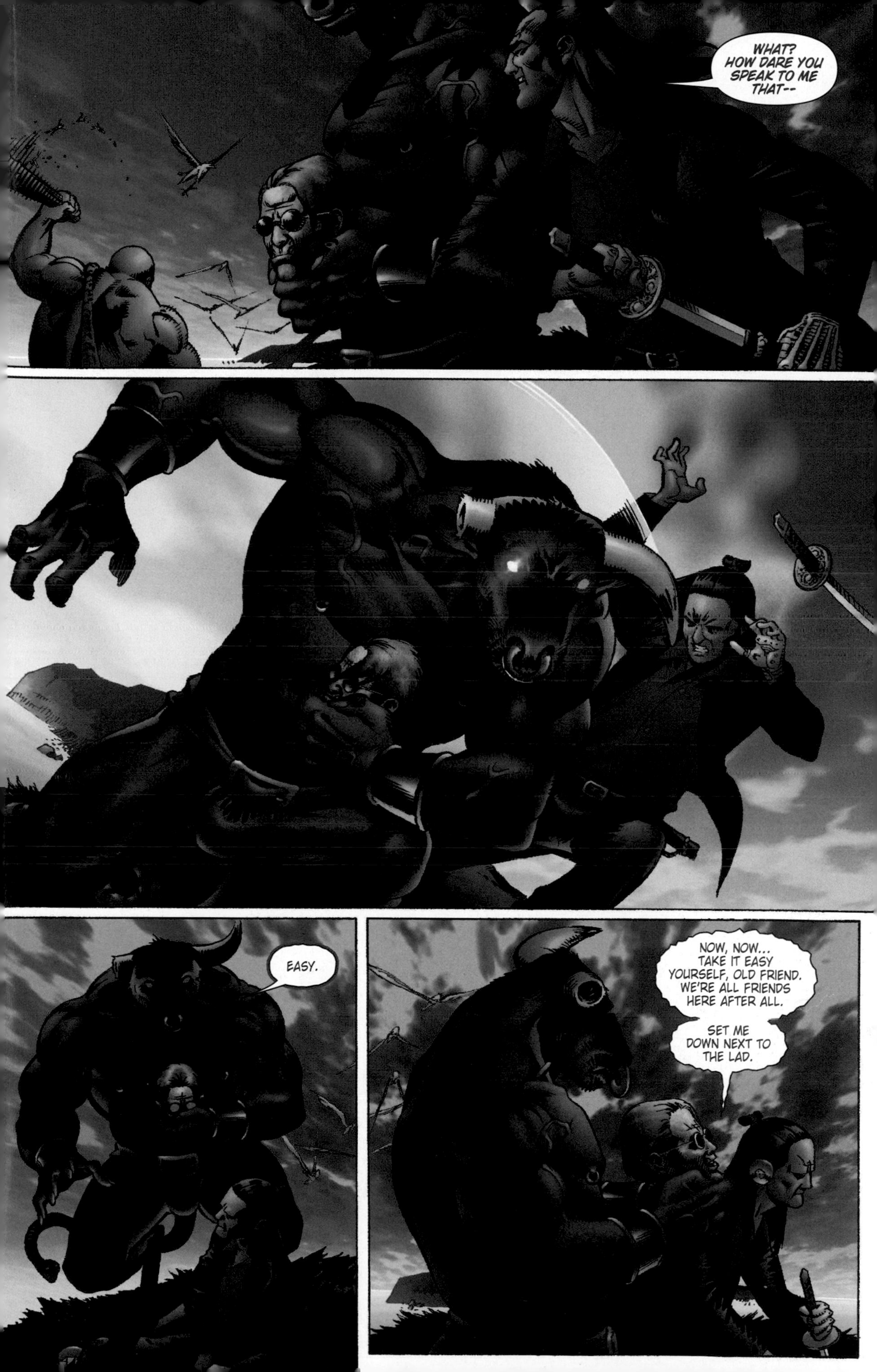
WHAT? HOW DARE YOU SPEAK TO ME THAT--
EASY.
NOW, NOW... TAKE IT EASY YOURSELF, OLD FRIEND. WE'RE ALL FRIENDS HERE AFTER ALL.
SET ME DOWN NEXT TO THE LAD.

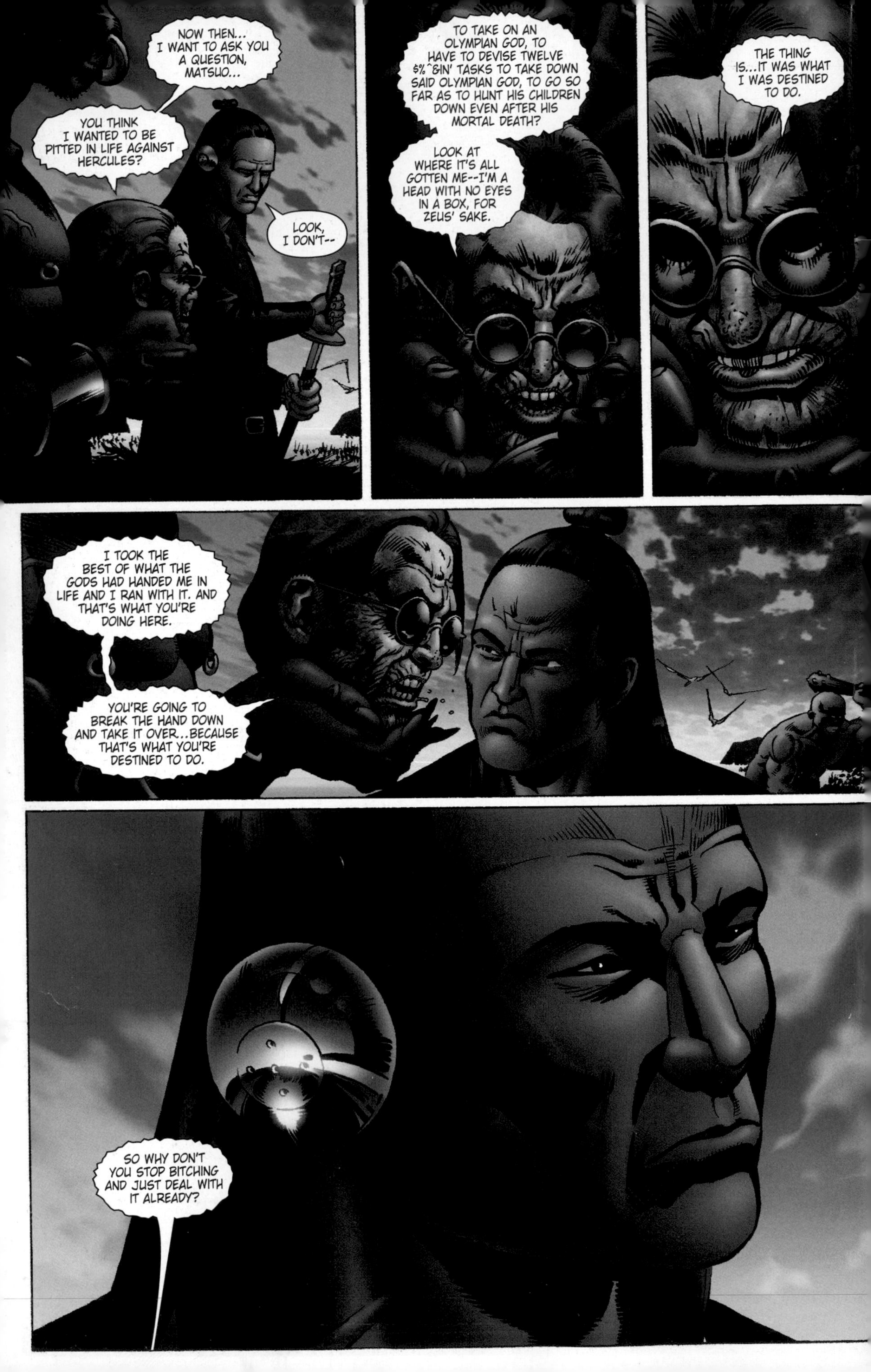

NOW THEN... I WANT TO ASK YOU A QUESTION, MATSUO...
YOU THINK I WANTED TO BE PITTED IN LIFE AGAINST HERCULES?
LOOK, I DON'T--
TO TAKE ON AN OLYMPIAN GOD, TO HAVE TO DEVISE TWELVE $%^&IN' TASKS TO TAKE DOWN SAID OLYMPIAN GOD, TO GO SO FAR AS TO HUNT HIS CHILDREN DOWN EVEN AFTER HIS MORTAL DEATH?
LOOK AT WHERE IT'S ALL GOTTEN ME--I'M A HEAD WITH NO EYES IN A BOX, FOR ZEUS' SAKE.
THE THING IS...IT WAS WHAT I WAS DESTINED TO DO.
I TOOK THE BEST OF WHAT THE GODS HAD HANDED ME IN LIFE AND I RAN WITH IT. AND THAT'S WHAT YOU'RE DOING HERE.
YOU'RE GOING TO BREAK THE HAND DOWN AND TAKE IT OVER...BECAUSE THAT'S WHAT YOU'RE DESTINED TO DO.
SO WHY DON'T YOU STOP BITCHING AND JUST DEAL WITH IT ALREADY?

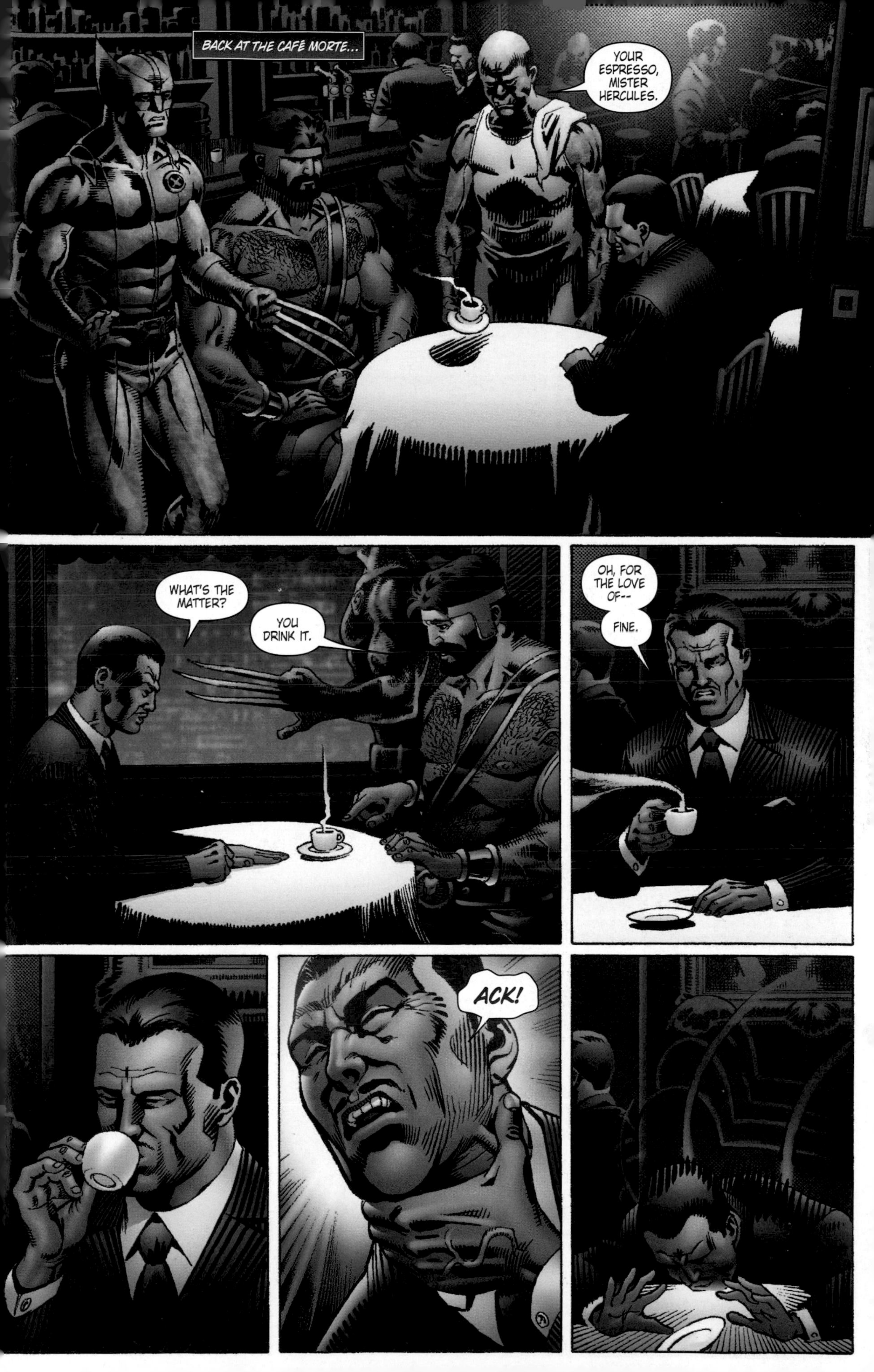
BACK AT THE CAFÉ MORTE...
YOUR ESPRESSO, MISTER HERCULES.
WHAT'S THE MATTER?
YOU DRINK IT.
OH, FOR THE LOVE OF--
FINE.
ACK!

I KNEW IT!

KNEW WHAT, YOU IDIOT. IF I WANTED TO KILL YOU, YOU'D BE DEAD ALREADY.

BESIDES, YOU HONESTLY THINK THERE'S A POISON THAT COULD AFFECT ME, THE GOD OF DEATH?

OH... YEAH. GOOD POINT.

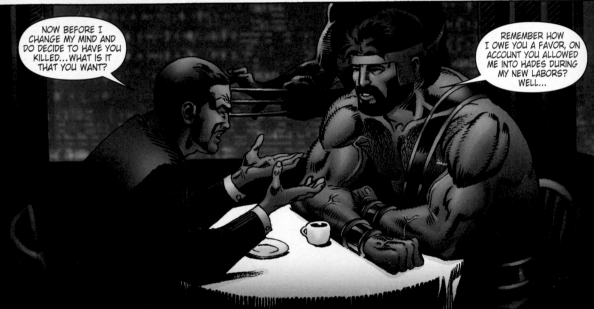

NOW BEFORE I CHANGE MY MIND AND DO DECIDE TO HAVE YOU KILLED...WHAT IS IT THAT YOU WANT?

REMEMBER HOW I OWE YOU A FAVOR, ON ACCOUNT YOU ALLOWED ME INTO HADES DURING MY NEW LABORS? WELL...

I'M HERE TO PAY UP.

HOW SO?

YOU'RE LOOKING AT HIM.

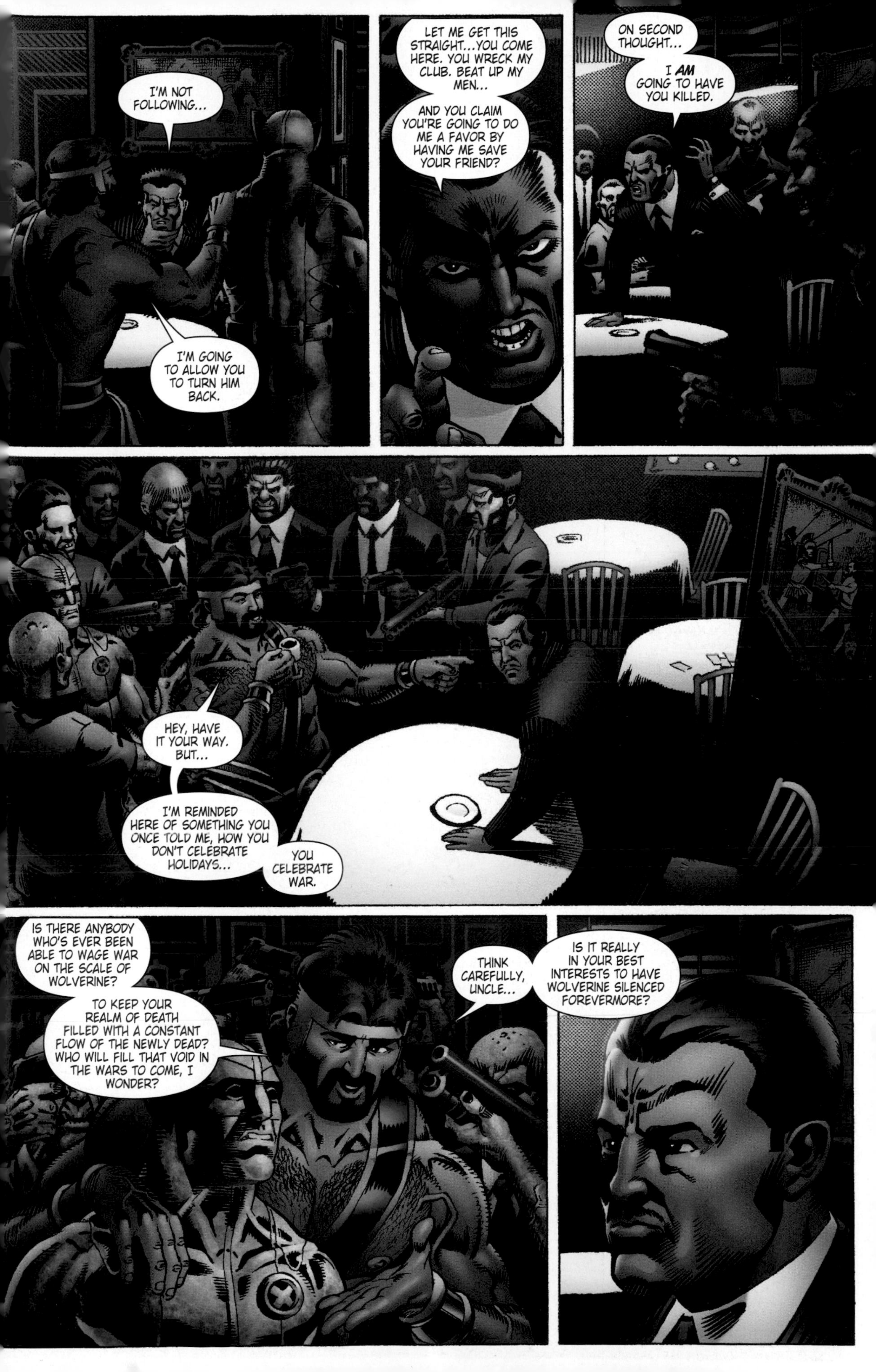
I'M NOT FOLLOWING...
I'M GOING TO ALLOW YOU TO TURN HIM BACK.
LET ME GET THIS STRAIGHT...YOU COME HERE. YOU WRECK MY CLUB. BEAT UP MY MEN...
AND YOU CLAIM YOU'RE GOING TO DO ME A FAVOR BY HAVING ME SAVE YOUR FRIEND?
ON SECOND THOUGHT...
I **AM** GOING TO HAVE YOU KILLED.
HEY, HAVE IT YOUR WAY. BUT...
I'M REMINDED HERE OF SOMETHING YOU ONCE TOLD ME, HOW YOU DON'T CELEBRATE HOLIDAYS...
YOU CELEBRATE WAR.
IS THERE ANYBODY WHO'S EVER BEEN ABLE TO WAGE WAR ON THE SCALE OF WOLVERINE?
TO KEEP YOUR REALM OF DEATH FILLED WITH A CONSTANT FLOW OF THE NEWLY DEAD? WHO WILL FILL THAT VOID IN THE WARS TO COME, I WONDER?
THINK CAREFULLY, UNCLE...
IS IT REALLY IN YOUR BEST INTERESTS TO HAVE WOLVERINE SILENCED FOREVERMORE?

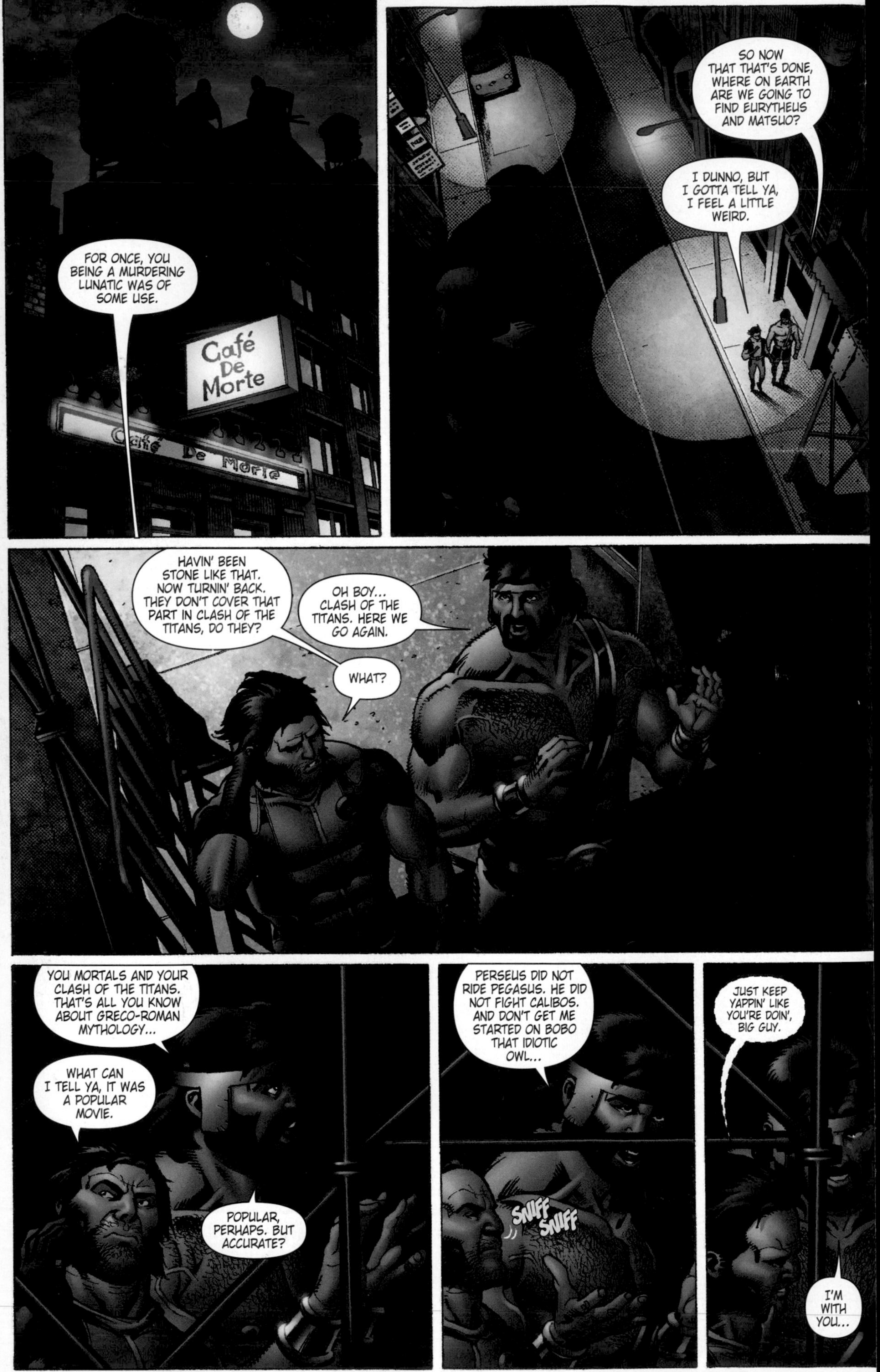

FOR ONCE, YOU BEING A MURDERING LUNATIC WAS OF SOME USE.
Café De Morte
Café De Morte
SO NOW THAT THAT'S DONE, WHERE ON EARTH ARE WE GOING TO FIND EURYTHEUS AND MATSUO?
I DUNNO, BUT I GOTTA TELL YA, I FEEL A LITTLE WEIRD.
HAVIN' BEEN STONE LIKE THAT. NOW TURNIN' BACK. THEY DON'T COVER THAT PART IN CLASH OF THE TITANS, DO THEY?
OH BOY... CLASH OF THE TITANS. HERE WE GO AGAIN.
WHAT?
YOU MORTALS AND YOUR CLASH OF THE TITANS. THAT'S ALL YOU KNOW ABOUT GRECO-ROMAN MYTHOLOGY...
WHAT CAN I TELL YA, IT WAS A POPULAR MOVIE.
POPULAR, PERHAPS. BUT ACCURATE?
PERSEUS DID NOT RIDE PEGASUS. HE DID NOT FIGHT CALIBOS. AND DON'T GET ME STARTED ON BOBO THAT IDIOTIC OWL...
SNIFF SNIFF
JUST KEEP YAPPIN' LIKE YOU'RE DOIN', BIG GUY.
I'M WITH YOU...

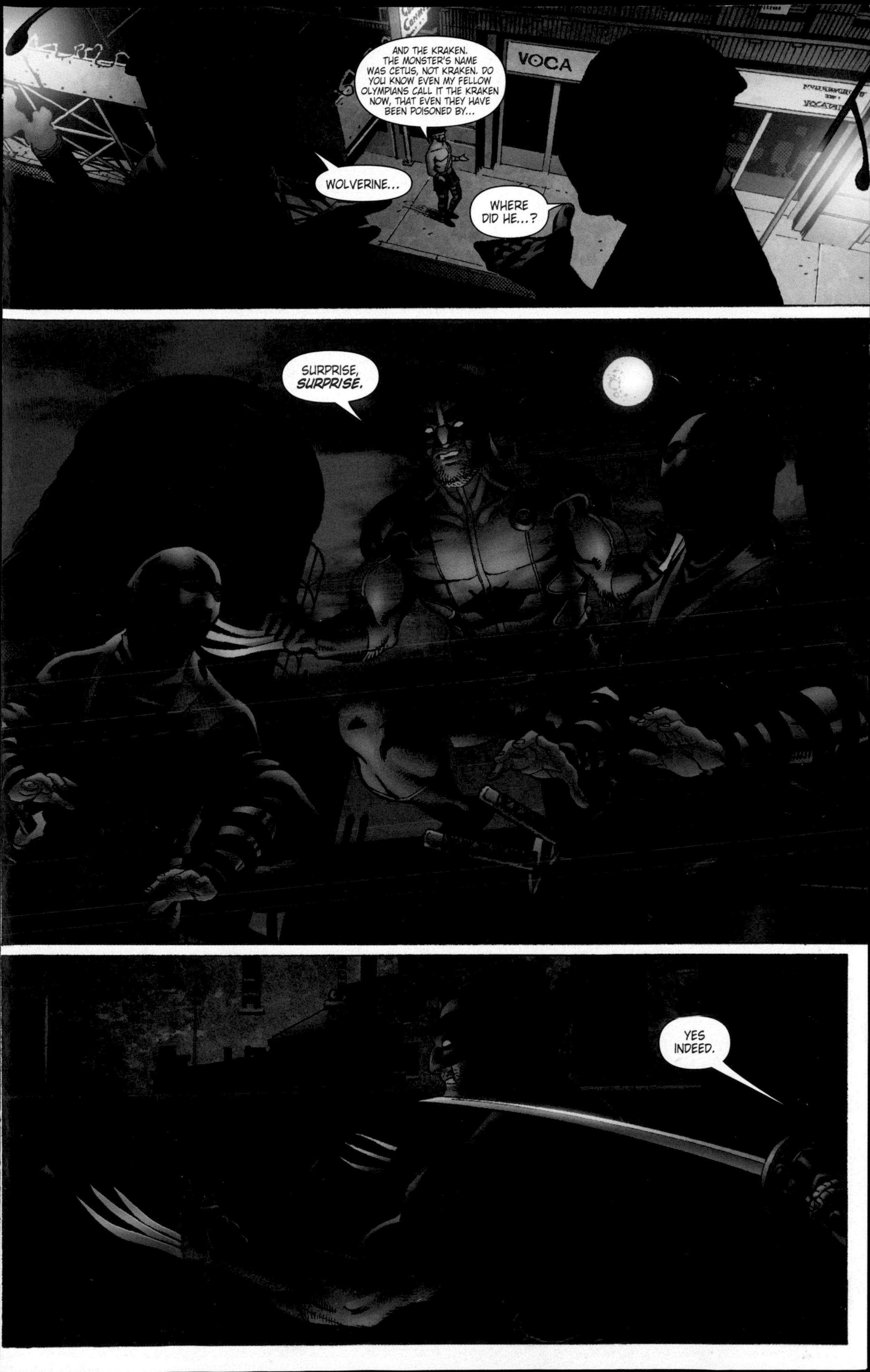
AND THE KRAKEN. THE MONSTER'S NAME WAS CETUS, NOT KRAKEN. DO YOU KNOW EVEN MY FELLOW OLYMPIANS CALL IT THE KRAKEN NOW, THAT EVEN THEY HAVE BEEN POISONED BY...
WOLVERINE...
WHERE DID HE...?
VOCA
SURPRISE, *SURPRISE.*
YES INDEED.

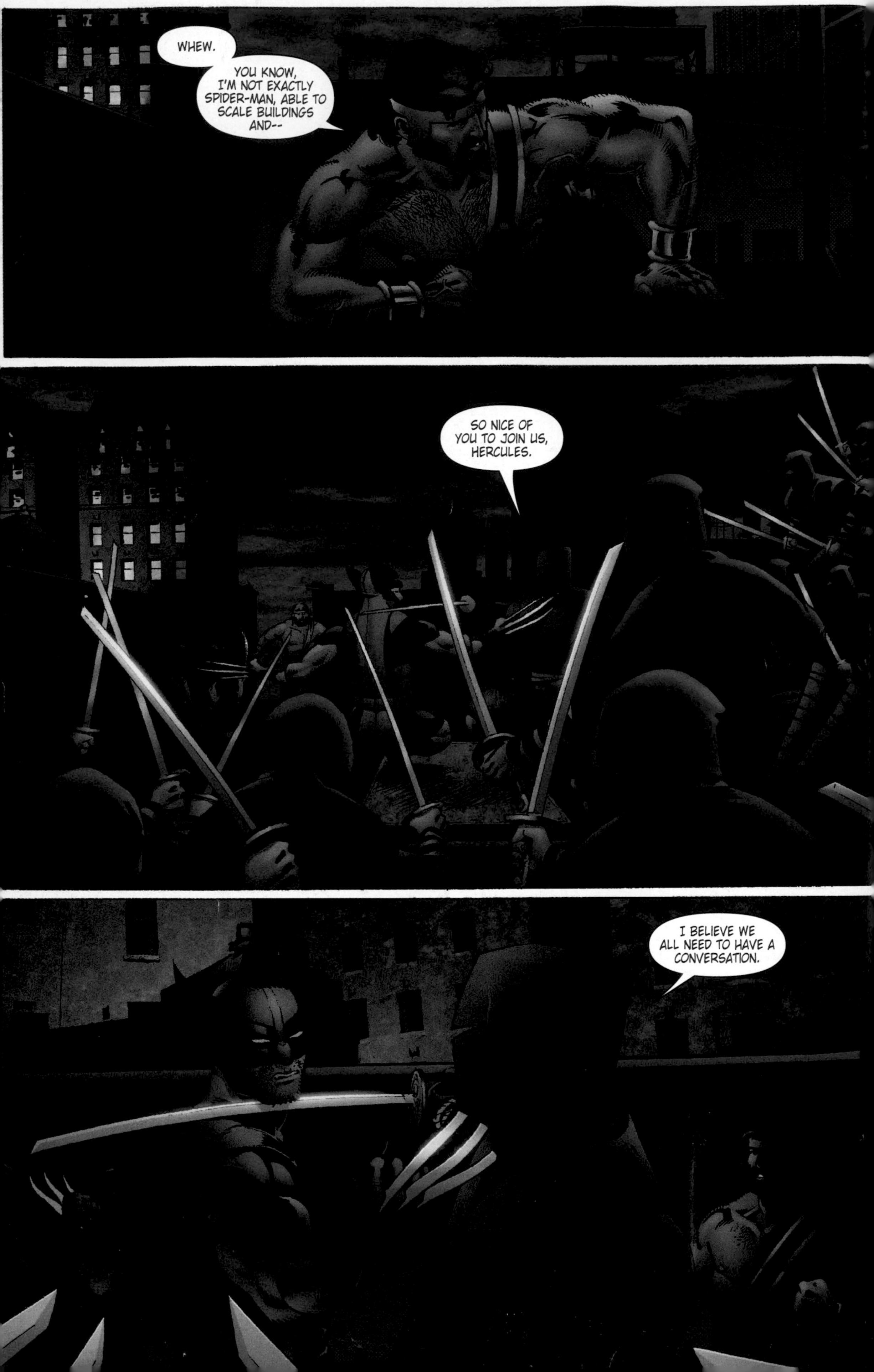
WHEW.
YOU KNOW, I'M NOT EXACTLY SPIDER-MAN, ABLE TO SCALE BUILDINGS AND--
SO NICE OF YOU TO JOIN US, HERCULES.
I BELIEVE WE ALL NEED TO HAVE A CONVERSATION.

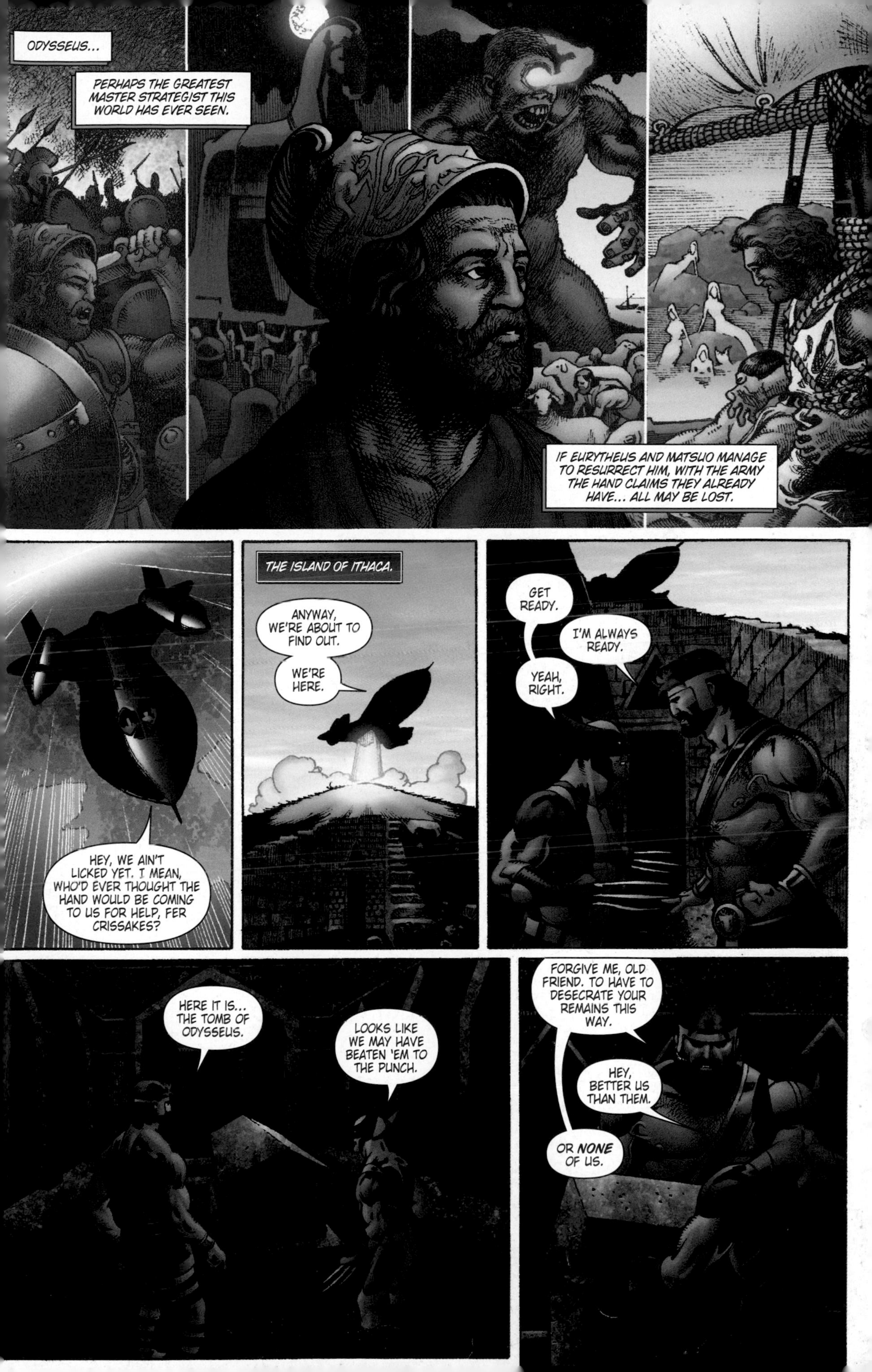

ODYSSEUS...
PERHAPS THE GREATEST MASTER STRATEGIST THIS WORLD HAS EVER SEEN.
IF EURYTHEUS AND MATSUO MANAGE TO RESURRECT HIM, WITH THE ARMY THE HAND CLAIMS THEY ALREADY HAVE... ALL MAY BE LOST.
HEY, WE AIN'T LICKED YET. I MEAN, WHO'D EVER THOUGHT THE HAND WOULD BE COMING TO US FOR HELP, FER CRISSAKES?
THE ISLAND OF ITHACA.
ANYWAY, WE'RE ABOUT TO FIND OUT.
WE'RE HERE.
GET READY.
I'M ALWAYS READY.
YEAH, RIGHT.
HERE IT IS... THE TOMB OF ODYSSEUS.
LOOKS LIKE WE MAY HAVE BEATEN 'EM TO THE PUNCH.
FORGIVE ME, OLD FRIEND. TO HAVE TO DESECRATE YOUR REMAINS THIS WAY.
HEY, BETTER US THAN THEM.
OR NONE OF US.

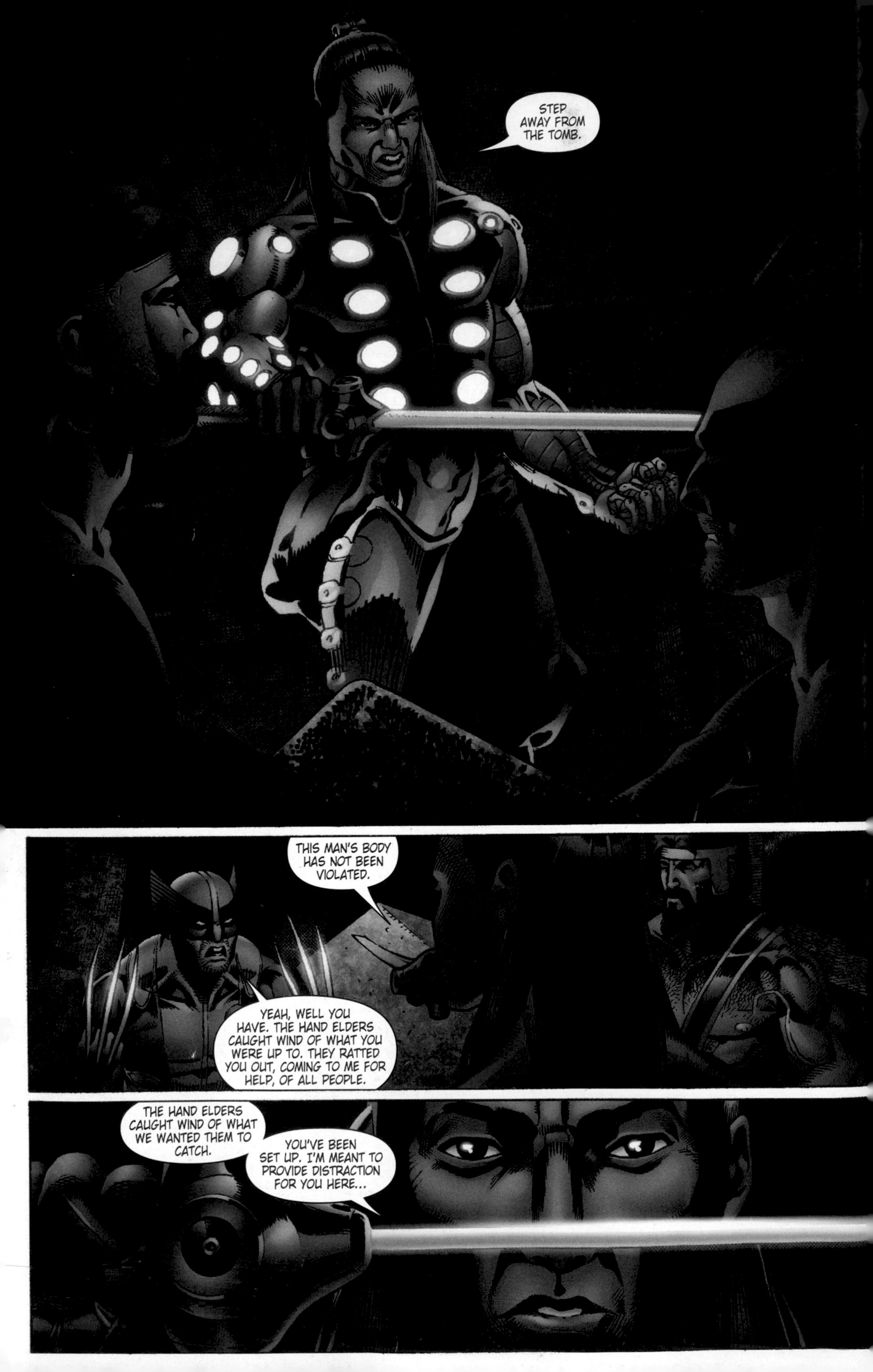
STEP AWAY FROM THE TOMB.
THIS MAN'S BODY HAS NOT BEEN VIOLATED.
YEAH, WELL YOU HAVE. THE HAND ELDERS CAUGHT WIND OF WHAT YOU WERE UP TO. THEY RATTED YOU OUT, COMING TO ME FOR HELP, OF ALL PEOPLE.
THE HAND ELDERS CAUGHT WIND OF WHAT WE WANTED THEM TO CATCH.
YOU'VE BEEN SET UP. I'M MEANT TO PROVIDE DISTRACTION FOR YOU HERE...

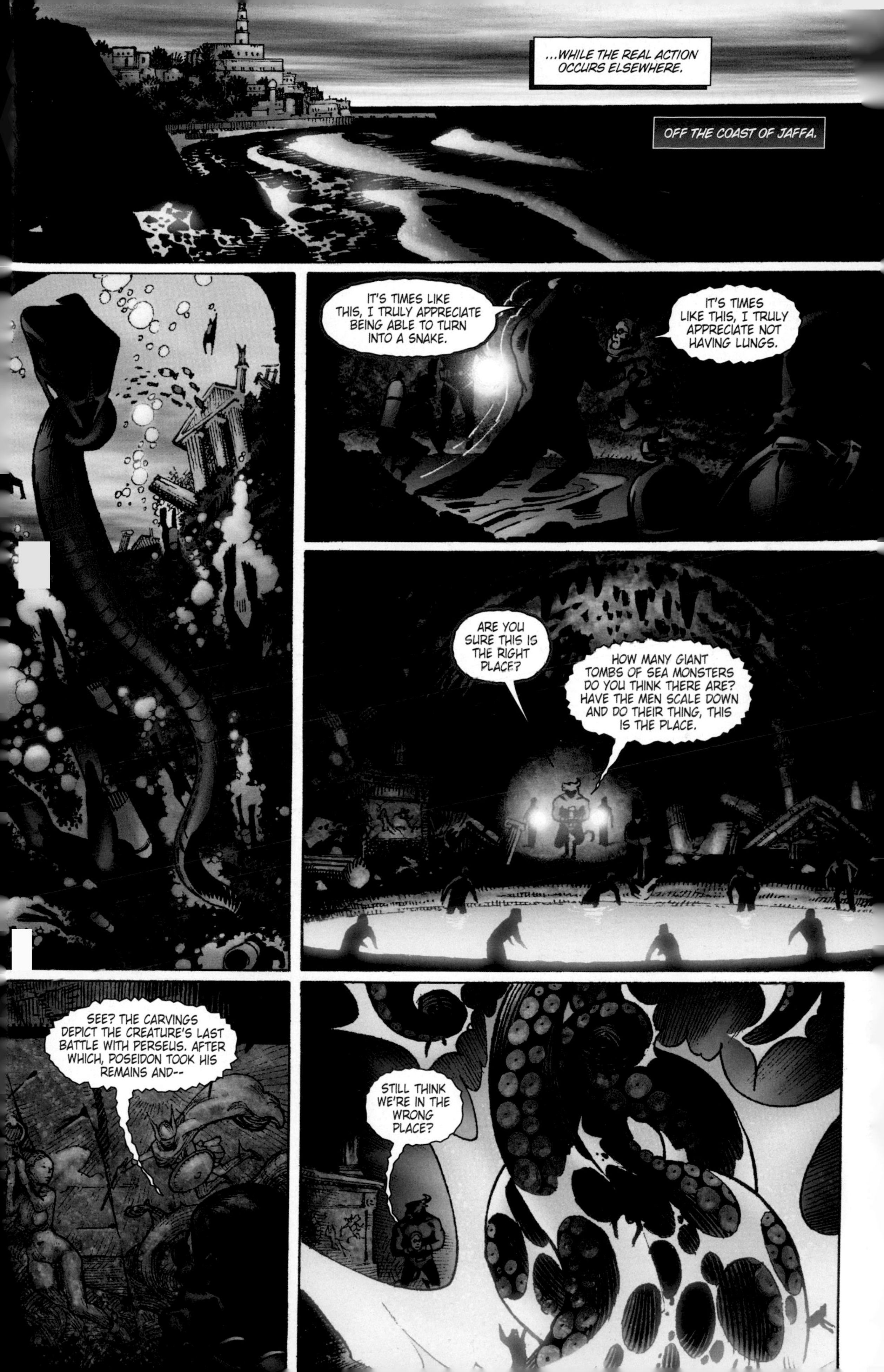

...WHILE THE REAL ACTION OCCURS ELSEWHERE.
OFF THE COAST OF JAFFA.
IT'S TIMES LIKE THIS, I TRULY APPRECIATE BEING ABLE TO TURN INTO A SNAKE.
IT'S TIMES LIKE THIS, I TRULY APPRECIATE NOT HAVING LUNGS.
ARE YOU SURE THIS IS THE RIGHT PLACE?
HOW MANY GIANT TOMBS OF SEA MONSTERS DO YOU THINK THERE ARE? HAVE THE MEN SCALE DOWN AND DO THEIR THING, THIS IS THE PLACE.
SEE? THE CARVINGS DEPICT THE CREATURE'S LAST BATTLE WITH PERSEUS. AFTER WHICH, POSEIDON TOOK HIS REMAINS AND--
STILL THINK WE'RE IN THE WRONG PLACE?

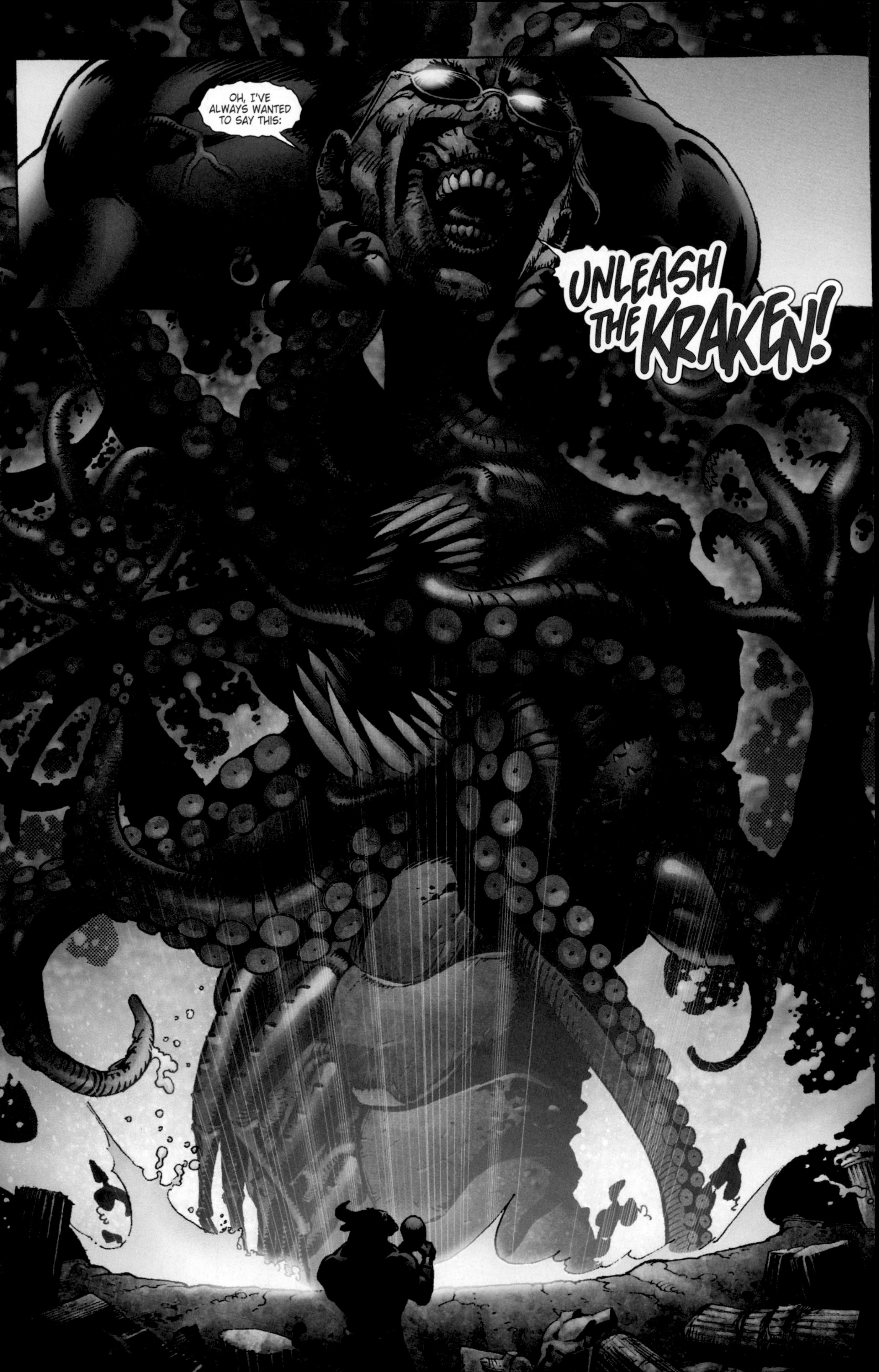
OH, I'VE ALWAYS WANTED TO SAY THIS:
UNLEASH THE KRAKEN!

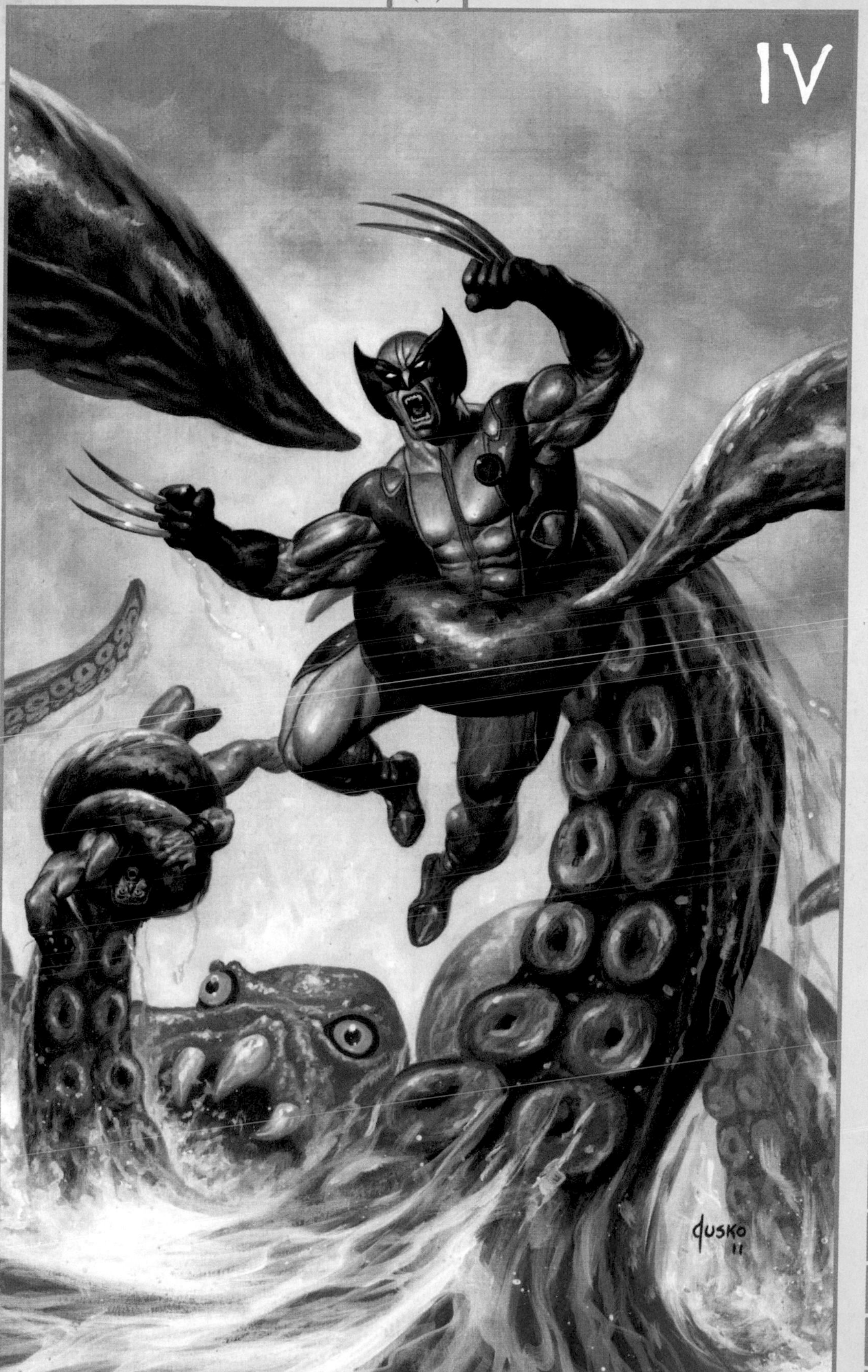
IV
JUSKO 11

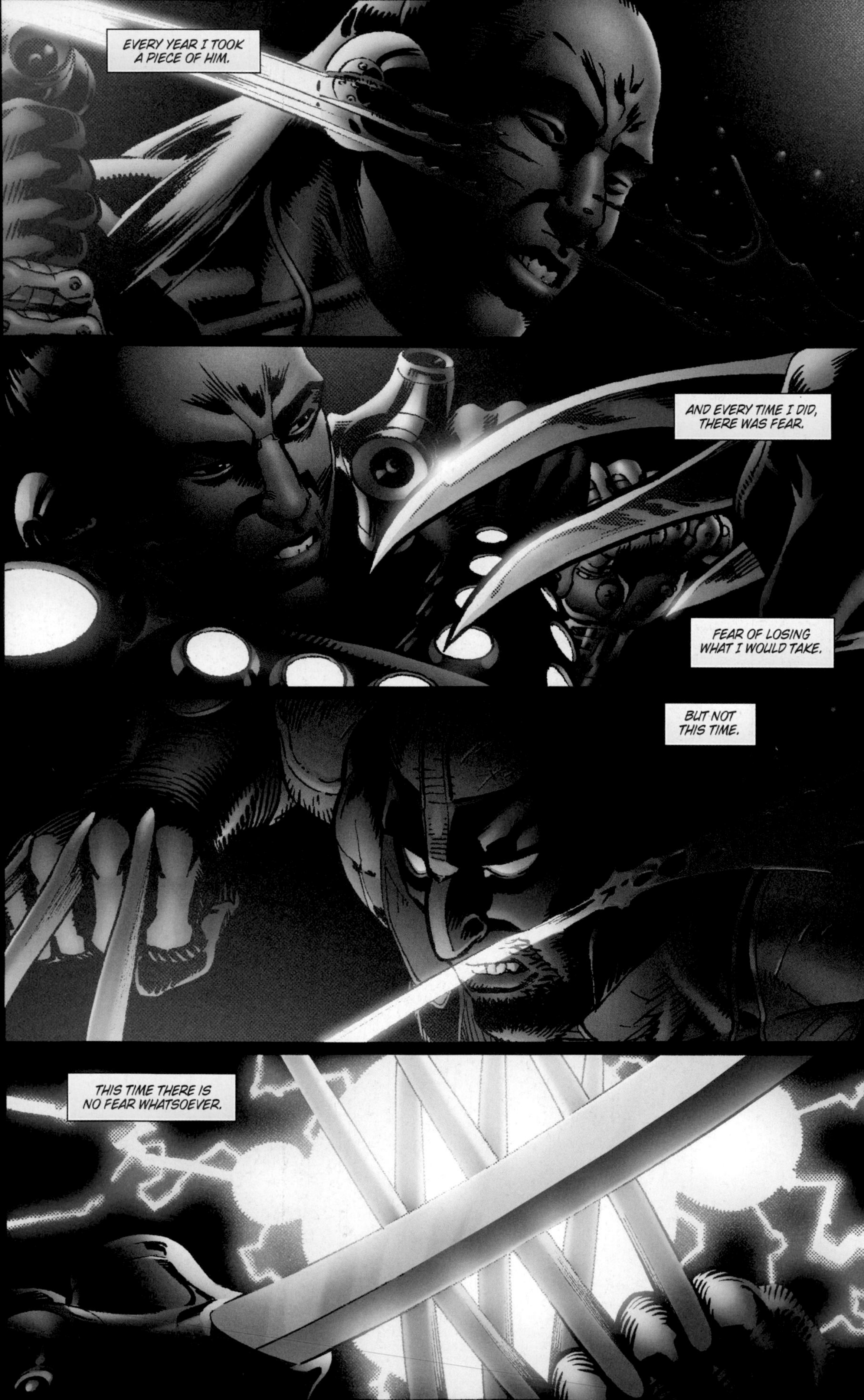
EVERY YEAR I TOOK A PIECE OF HIM.
AND EVERY TIME I DID, THERE WAS FEAR.
FEAR OF LOSING WHAT I WOULD TAKE.
BUT NOT THIS TIME.
THIS TIME THERE IS NO FEAR WHATSOEVER.

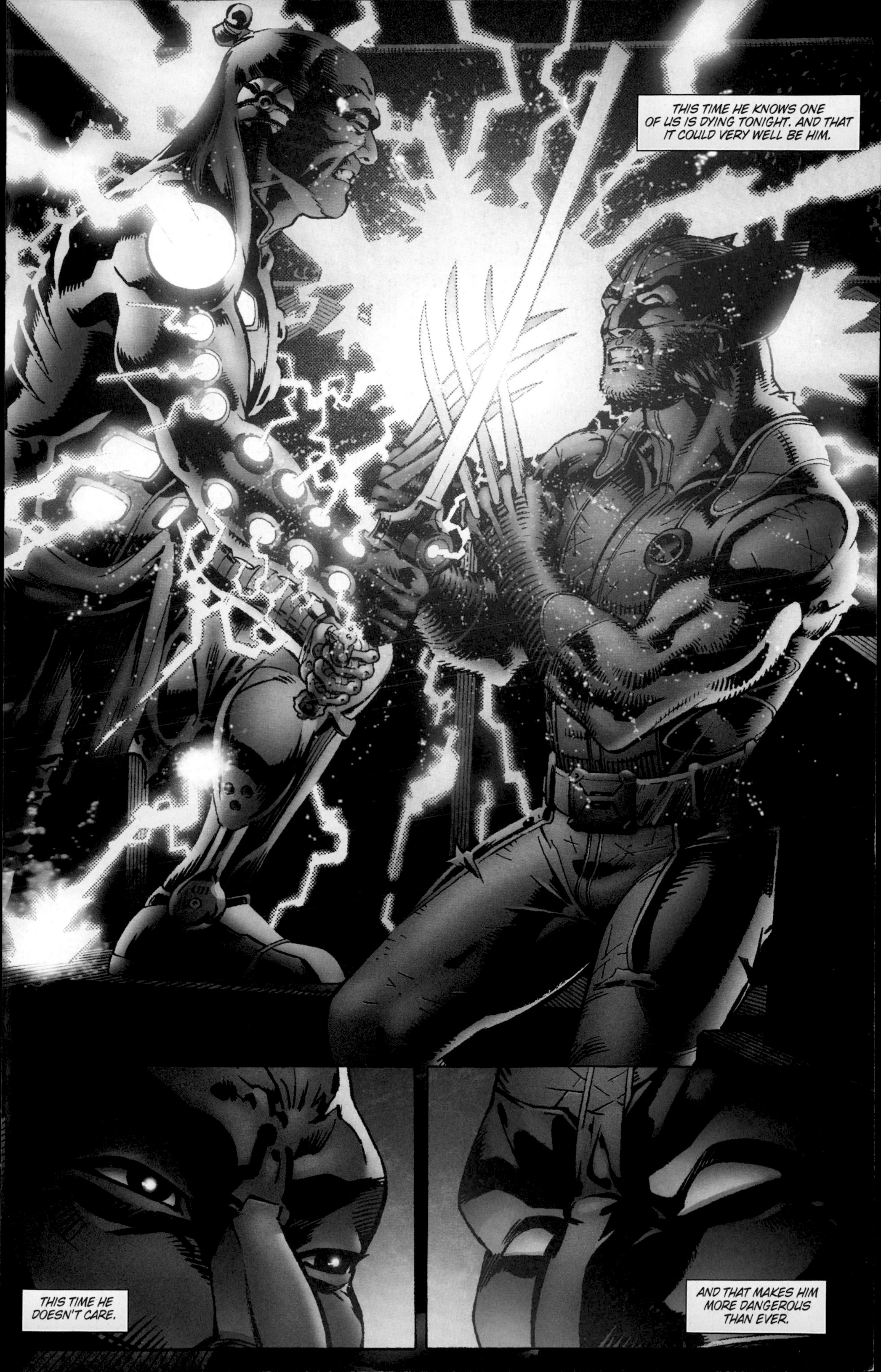
THIS TIME HE KNOWS ONE OF US IS DYING TONIGHT. AND THAT IT COULD VERY WELL BE HIM.
THIS TIME HE DOESN'T CARE.
AND THAT MAKES HIM MORE DANGEROUS THAN EVER.

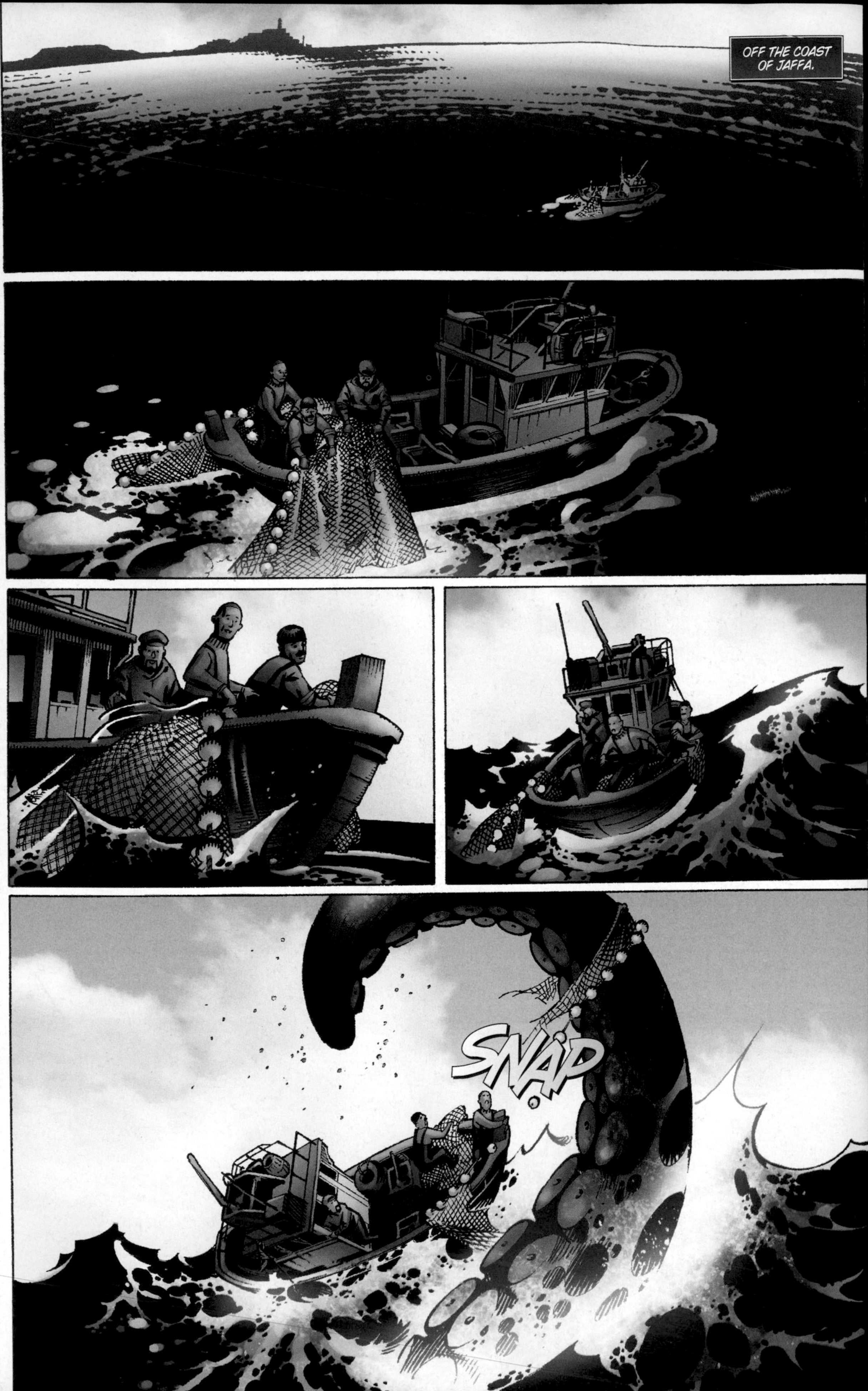
OFF THE COAST OF JAFFA.
SNAP

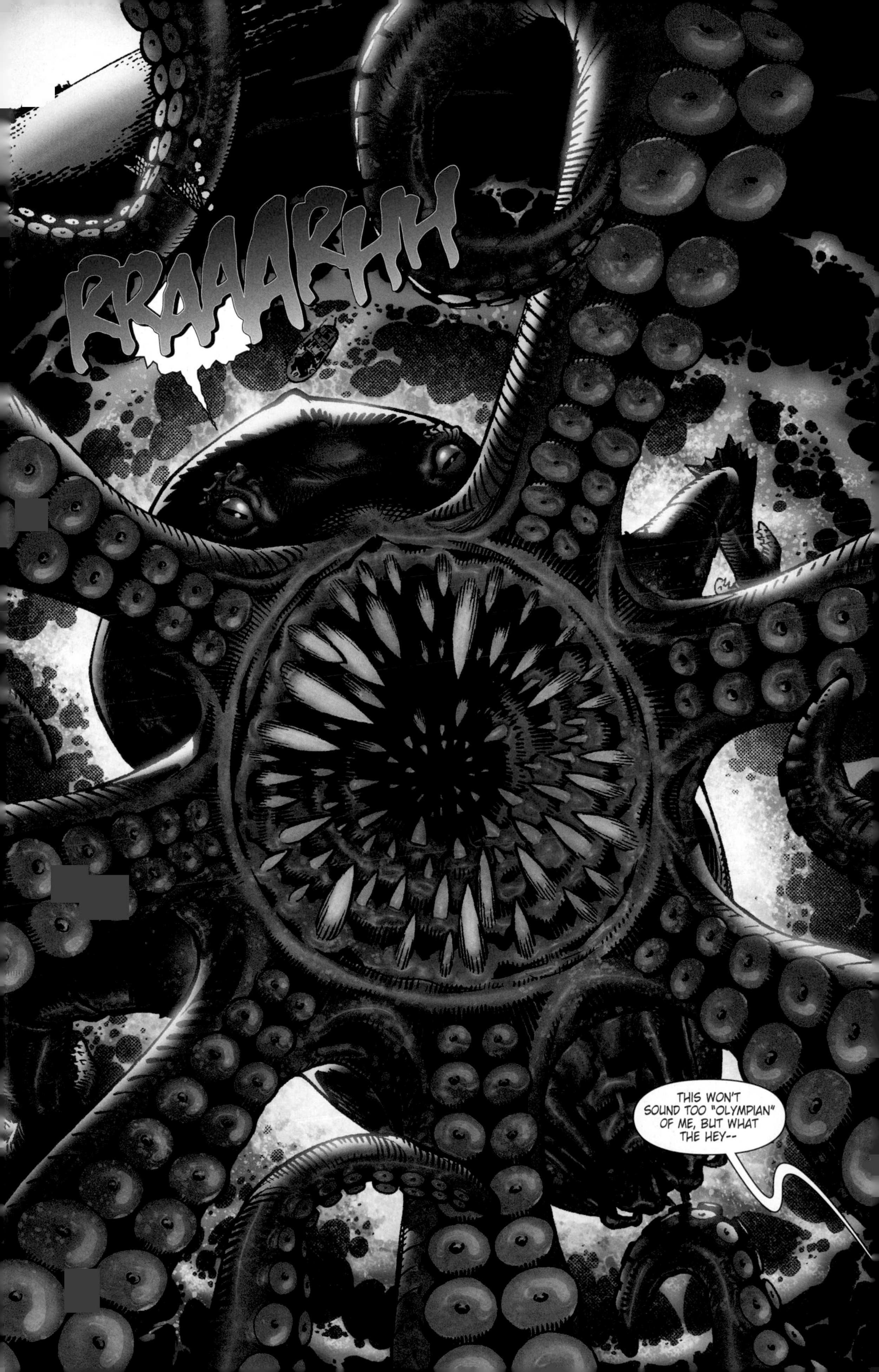
RRAAARHH
THIS WON'T SOUND TOO "OLYMPIAN" OF ME, BUT WHAT THE HEY--

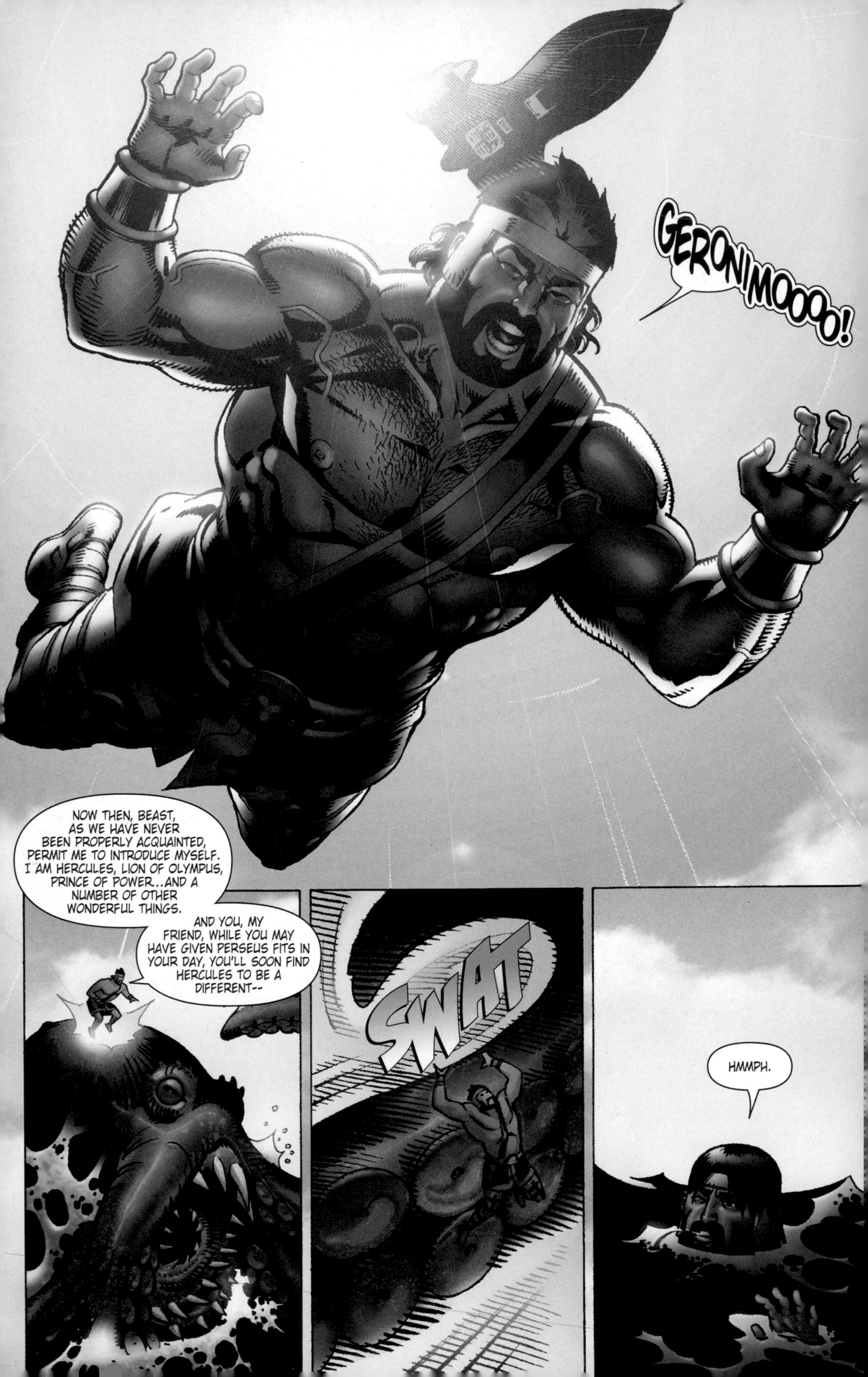
GERONIMOOOO!
NOW THEN, BEAST, AS WE HAVE NEVER BEEN PROPERLY ACQUAINTED, PERMIT ME TO INTRODUCE MYSELF. I AM HERCULES, LION OF OLYMPUS, PRINCE OF POWER...AND A NUMBER OF OTHER WONDERFUL THINGS.
AND YOU, MY FRIEND, WHILE YOU MAY HAVE GIVEN PERSEUS FITS IN YOUR DAY, YOU'LL SOON FIND HERCULES TO BE A DIFFERENT--
SWAT
HMMPH.

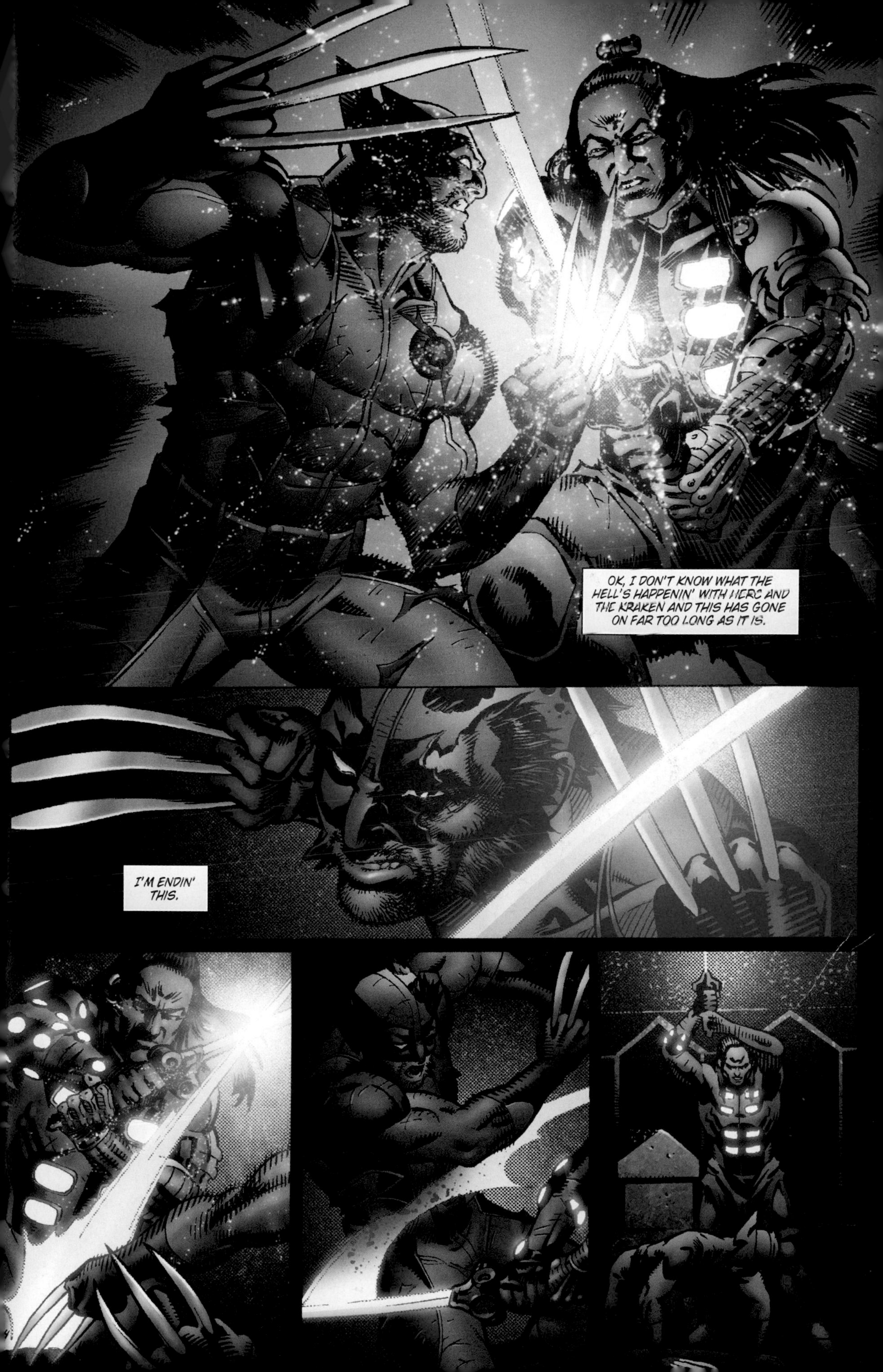
OK, I DON'T KNOW WHAT THE HELL'S HAPPENIN' WITH HERC AND THE KRAKEN AND THIS HAS GONE ON FAR TOO LONG AS IT IS.
I'M ENDIN' THIS.

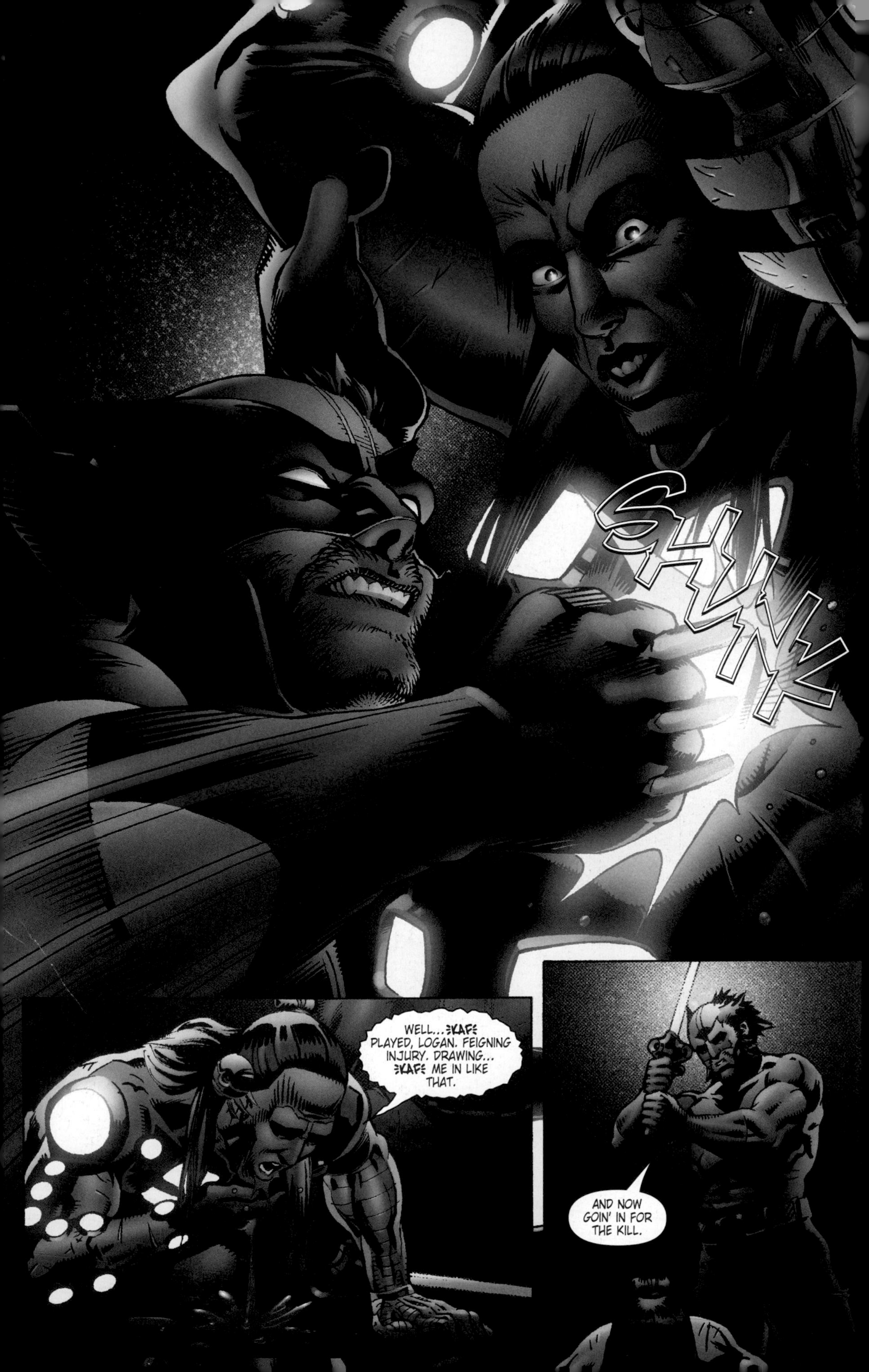
SHUNK
WELL... KAF PLAYED, LOGAN. FEIGNING INJURY. DRAWING... KAF ME IN LIKE THAT.
AND NOW GOIN' IN FOR THE KILL.

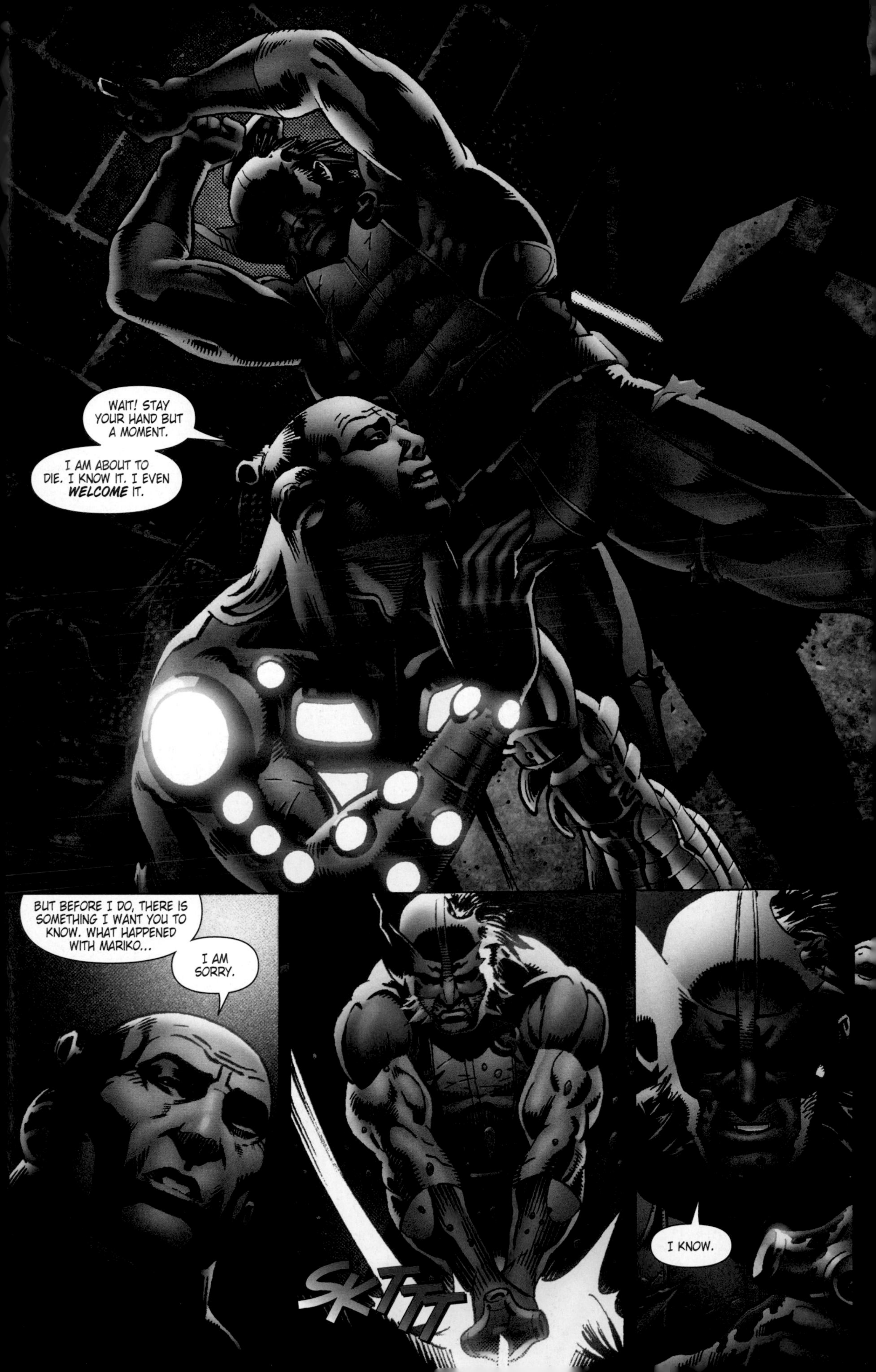
WAIT! STAY YOUR HAND BUT A MOMENT.
I AM ABOUT TO DIE. I KNOW IT. I EVEN WELCOME IT.
BUT BEFORE I DO, THERE IS SOMETHING I WANT YOU TO KNOW. WHAT HAPPENED WITH MARIKO...
I AM SORRY.
SKTTT
I KNOW.

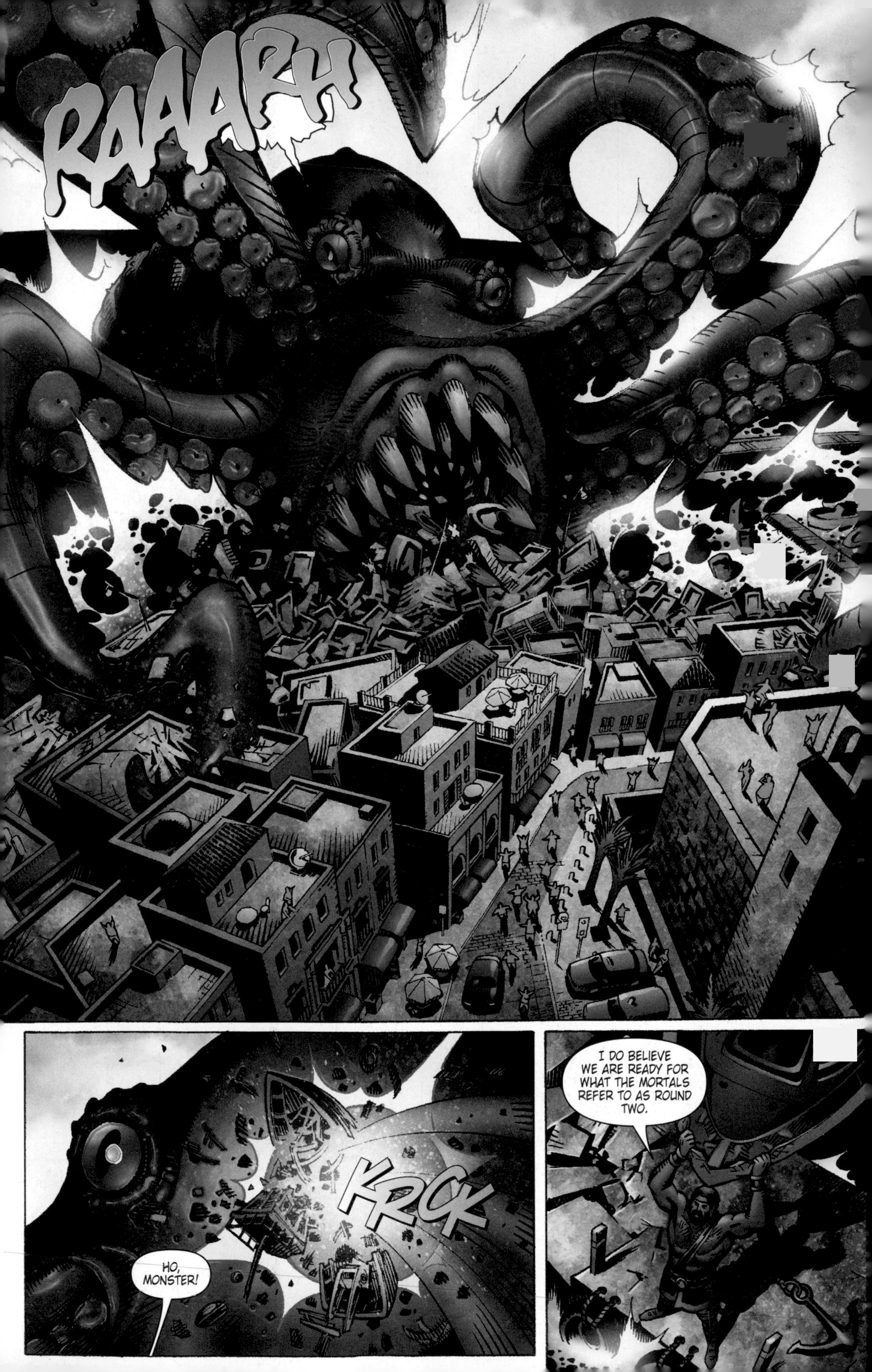
RAAARH
KRCK
HO, MONSTER!
I DO BELIEVE WE ARE READY FOR WHAT THE MORTALS REFER TO AS ROUND TWO.

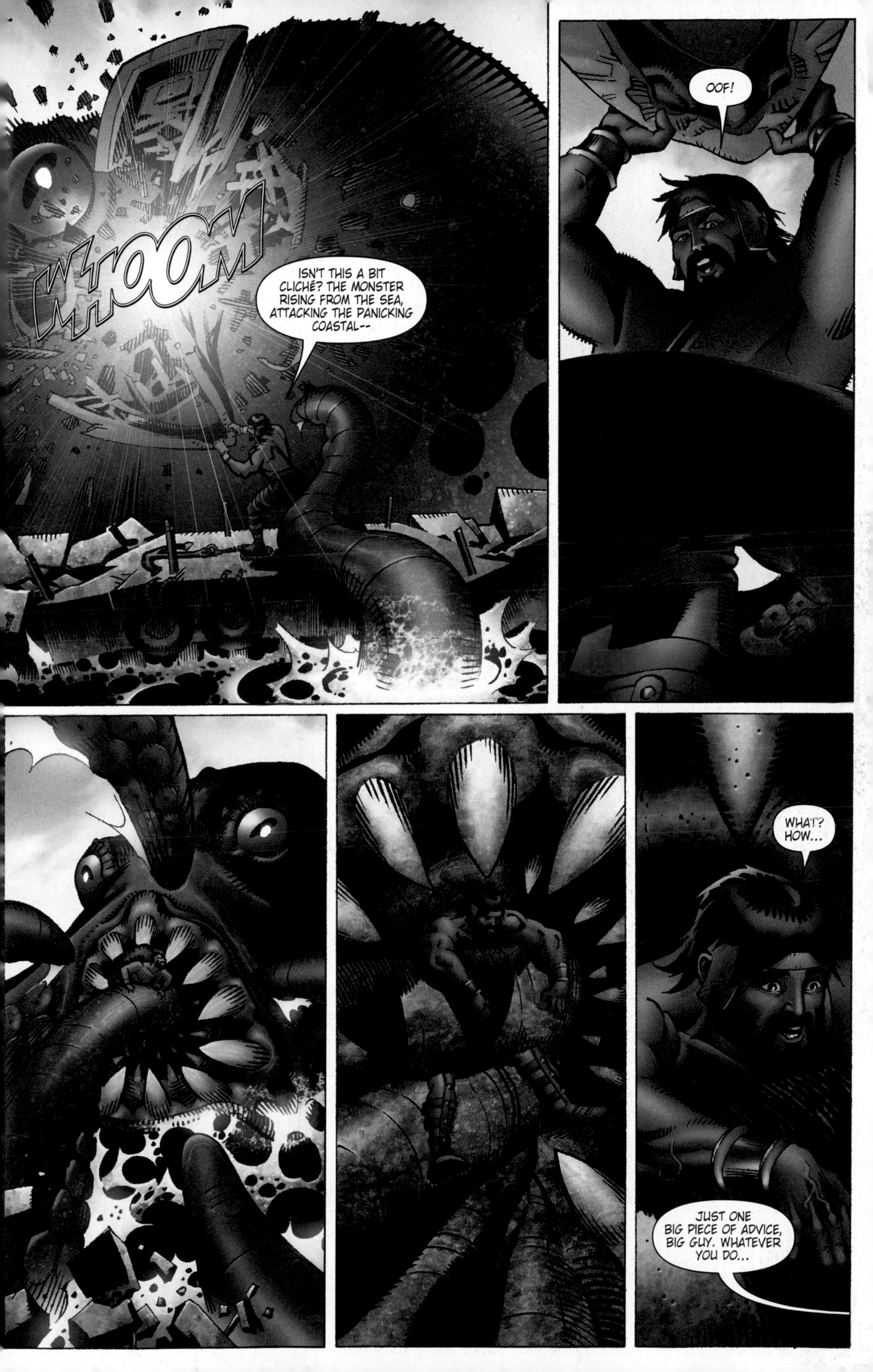
WHOOM
ISN'T THIS A BIT CLICHÉ? THE MONSTER RISING FROM THE SEA, ATTACKING THE PANICKING COASTAL--
OOF!
WHAT? HOW...
JUST ONE BIG PIECE OF ADVICE, BIG GUY. WHATEVER YOU DO...

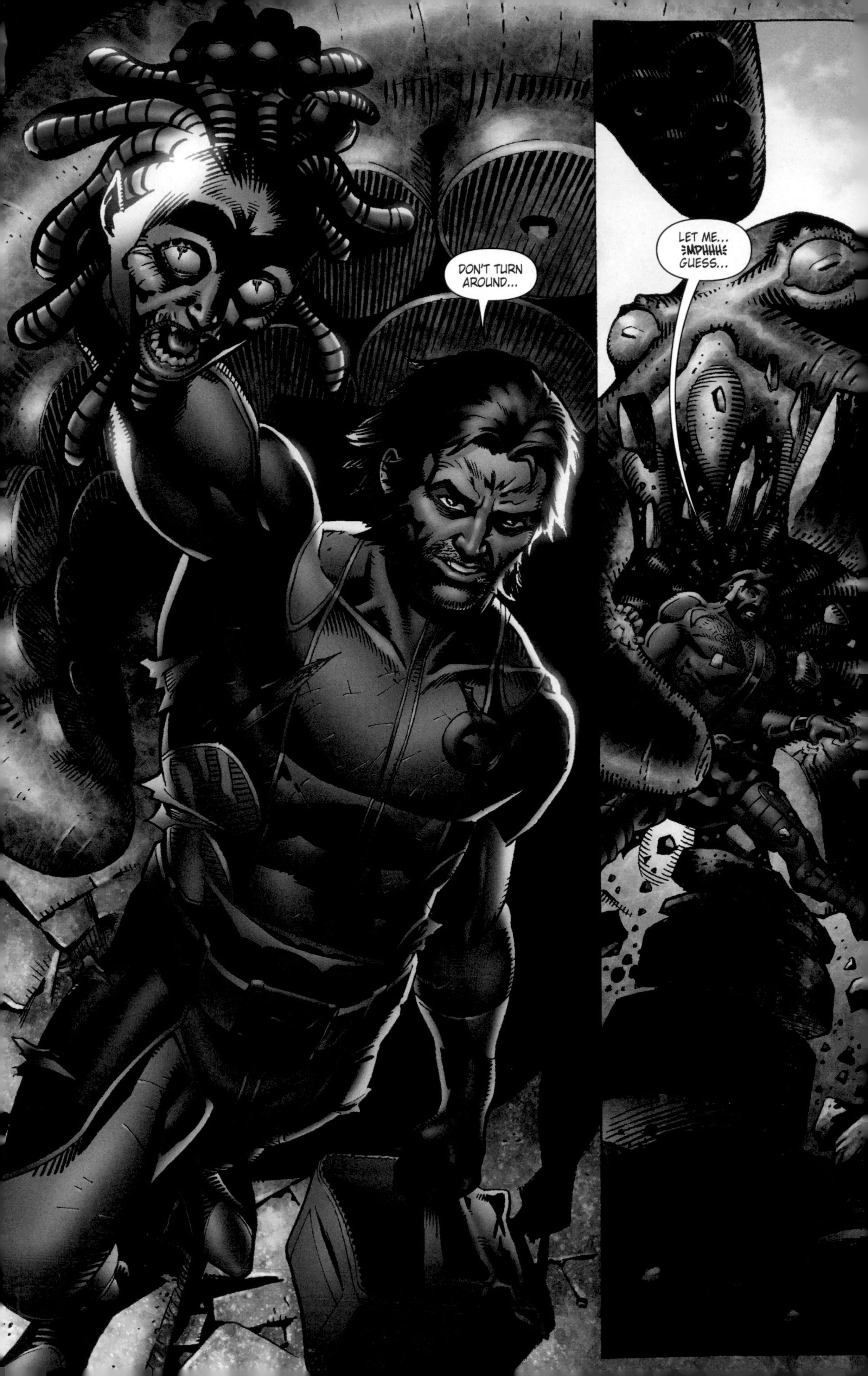
DON'T TURN AROUND...
LET ME... MPHHH GUESS...

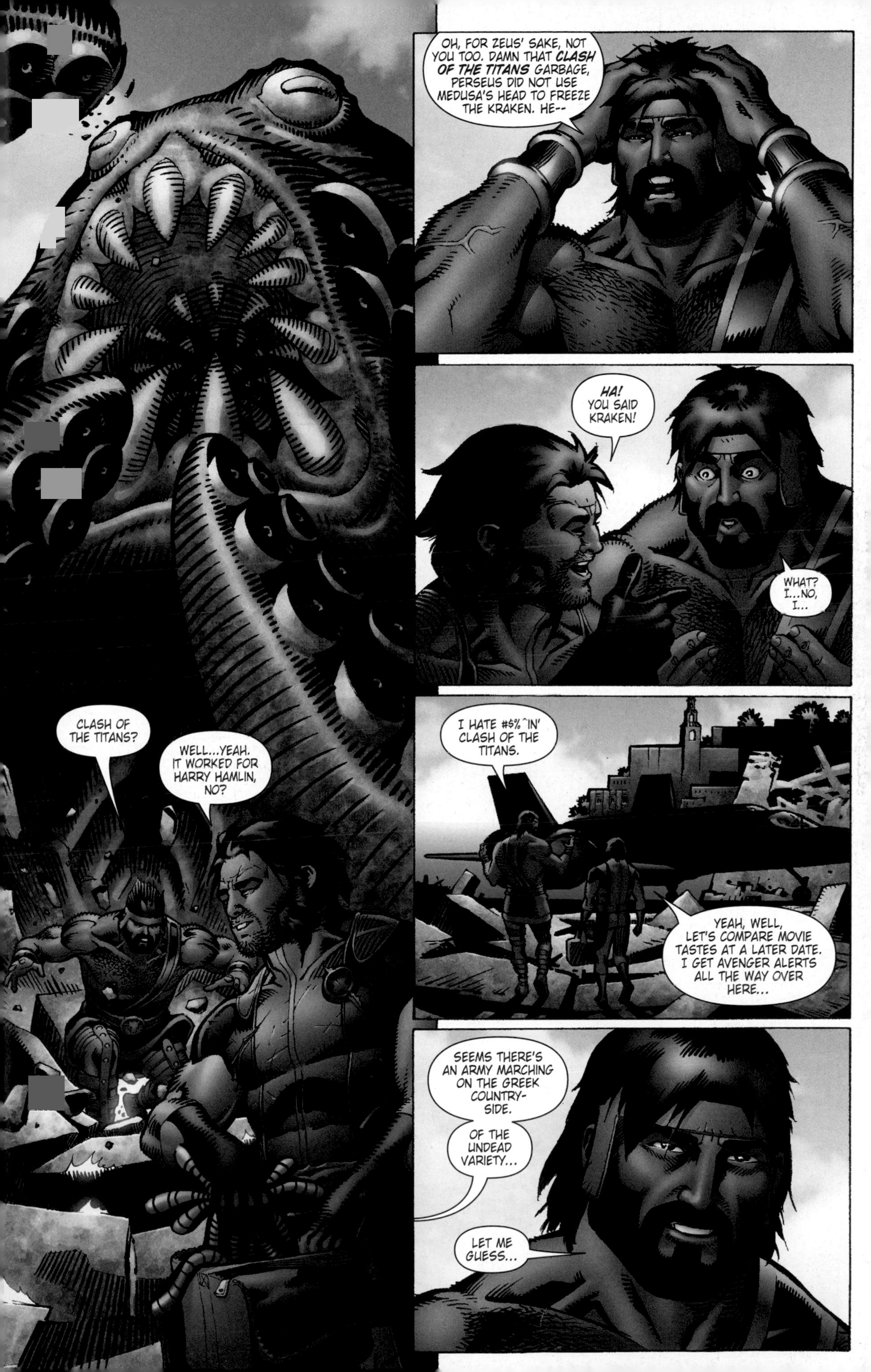
CLASH OF THE TITANS?
WELL...YEAH. IT WORKED FOR HARRY HAMLIN, NO?
OH, FOR ZEUS' SAKE, NOT YOU TOO. DAMN THAT CLASH OF THE TITANS GARBAGE, PERSEUS DID NOT USE MEDUSA'S HEAD TO FREEZE THE KRAKEN. HE--
HA! YOU SAID KRAKEN!
WHAT? I...NO, I...
I HATE #$%^IN' CLASH OF THE TITANS.
YEAH, WELL, LET'S COMPARE MOVIE TASTES AT A LATER DATE. I GET AVENGER ALERTS ALL THE WAY OVER HERE...
SEEMS THERE'S AN ARMY MARCHING ON THE GREEK COUNTRY-SIDE.
OF THE UNDEAD VARIETY...
LET ME GUESS...

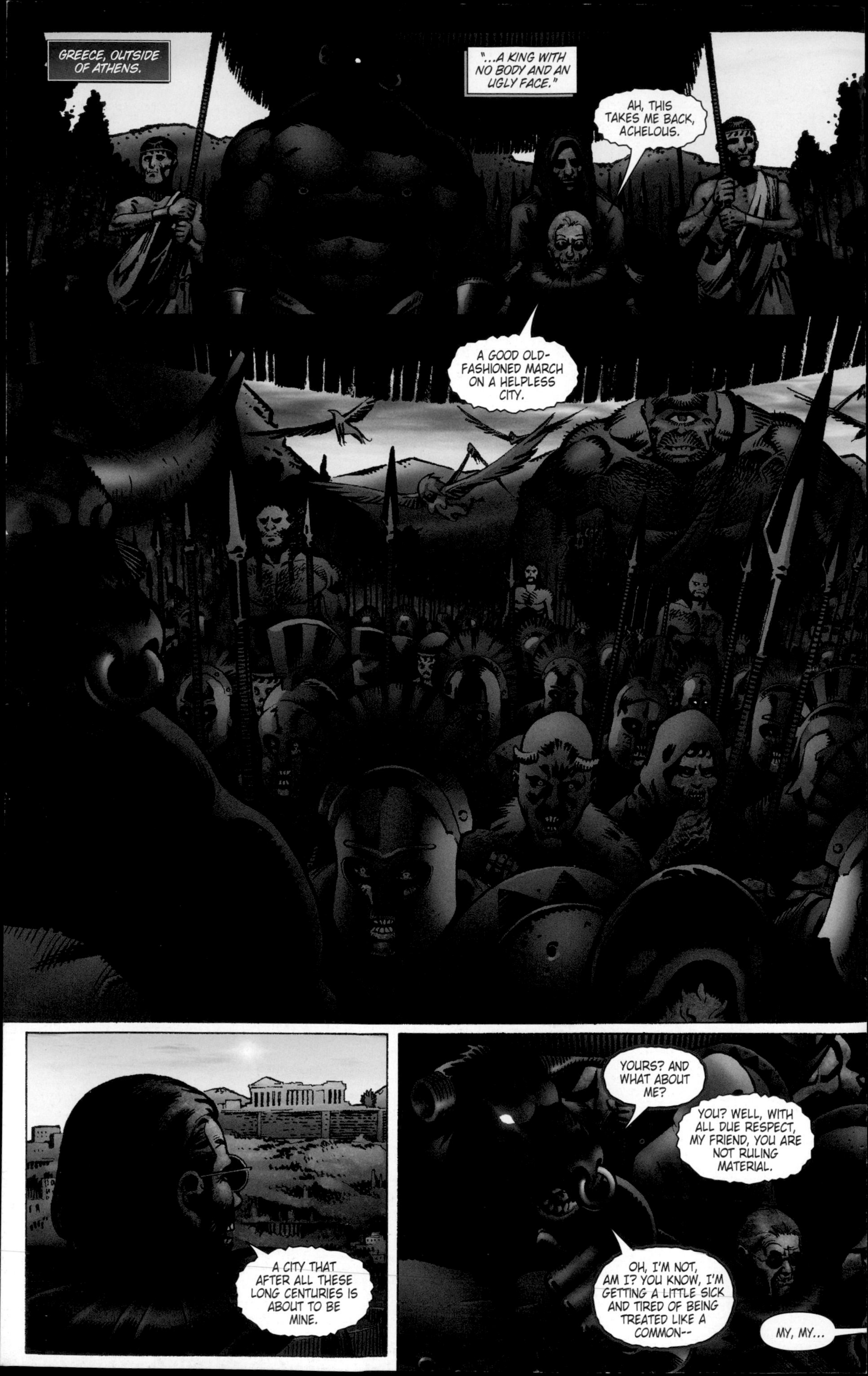
GREECE, OUTSIDE OF ATHENS.
"...A KING WITH NO BODY AND AN UGLY FACE."
AH, THIS TAKES ME BACK, ACHELOUS.
A GOOD OLD-FASHIONED MARCH ON A HELPLESS CITY.
A CITY THAT AFTER ALL THESE LONG CENTURIES IS ABOUT TO BE MINE.
YOURS? AND WHAT ABOUT ME?
YOU? WELL, WITH ALL DUE RESPECT, MY FRIEND, YOU ARE NOT RULING MATERIAL.
OH, I'M NOT, AM I? YOU KNOW, I'M GETTING A LITTLE SICK AND TIRED OF BEING TREATED LIKE A COMMON--
MY, MY...

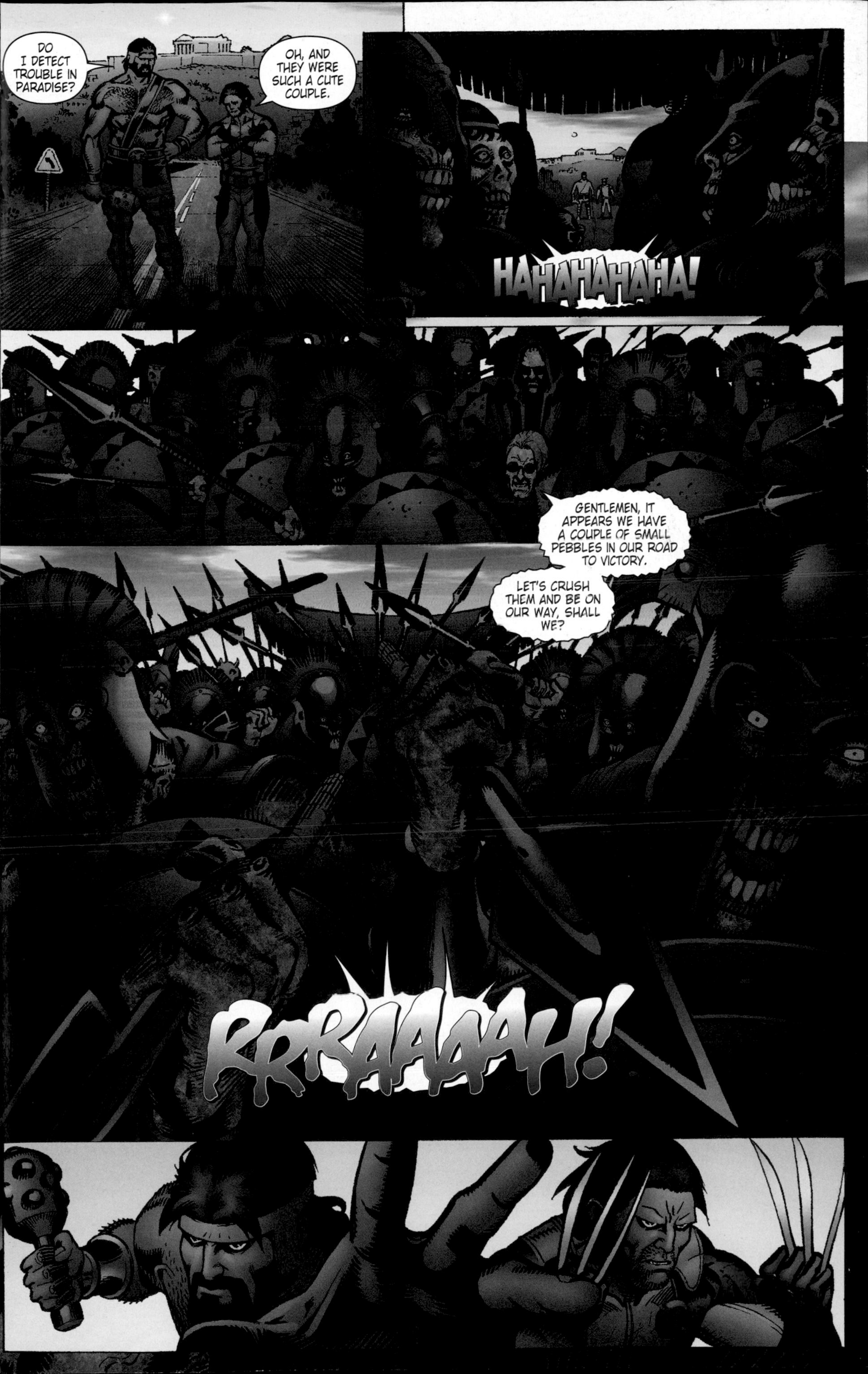
DO I DETECT TROUBLE IN PARADISE?
OH, AND THEY WERE SUCH A CUTE COUPLE.
HAHAHAHAHA!
GENTLEMEN, IT APPEARS WE HAVE A COUPLE OF SMALL PEBBLES IN OUR ROAD TO VICTORY.
LET'S CRUSH THEM AND BE ON OUR WAY, SHALL WE?
RRRAAAAH!

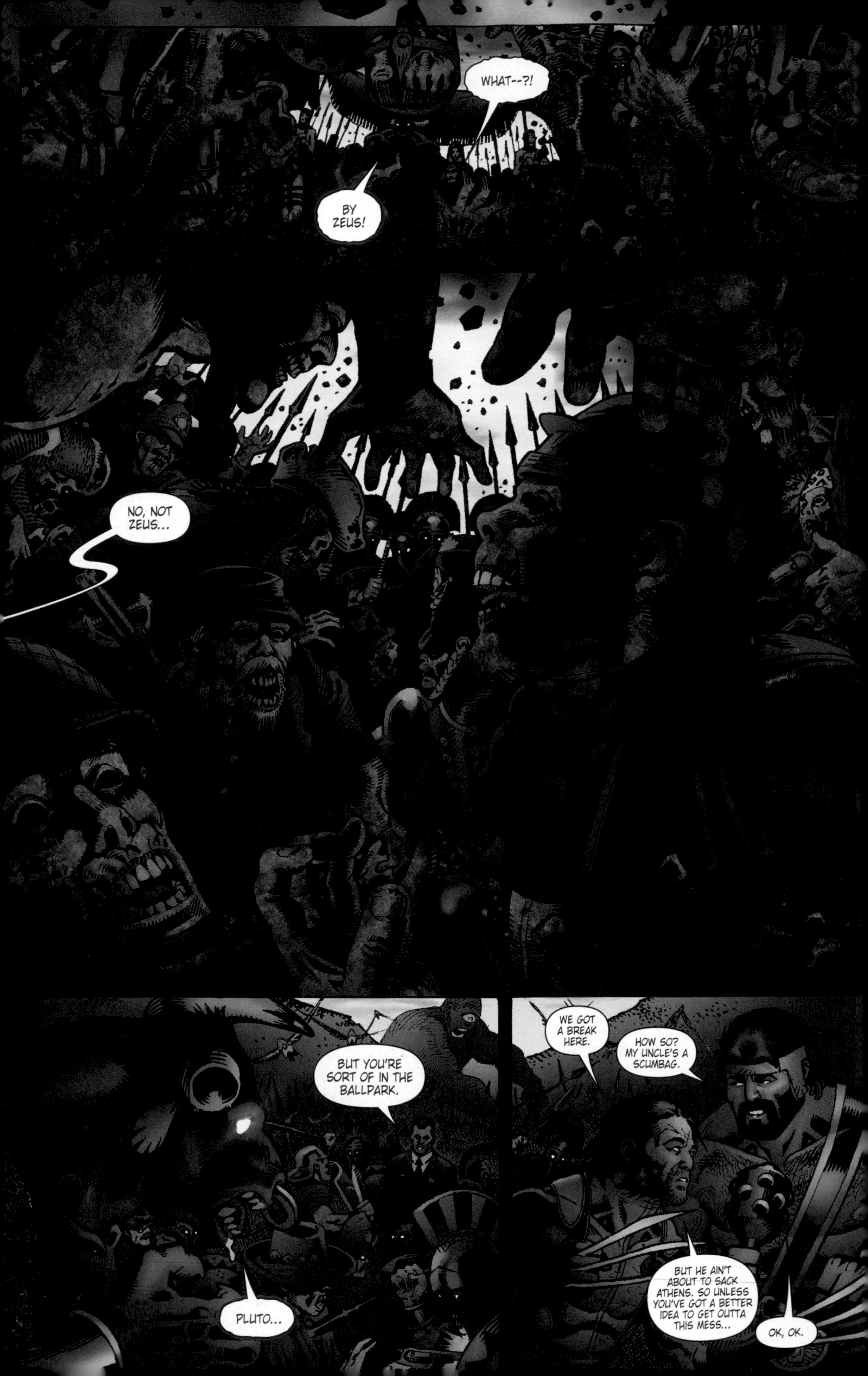
WHAT--?!
BY ZEUS!
NO, NOT ZEUS...
PLUTO...
BUT YOU'RE SORT OF IN THE BALLPARK.
WE GOT A BREAK HERE.
HOW SO? MY UNCLE'S A SCUMBAG.
BUT HE AIN'T ABOUT TO SACK ATHENS. SO UNLESS YOU'VE GOT A BETTER IDEA TO GET OUTTA THIS MESS...
OK, OK.

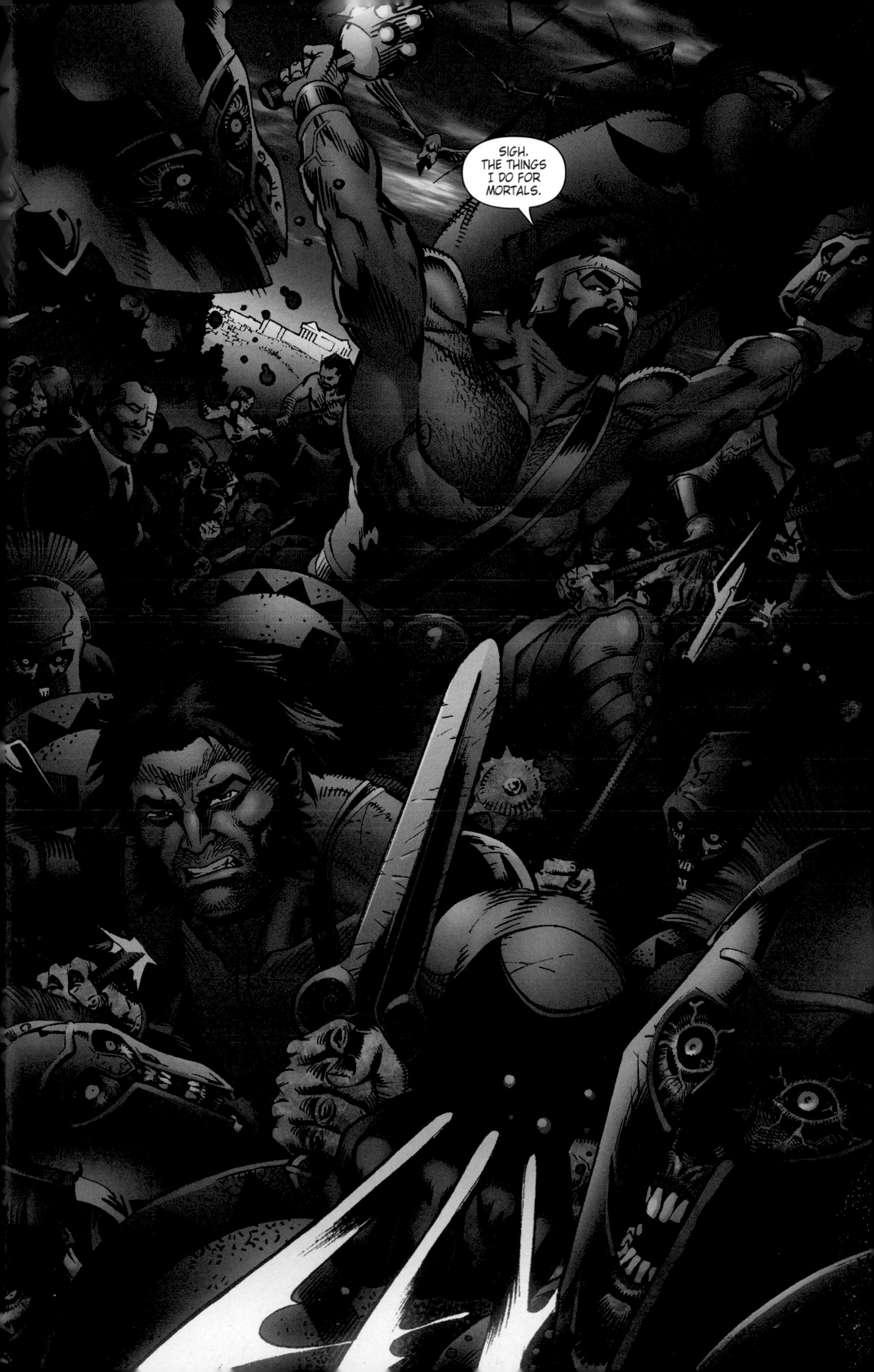
SIGH. THE THINGS I DO FOR MORTALS.

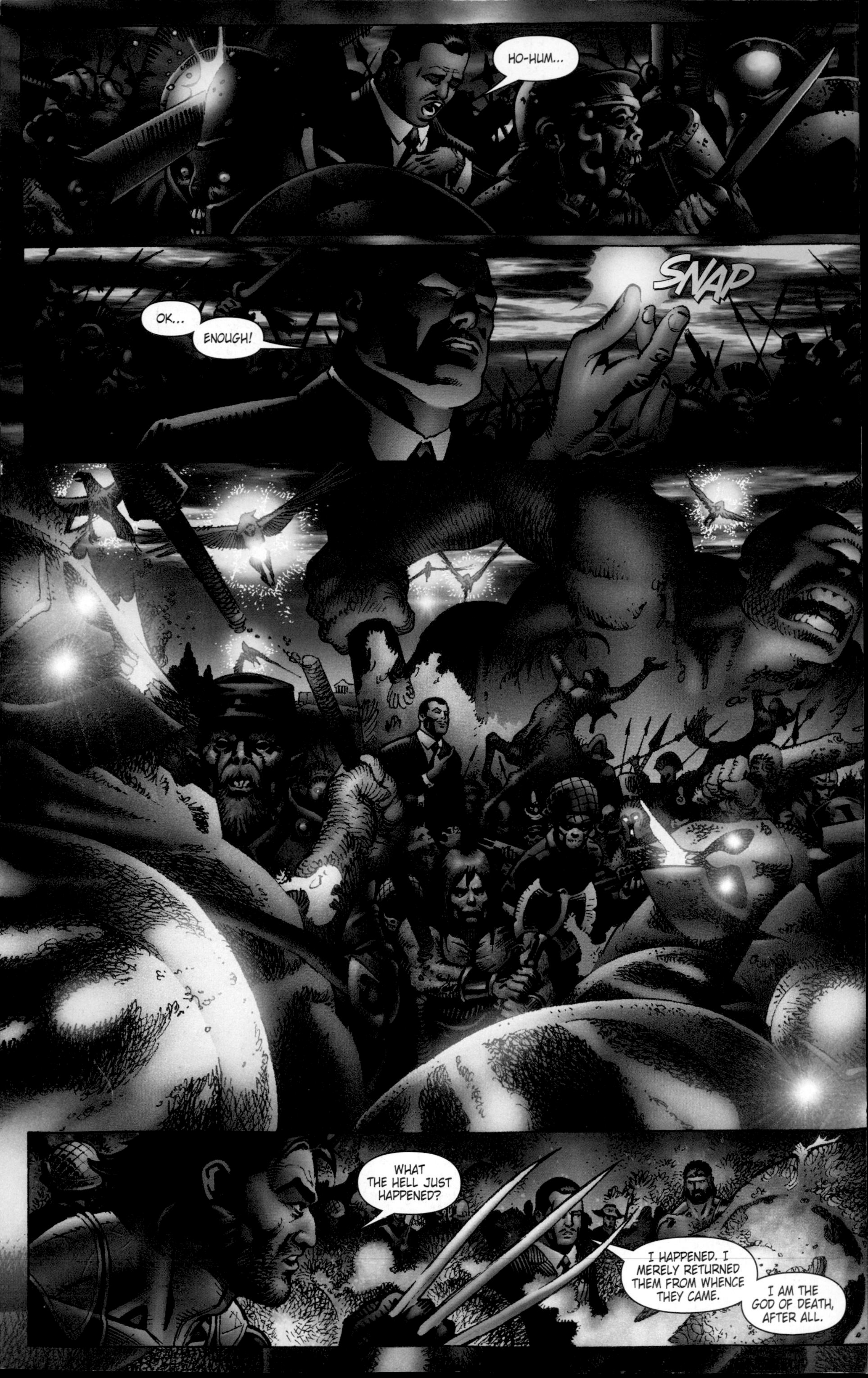
HO-HUM...
OK...
ENOUGH!
SNAP
WHAT THE HELL JUST HAPPENED?
I HAPPENED. I MERELY RETURNED THEM FROM WHENCE THEY CAME.
I AM THE GOD OF DEATH, AFTER ALL.

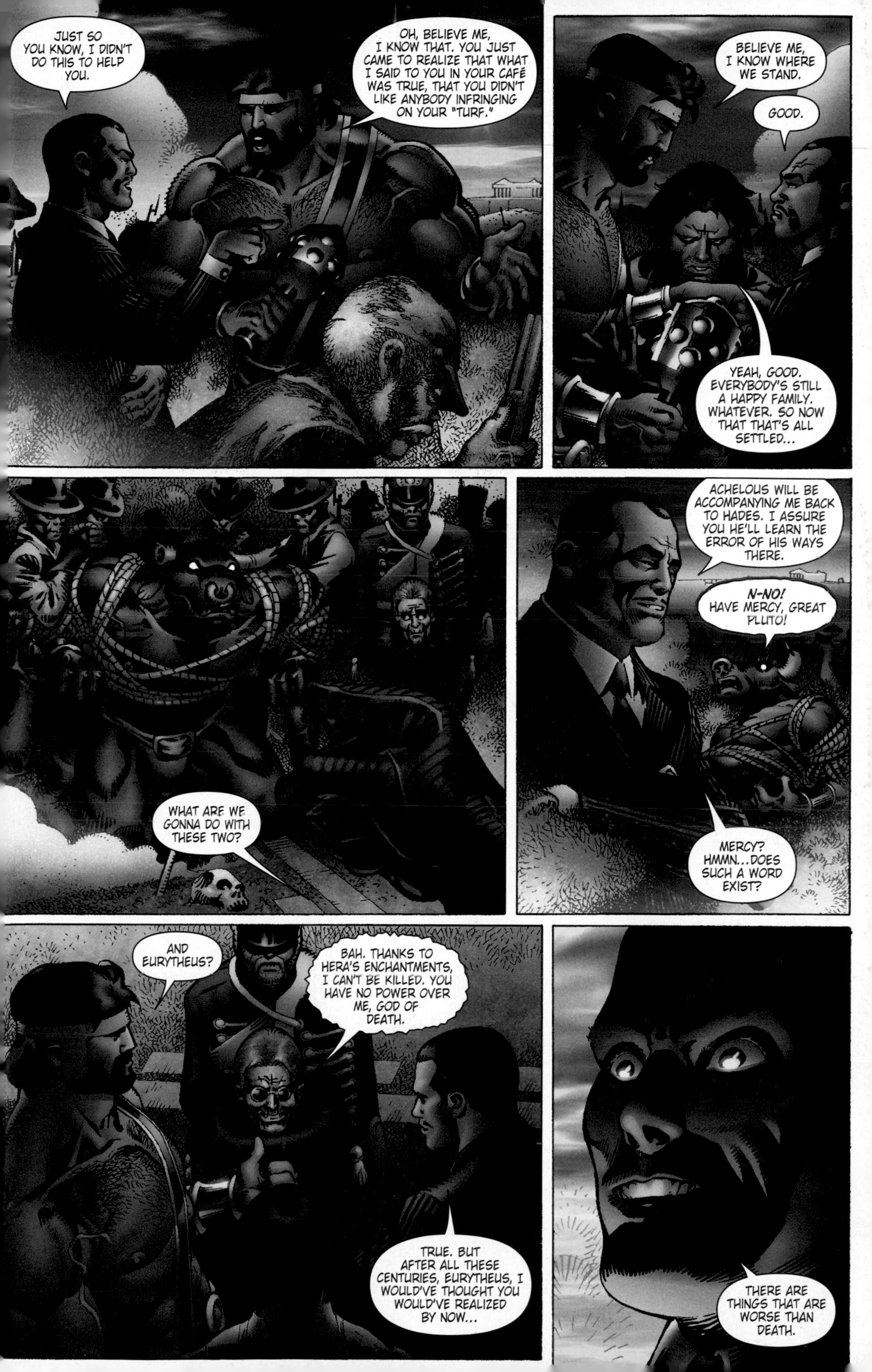
JUST SO YOU KNOW, I DIDN'T DO THIS TO HELP YOU.
OH, BELIEVE ME, I KNOW THAT. YOU JUST CAME TO REALIZE THAT WHAT I SAID TO YOU IN YOUR CAFÉ WAS TRUE, THAT YOU DIDN'T LIKE ANYBODY INFRINGING ON YOUR "TURF."
BELIEVE ME, I KNOW WHERE WE STAND.
GOOD.
YEAH, GOOD. EVERYBODY'S STILL A HAPPY FAMILY. WHATEVER. SO NOW THAT THAT'S ALL SETTLED...
WHAT ARE WE GONNA DO WITH THESE TWO?
ACHELOUS WILL BE ACCOMPANYING ME BACK TO HADES. I ASSURE YOU HE'LL LEARN THE ERROR OF HIS WAYS THERE.
N-NO! HAVE MERCY, GREAT PLUTO!
MERCY? HMMN...DOES SUCH A WORD EXIST?
AND EURYTHEUS?
BAH. THANKS TO HERA'S ENCHANTMENTS, I CAN'T BE KILLED. YOU HAVE NO POWER OVER ME, GOD OF DEATH.
TRUE. BUT AFTER ALL THESE CENTURIES, EURYTHEUS, I WOULD'VE THOUGHT YOU WOULD'VE REALIZED BY NOW...
THERE ARE THINGS THAT ARE WORSE THAN DEATH.

JAPAN.
FINALLY DECIDED TO END MY LITTLE GAME WITH MATSUO ONCE AND FOR ALL.
SO YEAH, IN OTHER WORDS, I GOT ME MY POUND OF FLESH.
WELL, SWEETHEART. IT'S OVER.
IT NEVER DOES.
DON'T MAKE ME MISS YA ANY LESS THOUGH.

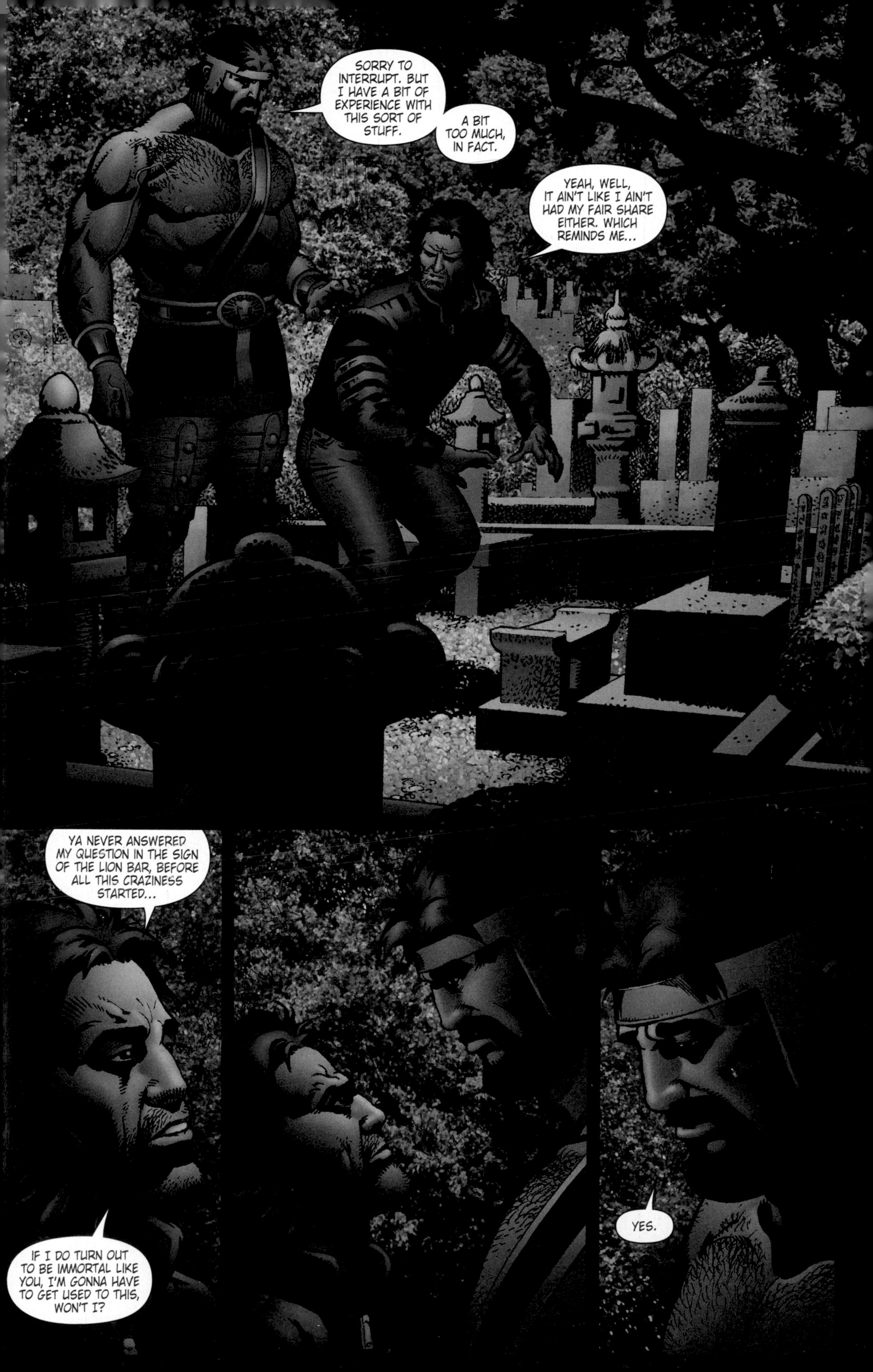
SORRY TO INTERRUPT. BUT I HAVE A BIT OF EXPERIENCE WITH THIS SORT OF STUFF.
A BIT TOO MUCH, IN FACT.
YEAH, WELL, IT AIN'T LIKE I AIN'T HAD MY FAIR SHARE EITHER. WHICH REMINDS ME...
YA NEVER ANSWERED MY QUESTION IN THE SIGN OF THE LION BAR, BEFORE ALL THIS CRAZINESS STARTED...
IF I DO TURN OUT TO BE IMMORTAL LIKE YOU, I'M GONNA HAVE TO GET USED TO THIS, WON'T I?
YES.

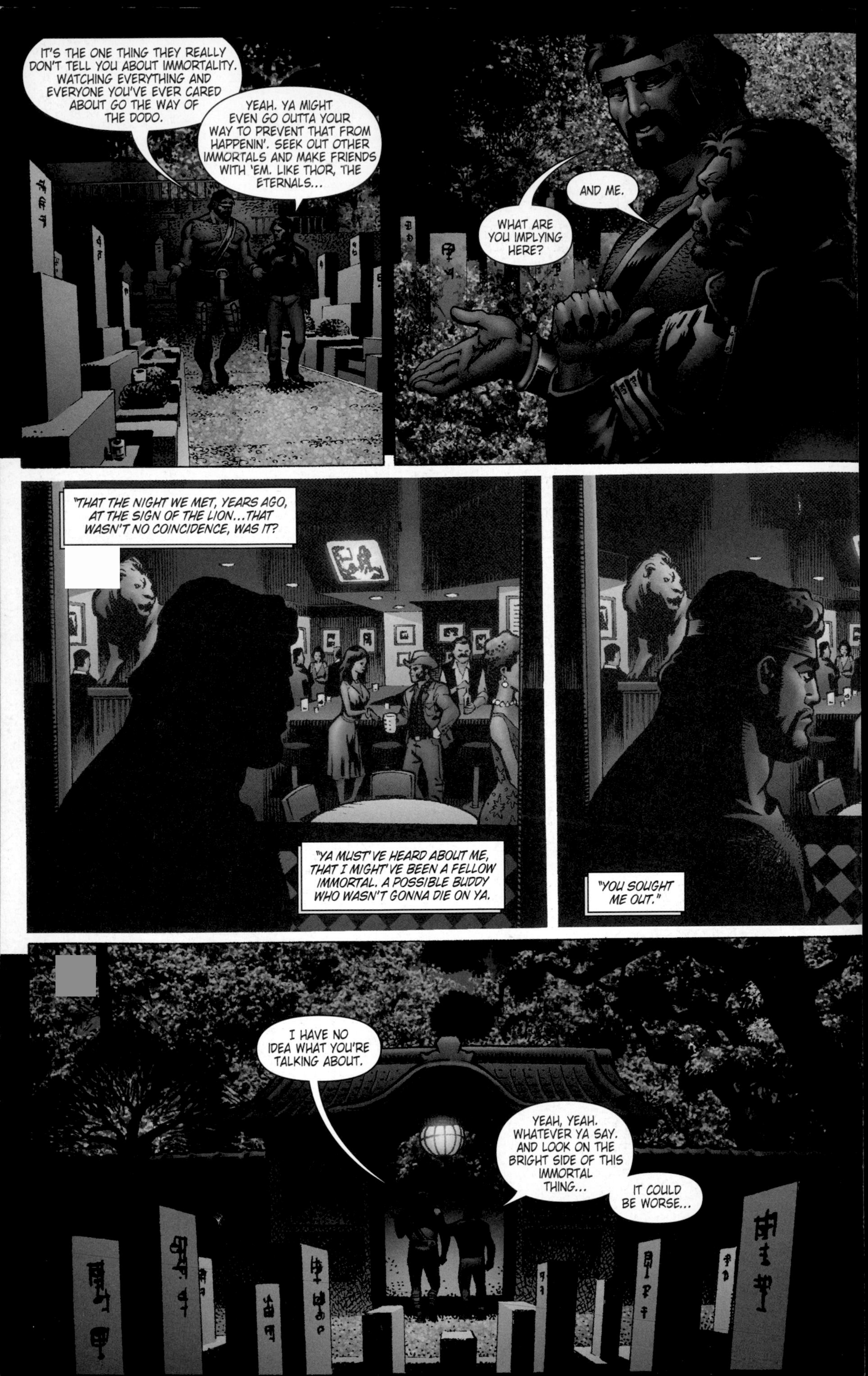
IT'S THE ONE THING THEY REALLY DON'T TELL YOU ABOUT IMMORTALITY. WATCHING EVERYTHING AND EVERYONE YOU'VE EVER CARED ABOUT GO THE WAY OF THE DODO.
YEAH. YA MIGHT EVEN GO OUTTA YOUR WAY TO PREVENT THAT FROM HAPPENIN'. SEEK OUT OTHER IMMORTALS AND MAKE FRIENDS WITH 'EM. LIKE THOR, THE ETERNALS...
AND ME.
WHAT ARE YOU IMPLYING HERE?
"THAT THE NIGHT WE MET, YEARS AGO, AT THE SIGN OF THE LION...THAT WASN'T NO COINCIDENCE, WAS IT?
"YA MUST'VE HEARD ABOUT ME, THAT I MIGHT'VE BEEN A FELLOW IMMORTAL. A POSSIBLE BUDDY WHO WASN'T GONNA DIE ON YA.
"YOU SOUGHT ME OUT."
I HAVE NO IDEA WHAT YOU'RE TALKING ABOUT.
YEAH, YEAH. WHATEVER YA SAY. AND LOOK ON THE BRIGHT SIDE OF THIS IMMORTAL THING...
IT COULD BE WORSE...

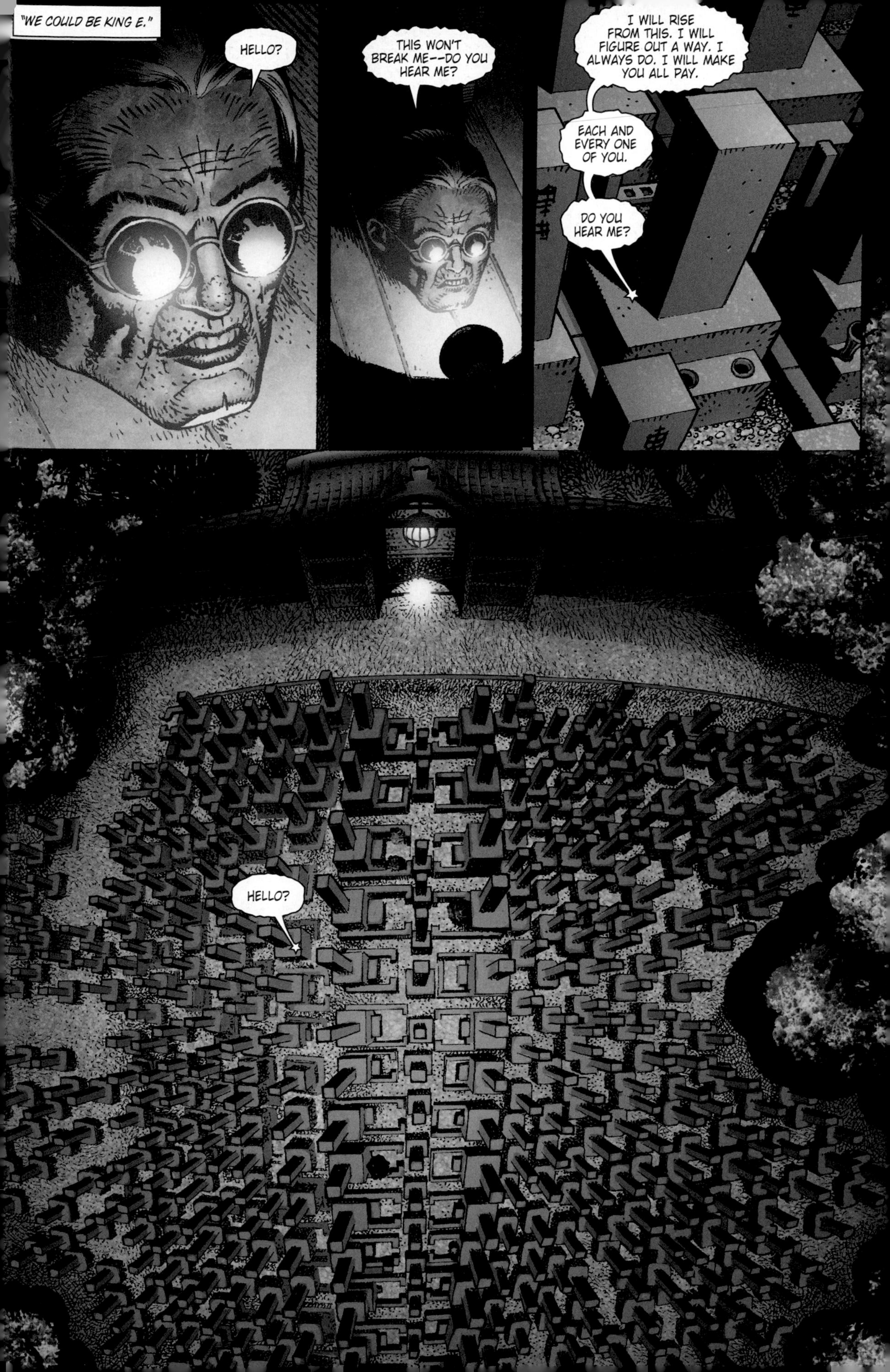
"WE COULD BE KING E."
HELLO?
THIS WON'T BREAK ME--DO YOU HEAR ME?
I WILL RISE FROM THIS. I WILL FIGURE OUT A WAY. I ALWAYS DO. I WILL MAKE YOU ALL PAY.
EACH AND EVERY ONE OF YOU.
DO YOU HEAR ME?
HELLO?

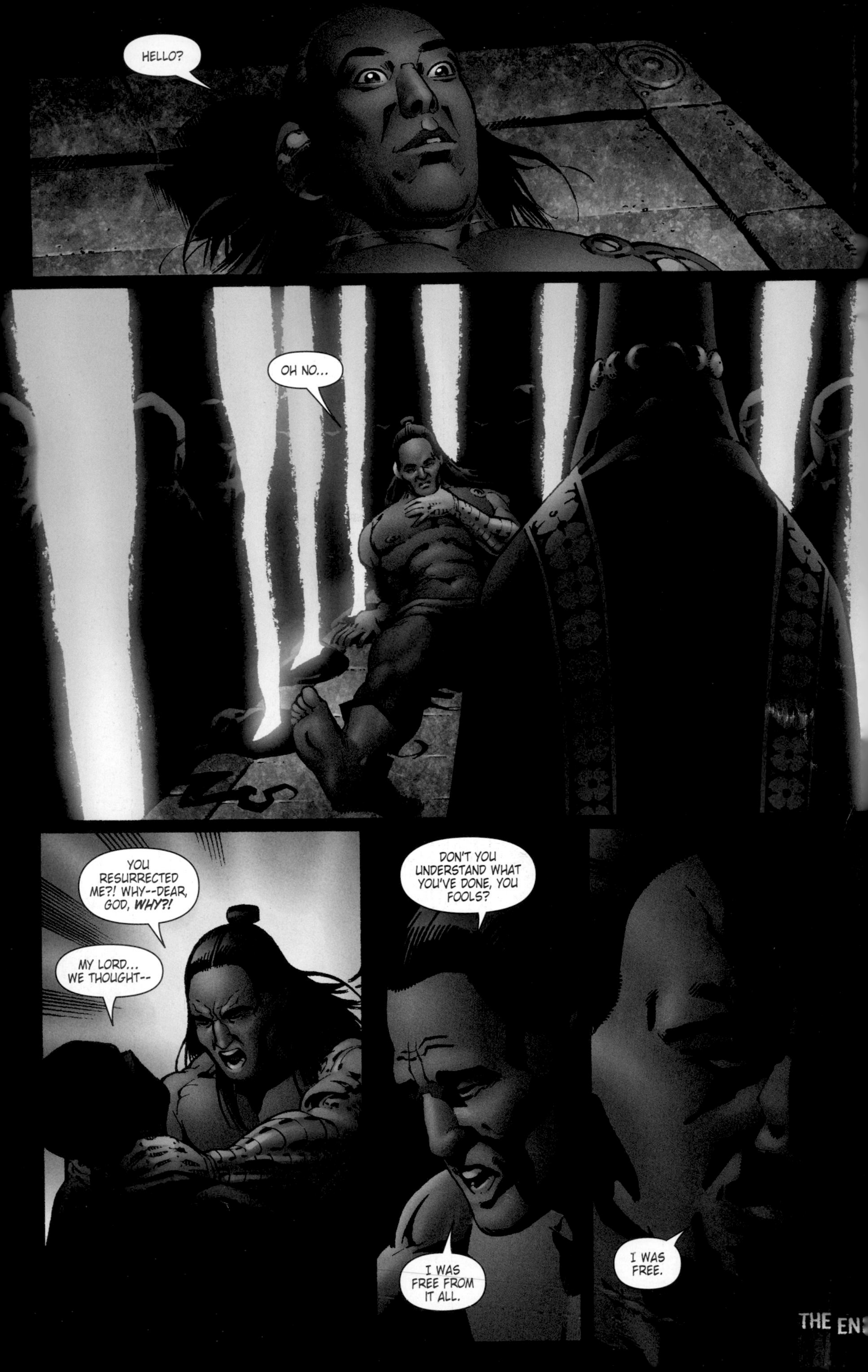
HELLO?
OH NO...
YOU RESURRECTED ME?! WHY--DEAR, GOD, ***WHY?!***
MY LORD... WE THOUGHT--
DON'T YOU UNDERSTAND WHAT YOU'VE DONE, YOU FOOLS?
I WAS FREE FROM IT ALL.
I WAS FREE.
THE EN

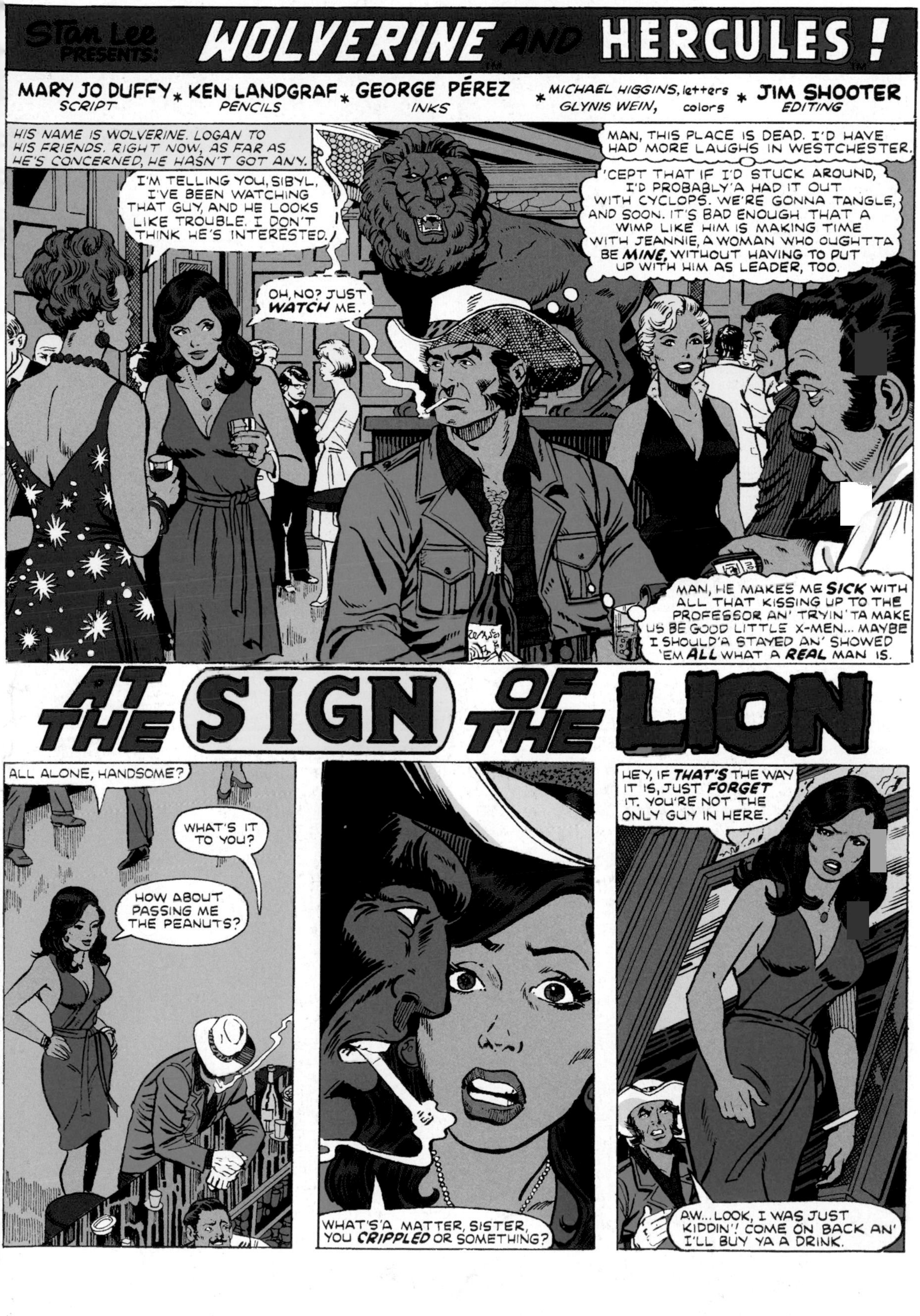
STAN LEE PRESENTS:
WOLVERINE AND HERCULES!
MARY JO DUFFY, SCRIPT * KEN LANDGRAF, PENCILS * GEORGE PÉREZ, INKS * MICHAEL HIGGINS, letters
GLYNIS WEIN, colors * JIM SHOOTER, EDITING
HIS NAME IS WOLVERINE. LOGAN TO HIS FRIENDS. RIGHT NOW, AS FAR AS HE'S CONCERNED, HE HASN'T GOT ANY.
I'M TELLING YOU, SIBYL, I'VE BEEN WATCHING THAT GUY, AND HE LOOKS LIKE TROUBLE. I DON'T THINK HE'S INTERESTED.
OH, NO? JUST WATCH ME.
MAN, THIS PLACE IS DEAD. I'D HAVE HAD MORE LAUGHS IN WESTCHESTER.
'CEPT THAT IF I'D STUCK AROUND, I'D PROBABLY'A HAD IT OUT WITH CYCLOPS. WE'RE GONNA TANGLE, AND SOON. IT'S BAD ENOUGH THAT A WIMP LIKE HIM IS MAKING TIME WITH JEANNIE, A WOMAN WHO OUGHTTA BE MINE, WITHOUT HAVING TO PUT UP WITH HIM AS LEADER, TOO.
MAN, HE MAKES ME SICK WITH ALL THAT KISSING UP TO THE PROFESSOR AN' TRYIN' TA MAKE US BE GOOD LITTLE X-MEN... MAYBE I SHOULD'A STAYED AN' SHOWED 'EM ALL WHAT A REAL MAN IS.
AT THE SIGN OF THE LION
ALL ALONE, HANDSOME?
WHAT'S IT TO YOU?
HOW ABOUT PASSING ME THE PEANUTS?
WHAT'S'A MATTER, SISTER, YOU CRIPPLED OR SOMETHING?
HEY, IF THAT'S THE WAY IT IS, JUST FORGET IT. YOU'RE NOT THE ONLY GUY IN HERE.
AW... LOOK, I WAS JUST KIDDIN'! COME ON BACK AN' I'LL BUY YA A DRINK.

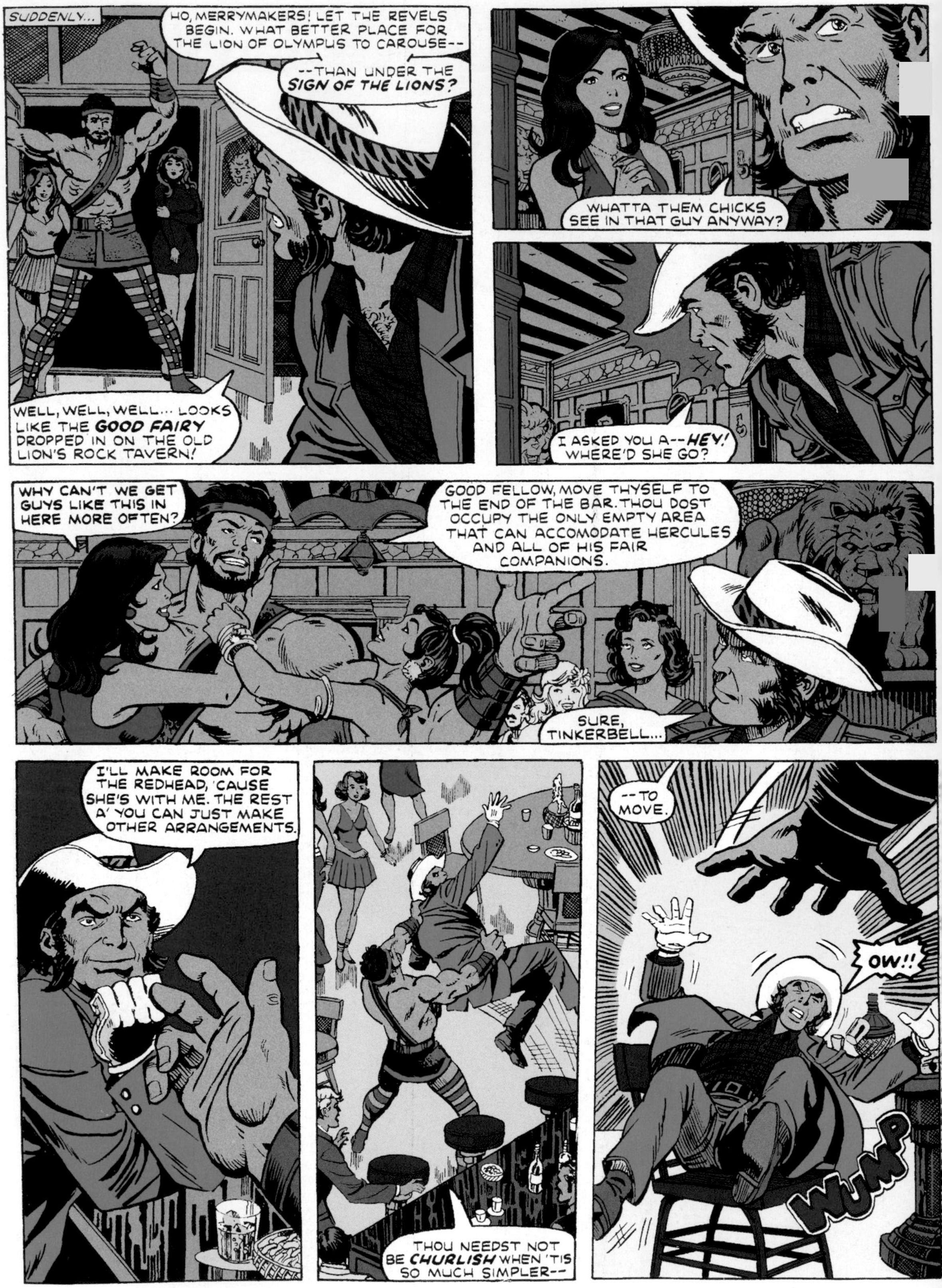
SUDDENLY...
HO, MERRYMAKERS! LET THE REVELS BEGIN. WHAT BETTER PLACE FOR THE LION OF OLYMPUS TO CAROUSE--
--THAN UNDER THE SIGN OF THE LIONS?
WELL, WELL, WELL... LOOKS LIKE THE GOOD FAIRY DROPPED IN ON THE OLD LION'S ROCK TAVERN!
WHATTA THEM CHICKS SEE IN THAT GUY ANYWAY?
I ASKED YOU A--HEY! WHERE'D SHE GO?
WHY CAN'T WE GET GUYS LIKE THIS IN HERE MORE OFTEN?
GOOD FELLOW, MOVE THYSELF TO THE END OF THE BAR. THOU DOST OCCUPY THE ONLY EMPTY AREA THAT CAN ACCOMODATE HERCULES AND ALL OF HIS FAIR COMPANIONS.
SURE, TINKERBELL...
I'LL MAKE ROOM FOR THE REDHEAD, 'CAUSE SHE'S WITH ME. THE REST A' YOU CAN JUST MAKE OTHER ARRANGEMENTS.
THOU NEEDST NOT BE CHURLISH WHEN 'TIS SO MUCH SIMPLER--
--TO MOVE.
OW!!
WUMP

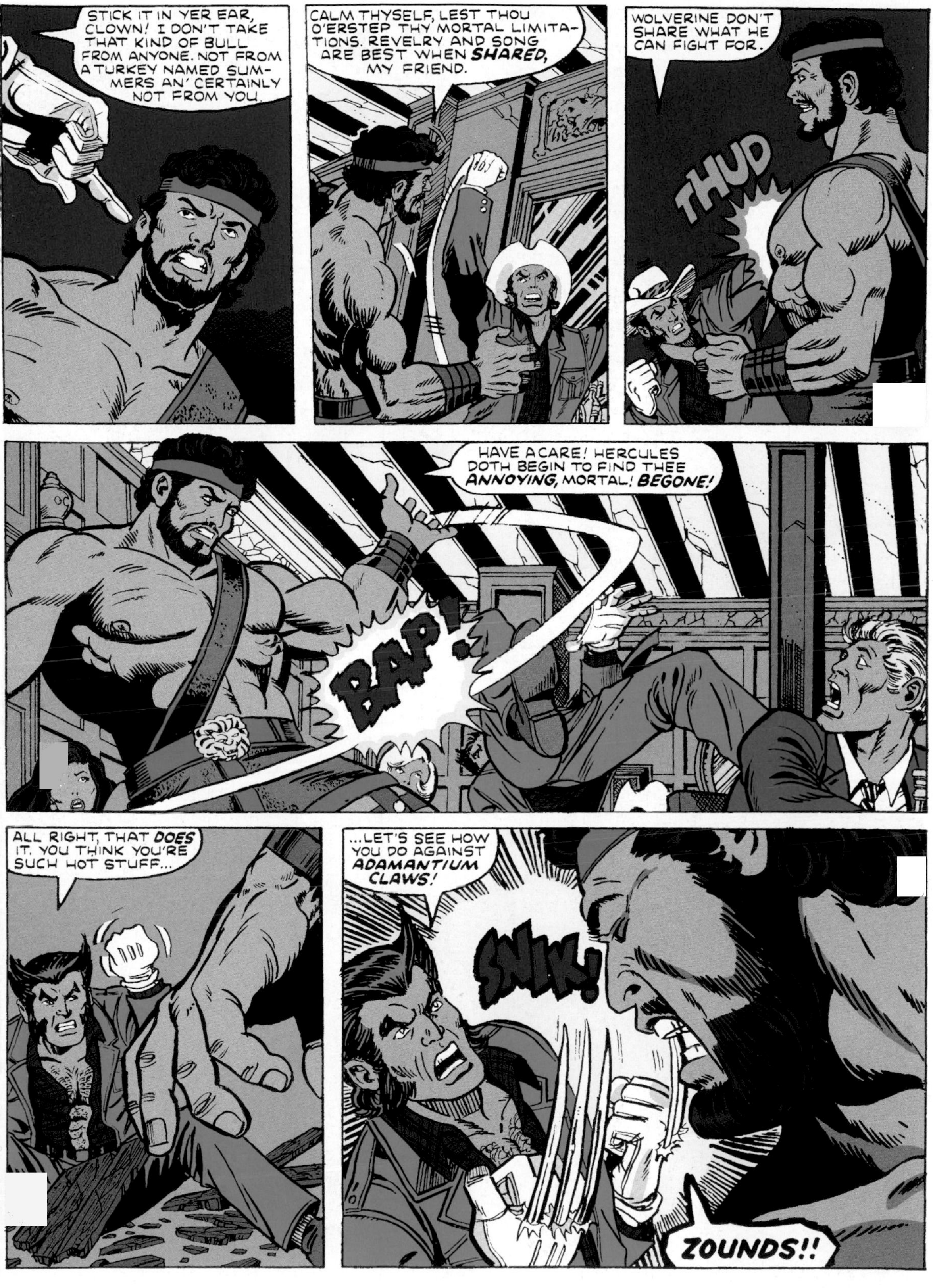
STICK IT IN YER EAR, CLOWN! I DON'T TAKE THAT KIND OF BULL FROM ANYONE. NOT FROM A TURKEY NAMED SUMMERS AN' CERTAINLY NOT FROM YOU.
CALM THYSELF, LEST THOU O'ERSTEP THY MORTAL LIMITATIONS. REVELRY AND SONG ARE BEST WHEN SHARED, MY FRIEND.
WOLVERINE DON'T SHARE WHAT HE CAN FIGHT FOR.
THUD
HAVE A CARE! HERCULES DOTH BEGIN TO FIND THEE ANNOYING, MORTAL! BEGONE!
BAP!
ALL RIGHT, THAT DOES IT. YOU THINK YOU'RE SUCH HOT STUFF...
...LET'S SEE HOW YOU DO AGAINST ADAMANTIUM CLAWS!
SNIK!
ZOUNDS!!

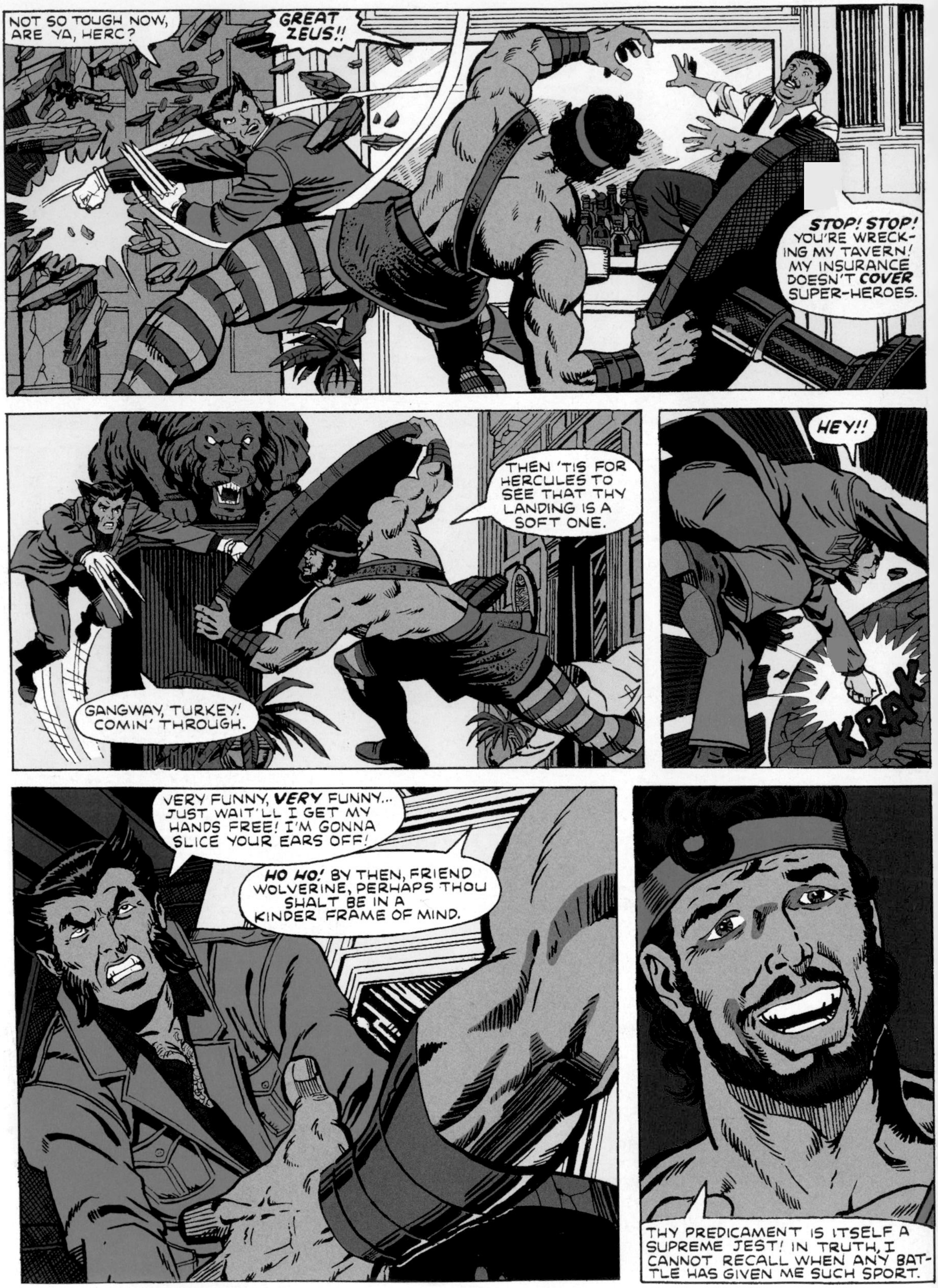
NOT SO TOUGH NOW, ARE YA, HERC?
GREAT ZEUS!!
STOP! STOP! YOU'RE WRECKING MY TAVERN! MY INSURANCE DOESN'T COVER SUPER-HEROES.
THEN 'TIS FOR HERCULES TO SEE THAT THY LANDING IS A SOFT ONE.
GANGWAY, TURKEY! COMIN' THROUGH.
HEY!!
KRAK
VERY FUNNY, VERY FUNNY... JUST WAIT'LL I GET MY HANDS FREE! I'M GONNA SLICE YOUR EARS OFF!
HO HO! BY THEN, FRIEND WOLVERINE, PERHAPS THOU SHALT BE IN A KINDER FRAME OF MIND.
THY PREDICAMENT IS ITSELF A SUPREME JEST! IN TRUTH, I CANNOT RECALL WHEN ANY BATTLE HAS GIVEN ME SUCH SPORT.

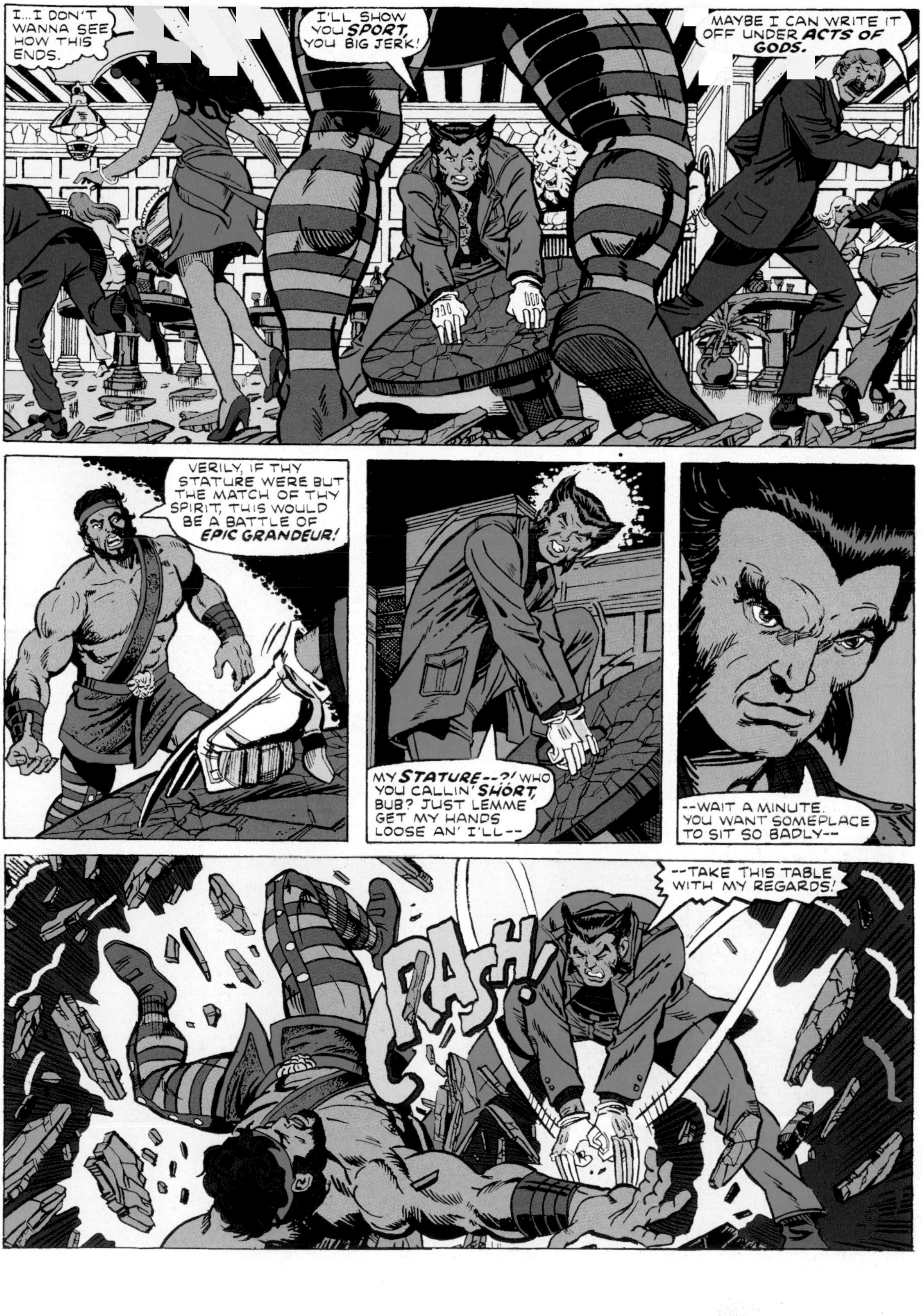

I... I DON'T WANNA SEE HOW THIS ENDS.
I'LL SHOW YOU **SPORT**, YOU BIG JERK!
MAYBE I CAN WRITE IT OFF UNDER **ACTS OF GODS.**
VERILY, IF THY STATURE WERE BUT THE MATCH OF THY SPIRIT, THIS WOULD BE A BATTLE OF **EPIC GRANDEUR!**
MY **STATURE--?!** WHO YOU CALLIN' **SHORT,** BUB? JUST LEMME GET MY HANDS LOOSE AN' I'LL--
--WAIT A MINUTE. YOU WANT SOMEPLACE TO SIT SO BADLY--
--TAKE THIS TABLE WITH MY REGARDS!
CRASH!

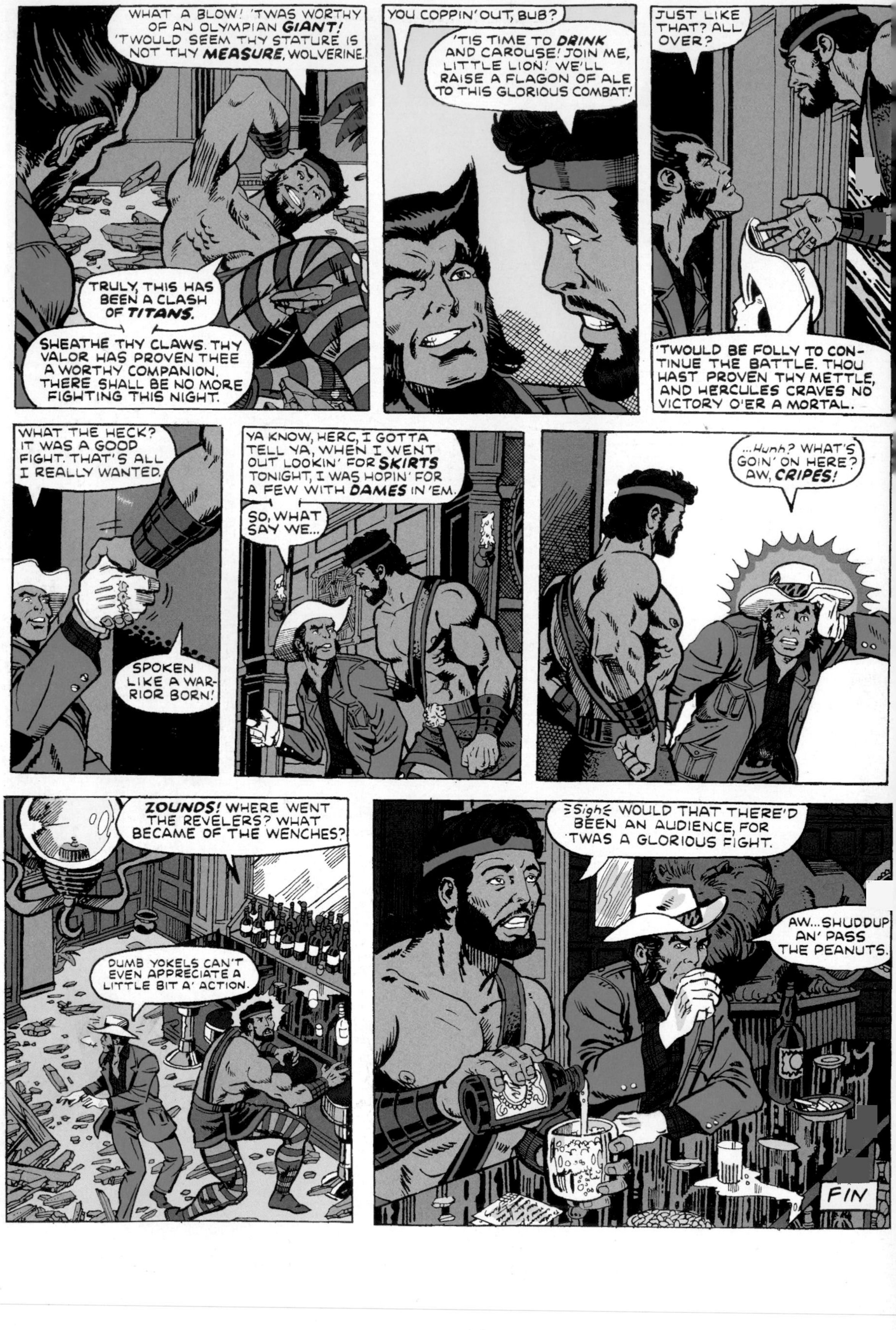
WHAT A BLOW! 'TWAS WORTHY OF AN OLYMPIAN GIANT! 'TWOULD SEEM THY STATURE IS NOT THY MEASURE, WOLVERINE.
TRULY, THIS HAS BEEN A CLASH OF TITANS.
SHEATHE THY CLAWS. THY VALOR HAS PROVEN THEE A WORTHY COMPANION. THERE SHALL BE NO MORE FIGHTING THIS NIGHT.
YOU COPPIN' OUT, BUB?
'TIS TIME TO DRINK AND CAROUSE! JOIN ME, LITTLE LION! WE'LL RAISE A FLAGON OF ALE TO THIS GLORIOUS COMBAT!
JUST LIKE THAT? ALL OVER?
'TWOULD BE FOLLY TO CONTINUE THE BATTLE. THOU HAST PROVEN THY METTLE, AND HERCULES CRAVES NO VICTORY O'ER A MORTAL.
WHAT THE HECK? IT WAS A GOOD FIGHT. THAT'S ALL I REALLY WANTED.
SPOKEN LIKE A WARRIOR BORN!
YA KNOW, HERC, I GOTTA TELL YA, WHEN I WENT OUT LOOKIN' FOR SKIRTS TONIGHT, I WAS HOPIN' FOR A FEW WITH DAMES IN 'EM.
SO, WHAT SAY WE...
...Hunh? WHAT'S GOIN' ON HERE? AW, CRIPES!
ZOUNDS! WHERE WENT THE REVELERS? WHAT BECAME OF THE WENCHES?
DUMB YOKELS CAN'T EVEN APPRECIATE A LITTLE BIT A' ACTION.
Sigh WOULD THAT THERE'D BEEN AN AUDIENCE, FOR TWAS A GLORIOUS FIGHT.
AW...SHUDDUP AN' PASS THE PEANUTS.
FIN